Interprofessional Ethics

Collaboration in the social, health and human services

Organisations in the social, health and human services sectors employ a range of professionals to provide dynamic and quality service and care to people across the lifespan. *Interprofessional Ethics* recognises that multidisciplinary teams exist in many health, government and community-based workplaces. It explores the ethical frameworks, policies and procedures of professional practice, in order to equip readers with the knowledge and skills to work within collaborative teams, and to better understand and consider the perspectives, approaches and values of others.

Each chapter features:

- *Reflection points* – reflective activities to encourage readers to focus on their own experiences and values
- *Through the eyes of a practitioner* – reflections from practitioners on their professional experiences
- *Learning objectives* – encourage readers to engage with core ideas and concepts

As the professional practice context has become more complex and concerned with risk management, there is an increasing need for practitioners to be skilled in ethical decision-making. *Interprofessional Ethics* provides a sound introduction to moral philosophy and ethical theory, professional regulation, ethical decision-making, activism, e-professionalism, and personal and professional responsibilities.

Donna McAuliffe is Associate Professor, School of Human Services and Social Work at Griffith University, Queensland.

Interprofessional Ethics

Collaboration in the social, health and human services

Donna McAuliffe

CAMBRIDGE
UNIVERSITY PRESS

477 Williamstown Road, Port Melbourne, VIC 3207, Australia

Cambridge University Press is part of the University of Cambridge.

It furthers the University's mission by disseminating knowledge in the pursuit of education, learning and research at the highest international levels of excellence.

www.cambridge.org
Information on this title: www.cambridge.org/9781107650466

© Cambridge University Press 2014

First published 2014

Cover designed by Marianna Berek-Lewis
Typeset by Integra Software Services Pvt. Ltd.
Printed in Singapore by C.O.S Printers Pte Ltd.

A catalogue record for this publication is available from the British Library

A Cataloguing-in-Publication entry is available from the catalogue of the National Library of Australia at www.nla.gov.au

ISBN 978-1-107-65046-6 Paperback

To Lesley Chenoweth – my mentor and colleague –
'wise, brave and human'

Contents

Acknowledgements

The process involved in writing any book is long and arduous and involves many people deserving of thanks. This particular interprofessional ethics text was written during a period of study leave supported by Griffith University, and my appreciation is extended to my colleagues for shouldering my teaching and administrative load while I was writing off-campus. Special thanks must go to Dr Lyndal Greenslade, my co-educator in ethics, who willingly read each chapter as the book progressed, gave invaluable feedback and incisive edits, and contributed many ideas about how to make the content more accessible for students. Her knowledge of eastern philosophies was particularly useful. I also extend thanks to Kathryn Beard, who painstakingly formatted the chapters and checked references for accuracy. Her attention to detail is unmatched. I was fortunate to have many people whom I could approach to contribute practitioner stories that are found in each chapter. Of the 24 who generously assisted, some are practitioners and former students who have studied ethics with me in the past; others are colleagues whom I respect and admire within academia and practice. Their contributions bring life to the chapters and inject a taste of reality into what can at times be a dense subject. My ethics colleagues at the AASW, Kym Daly, Sharlene Nipperess, Kerryn Pennell and Fran Hardcastle, have provided inspiration through their commitment to exemplary ethical practice. Thanks also to Isabella Mead and Tara Peck from Cambridge University Press, who have been exceedingly patient as the chapters slowly emerged, and to Katy McDevitt for making what could have been a painful copyediting task quite enjoyable.

Outside work, there is the support system of family and friends that sustains any writer. My sincere thanks to Sallyanne, Jaida and Reuben for keeping my feet on the ground and reminding me that I am 'mum' first and everything else second. Thanks to my bootcamp companions for training me to stay focused and consistent in body, mind and spirit. Finally, thanks to all my students, who are not afraid to ask the hard questions and rightly expect that I will give responses that uphold professional ethical practice, even if most times my response is simply 'it depends'.

Introduction

This book is testament to many years of work in social work, health, human services and academia, through which it has become apparent that tertiary education has missed the mark in not, as a matter of principle, bringing together students from different disciplines to learn with, from and about each other. The concept of interprofessional education (IPE) has emerged over the past decade as an eminently sensible way to prepare graduates for the realities of working life, where organisations generally are not set up to employ only one discipline. Imagine a hospital that employed only doctors, or a disability service office that had only psychologists. A school that employs only teachers will neglect the issues that a guidance officer needs to address. A community legal service that is only staffed by lawyers may not be able to extend to advocacy for older people at risk of elder abuse who need a social worker for family intervention. A youth service that employs only recreational staff may miss out on the benefits of having a sexual-health nurse as part of the team. Evidence shows that collaborative care involving different skill sets and knowledge will ultimately provide better outcomes. Multidisciplinary teams have provided a model in health care for decades and have now extended into many other government and community-based workplaces. Tertiary education now needs to catch up with what has been happening in practice so that graduates are better able to move into work prepared and ready for collaborative team approaches to care and service provision.

This book has been inspired by two initiatives that have provided evidence of the benefits of interprofessional approaches to exploring professional ethics. The first was the development of a postgraduate interdisciplinary professional ethics course, taught online since 2009 at Griffith University, where students enrolled in social work, public health, mental health, and human service programs explored ethics together. As postgraduates, these students came from a broad range of disciplinary backgrounds, including psychology, nursing, law, education, communication and media studies, criminology and policing. Part of their course assessment was to develop an ethical question and explore it through dialogue with two others from disciplinary backgrounds different from their own. This experience provided an opportunity for engagement with different perspectives on controversial issues and opened up a space for learning that is not often afforded when students stay within their own discipline. Students reported in course evaluation comments that they had a much greater appreciation of the differences in ethical perspectives of others and a better awareness of the provisions of ethical codes from different professions, and that they would feel more confident engaging in ethical decision-making as a member of a multidisciplinary team.

The second initiative that has influenced this book was a leadership project funded by the (then) Australian Learning and Teaching Council (ALTC), in which a workshop and learning resources were developed to bring students together to focus on multidisciplinary practice in mental health. In these workshops, students from social work, psychology, medicine and nursing came together to learn from and with each other. The first part of the workshop was exploration of each discipline's 'POEM'; that is, its philosophy, ontology, epistemology and method. Students first identified their own POEM and then moved on to identify the POEM of other disciplines. The potential for transformative learning from designing IPE in this way was clear (McAllister et al., 2011). The POEM activity clearly showed that students carry stereotypes about other disciplines and may lack awareness of what others have a legitimate mandate to do in practice. One of the greatest barriers to people working effectively together is the build-up of territorial walls, which can inhibit collaborative partnerships. Gaining an understanding of what colleagues from different disciplines know and can do is important, as is an understanding of what theoretical positions may be dominant within different professions. The role of the nurse is so much broader than just dispensing medication, for example, and psychologists do more than psychometric testing. Social workers do more than place people in nursing homes and fill out forms to secure income, and doctors have an eye to social factors as well as physical ones. This text is not suggesting that professional practitioners should encroach on discipline-specific roles, but rather that professional practice plays to the strengths and recognised disciplinary expertise in a spirit of shared learning with and about others.

This book, then, is about interprofessional practice and also about interdisciplinary professional ethics. It is argued in Chapter 1 that ethics and professional practice courses provide the best learning space for discussion of the myriad of complex practice issues that will inevitably confront workers in the field, as broad and diverse as it is. The opportunity for engaged dialogue about sensitive and morally controversial issues paves the way for more respectful relationships. Learning to listen to different opinions and perspectives is an important skill for anyone working in social, health or human services. The codes of ethics for all professional disciplines – from medicine and nursing to psychology, social work, teaching, law, physiotherapy, occupational therapy, dietetics, pharmacy and journalism – embed respect for others as a primary ethical concern. When we respect another, we agree to treat that person well, afford them autonomy in making decisions that affect their life, pay attention to the issues that concern them, and allow them to hold views that may differ from our own. Throughout this book, we will explore the differences between truly respecting others and 'tolerating' them. The concept of 'ethical literacy' is explored within the context of interprofessional practice.

Chapter 2 provides solid information about moral philosophy and ethical theory, and explore why it is important that we understand the rationales that we commonly use when we make decisions. We live in a time where political and economic imperatives override moral arguments, and we see this playing out in a range of ways. We see time and again that the world's most disempowered and most vulnerable are used as political footballs. When goals need to be scored, it is refugees and asylum seekers, people with mental illness and disabilities, neglected and abused children, and homeless families who take the spotlight. Questions of who is 'deserving' or 'not deserving' constantly play out in decisions about how resources are allocated. Behind all of these people are professional workers who battle unfair and inequitable systems to ensure that basic human rights are observed.

The exploration of how professionals can work together to support each other in the pursuit of social justice and human rights is the focus of Chapter 3. This chapter also explores the concept of activism. How do we stand up and be counted, make our voices heard, and demand changes to social structures, laws and policies that disempower, discriminate and oppress? More importantly, how do we band together to do this? Readers are challenged to consider ways in which activism can be used to advocate and lobby to address structural disadvantage. The chapter also considers the intersection of ethics and law using examples from recent government policy initiatives, before opening up the topic of resource allocation and questioning the impact of economic rationales for division of resources on the moral imperatives of fairness and justice. We will explore examples of implications of the 'deserving/undeserving' dualism and how different ethical theories support different ways of dividing resources in a climate of economic austerity. Content in this chapter takes a more global view of distribution and focuses on both macro and micro levels when looking at how economic imperatives and political ideologies influence resource allocation.

Chapter 4 focuses on the way that professions are regulated, how complaints are managed within different disciplines, and how codes of ethics, practice standards and codes of conduct are constructed and kept relevant. The system of regulation of professions in Australia is highly dependent on political will, and there are many inequities in the management of regulated and unregulated professions. The Australian Health Practitioner Regulation Agency (AHPRA), which sits within the National Registration and Accreditation Scheme (NRAS), is continuously under review and many professions continue to lobby for inclusion under this scheme so that vulnerable clients may be afforded better protection. The chapter explores how professions can cause harm, and what structures need to be in place to safeguard people from harm. Chapter 5 begins with the proposition that ethical decision-making is a skill required by all who work in a professional capacity in social, health or human services. Ethics is at the centre of what we do and cannot be avoided; ethical dilemmas are commonplace in all fields of practice. Individual practitioners will have their own personal values, and most times these will align well with professional values. There will, however, be many times when values (personal and professional) collide and conflict. The ability to use ethical decision-making models and reach well-justified decisions is a critical part of ethical practice. Attention to principles of respect for diversity, cultural sensitivity, autonomy and privacy may be important, as is a willingness to consult appropriately with others, consider the range of accountabilities and remain critically reflective.

Chapter 6 moves on to explore ethical principles in practice, including autonomy, informed consent, confidentiality and privacy. There is also discussion of obligations as these relate to duty of care, and duty to warn within the context of the justice/care debates. A number of cases will be used to highlight ethical dilemmas across different fields of practice. Management of information, documentation and keeping of records will also be covered in this chapter, as they relate to the other principles. The theme of professional integrity continues into Chapter 7, where content covers the differences between personal and professional relationships and explores issues of sexual-boundary violations, dual and multiple relationships and personal self-disclosures. These are all issues that require clarity so that expectations about professional conduct across different disciplines are transparent. Given significant advances in technology and the impact of such advances on the delivery of services, it is important to address the emerging issue of 'e-professionalism'. Essentially, this is the way that people construct their online persona and engage in online communications in a way that is consistent with professional expectations. Implications for engagement with social media and social networking are explored, as are guidelines and protocols for online behaviour.

Chapter 8 explores interprofessional and collegial relationships and the strategies that practitioners use to manage workplace tensions, value differences and avert conflict. The role of organisational policies and industrial protocols is discussed as well as the responsibilities of management and the place of professional supervision, mentoring and peer support. The chapter builds on earlier chapters to explore further the place of activism, particularly whistleblowing, and highlights the ethical responsibilities of self-care and collegial support. Finally, Chapter 9 sets out the 'ethics agenda' for organisations that employ professional staff, and proposes a number of strategies that individual practitioners, groups of co-workers, and organisations can employ to enhance interprofessional ethics literacy. Continuing professional development, the role of critical reflection, and the construction of practice frameworks that incorporate an ethical dimension are discussed. The need to keep ethics on the agenda for the professions is a strong message threaded through this book.

The book aims to provide a synthesis of theory, research and practice, so that a sound foundation can be built for interprofessional collaborations. Learning objectives at the beginning of each chapter provide the blueprint for the overall structure of the book. The voices of practitioners are woven throughout the structure of the book in inserts labelled 'Through the eyes of a practitioner', and these give examples of insights, reflections and situations that have resulted in learning from experience. Colleagues have contributed these examples at our request, providing valuable signposts to illustrate themes in the book. Case examples, provided to demonstrate the application of particular principles, have been gleaned from practice experiences as well as literature. The final aim is to ensure that professional practitioners can attain greater confidence in their own value positions, understand more clearly what professional expectations exist around ethical issues, and engage more consciously in ethical dialogue with colleagues from different disciplines. Ultimately, it is hoped, this will improve the quality of care for clients, patients and users of social, health and human services.

1

Ethics in professional practice: an interprofessional perspective

■ Learning objectives

- **TO ESTABLISH** the context of interprofessional practice and identify the need for interprofessional education (IPE)

- **TO DEFINE** what is meant by a 'profession', identify common perceptions of different disciplines, their value positions and ethical foundations

- **TO EXPLORE** interprofessional ethics education and the need for ethical literacy within the professions

■ Introduction

WHEN WE THINK about contemporary workplaces in the broad human services, health and social care industries, and consider who works alongside each other on a daily basis in the delivery of services, it is not difficult to see the interprofessional context in action. Casting an eye across the vast terrain of social, health and human services in Australian and international contexts, it is clear that members of the professionally trained workforce rarely work in isolation, unless we are in a very remote area. If workers are isolated by geography, connections are now more possible due to advances in technologies. In hospitals, health and community centres, mental health agencies, income security organisations, schools, prisons, aged-care facilities, and childcare centres, staff from a wide range of disciplines work together in close proximity. When students graduate from professional programs and move into the social, health and human service workforce, they will inevitably find themselves sitting alongside colleagues from different discipline backgrounds. A social worker employed in a community mental health team will work closely with psychiatrists, medical registrars, nursing staff, recreational officers, dieticians and occupational therapists. A nurse working in a paediatric setting may work closely with a speech therapist, psychologist, pharmacist and chaplain. A police officer will work daily with lawyers, correctional staff with training in criminology, and human service workers. A teacher in a typical school may work with a librarian, a guidance officer and a multicultural liaison worker. The complementarity of many professional disciplines is what gives strength and coherence to the workforce, just as the differences between professions gives each a unique place and prevents duplication of service delivery.

■ Negotiating working together

Clark, Cott and Drinka (2007) propose that different professionals who work together in teams must learn to negotiate and understand three important elements: (1) principles (guidelines for behaviour); (2) structures (established forms of knowledge and patterns of behaviour); and (3) processes (how things are done). As new practitioners, the difficulty many of us face when we first enter the workforce is the lack of understanding about fundamental differences in roles and responsibilities, and value positions between different professional staff. We need to learn quickly what defines the roles of others and what they are trained to do. We may not necessarily have gained this knowledge from our own studies, and we may have had little to do with different professions unless we have personal experience of them. For example, the role of a teacher will be clear enough because most of us have been to a school of some description; in the same way, most of us will have been to a doctor, an optometrist or a dentist, and most will have come to understand the roles played by police, lawyers, nurses and journalists. However, unless there has been cause in our lives to encounter a psychologist, social worker, occupational therapist, audiologist, acupuncturist, osteopath or podiatrist, we may have much more limited knowledge of what defines these professions. It is common for us to build up stereotypes of what we think different professions are about, and popular media largely contributes to these stereotypes. When moving into the professional workforce, these stereotypes can be carried along and may cause a degree of confusion if they are skewed or inaccurate. One of the common perceptions of social workers, as an example, is that they are either 'bleeding heart do-gooders' or 'Rottweilers' who snatch children away from their families. The media has largely contributed to these quite inaccurate public perceptions. There is often little understanding that social workers train for four years to obtain a degree that gives them deep understanding of individuals, groups and communities, and the social context within which social issues and problems occur, as well as skills in assessment and intervention guided by an extensive code of ethics and values. Perceptions of occupational therapists, as another example, have traditionally been of 'basket weavers' or people who help others to engage in crafts or recreational activities. Like social work, occupational therapy is an extensive degree program focused on knowledge of anatomy and physiology with a view to assisting rehabilitation and assessment of activities of daily living and specific interventions designed towards recovery and re-engagement with optimal functioning. It is important, then, as a starting point to considering how professions work together, to examine what knowledge and stereotypes we already hold about different disciplines, and identify those professions about whom we realise we have very little knowledge at all. In considering the range of professions, we can be guided by the following definition provided by Professions Australia (2013):

> A disciplined group of individuals who adhere to ethical standards and who hold themselves out as, and are accepted by the public as possessing special knowledge and skills in a widely recognised body of learning derived from research, education and training at a high level, and who are prepared to apply this knowledge and exercise these skills in the interest of others. It is inherent in the definition of a profession that a code of ethics governs the activities of each profession. Such codes require behaviour and practice beyond the personal moral obligations of an individual. They define and demand high standards of behaviour in respect to the services provided to the public and in dealing with professional colleagues. Further, these codes are enforced by the profession and are acknowledged and accepted by the community.

■ Ethical difference: tensions between the professions

In noting the explicit mention of the importance of ethical standards and moral obligations in the definition of professions, it is important to understand that this is the area that can often contribute to tensions between professions. These ethical differences may not become apparent until a situation arises in which decisions need to be made that call on practitioners to take a stance on a contentious issue.

In daily life, we are all confronted with moral questions and will have developed individual responses to these. Our socialised experiences, religious and spiritual beliefs, cultural backgrounds and political leanings will all influence our attitudes towards issues as diverse as euthanasia, capital punishment, termination of pregnancy and mandatory reporting of child abuse. While we can hold these beliefs at a personal level, it is when the professional context intersects that challenges may arise. The concept of people from different disciplines working together and needing to find common ground in the interests of continuity of care and consistency of standards is certainly not new. Multidisciplinary teams, particularly in health care, have been in existence for many decades, and the difficulties inherent in this model due to professional differences, status and hierarchy are well documented. The fact that people have continued to work together reasonably well despite professional tensions implies that the benefits of this model may outweigh the costs. Organisational structures and culture can promote or impede constructive working relationships, which is why it is so important to have a good understanding of roles, responsibilities, duties and obligations, not just within our own discipline but also in those of colleagues. Understanding the professionalisation or socialisation of others is also important so that behaviour can be understood within a context. Hall (2005) explains, for example, that medical education focuses on educating doctors to be authoritarian, take charge of decisions, and give preference to maintaining life over quality of life. Clergy are trained to preserve absolute confidentiality. Nurses and social workers will value the narrative and story of the patient and his or her family. One of the essential goals of this book is to help readers understand why it is important to pay attention to others.

D'Cruz, Jacobs and Schoo (2009, p. 3) provide a useful analysis of why professions are different. They state:

> the most salient differences between professions relate to the substantive disciplines and knowledge informing professional education. These disciplines are, broadly, the natural sciences (including biology) and the social sciences (including the humanities). Further differences include concepts, theories and practices that are peculiar to a profession; the extent to which professionals use technology as part of their helping repertoire; and the degree of visibility afforded to the interventions offered, for example through medication or testing, as opposed to counselling or 'talk' therapies. Differences between professions may also relate to the rigour with which their claims about the efficacy of interventions – problem, intervention, outcome – can be assessed empirically.

(Reproduced with permission of Ashgate Publishers. Copyright © 2009.)

REFLECTION 1.1
Review this list of professional disciplines.
- Acupuncturist
- Audiologist
- Chiropractor
- Dentist
- Dietician
- Doctor
- Human resource manager
- Journalist
- Lawyer
- Midwife
- Nurse
- Occupational therapist

- Optometrist
- Osteopath
- Pharmacist
- Physiotherapist
- Podiatrist
- Police officer
- Psychiatrist
- Psychologist
- Social worker
- Speech therapist
- Teacher

1   Think about the first three words that come to mind when you think about each of these professional disciplines. Which discipline was the hardest to describe, and which the easiest? Why do you think this is?
2   Does any discipline bring up positive or negative imagery for you and, if so, why? It may be helpful to consider any personal experience you have of being treated by, or having a connection with, someone from another professional discipline.
3   Looking again at the list, can you describe in fewer than 10 words what practitioners of each discipline do?

■ What makes a profession?

The understanding of what it is to be a 'professional' has developed over time from a singular notion of a group of like-minded people working towards a common goal, to that of groups of people (not necessarily like-minded) being able to work together to achieve a reasonable compromise. Human nature being what it is means that, in realistic terms, people are not always going to agree, or even agree to disagree. Part of the hallmark of belonging to a professional discipline is the baseline that professionals 'profess' to hold knowledge and wisdom that gives them the edge in their territory. A professional strives to have the knowledge to be 'right', and with this often comes arrogance that if one is right, then others have to be wrong. Many longstanding professional rivalries have been based on this contention. In efforts to secure territory and status, professional disciplines generate their own knowledge, conduct their own research, and promote their own evidence base. This evidence gives legitimacy, on the basis of which the public trusts that people who belong to this professional discipline will act with integrity. The goal of every professional's discipline is to hold expertise in his or her field, to be sure of what he or she is doing and of the effectiveness of his or her interventions, and to have good faith in outcomes. When we work together, there is opportunity for scrutiny of the practice of others, which can lead to either respect for the work of others, or hostility and tension if professional rivalry takes the upper hand. Good management is needed to ensure that a workplace does not disintegrate into disharmony and develop what is often known as a 'toxic culture'. The example given in the 'Through the eyes of a practitioner' insert shows what can happen when communication is not as clear as it perhaps could be.

THROUGH THE EYES OF A PRACTITIONER

I work in a rehabilitation unit within a tertiary teaching hospital. Social workers can sometimes be the 'conscience' of multidisciplinary health teams. The unit had a patient who was dying of a condition that could have been treated if he had not suffered from a range of other co-existing conditions making surgery impossible. I developed a supportive relationship with this man and his loving family who lived a distance away and could only visit once weekly. Every day it was obvious that his condition was worsening. The doctor had discussed nursing home placement with the family and they were busy trying to locate a suitable facility but the time needed to make these arrangements was impeding their ability to visit their father. With the medical focus on rehabilitation, it was difficult for the medical and therapy staff to acknowledge that he was not going to be a 'success' and the patient was by this time disoriented. I requested that the doctor convey the imminence of his death to the family. The doctor brushed aside my request, stating to me that the family knew that the end was close. I knew that they did not but could not convey this to the family as it was medical advice. Eventually the doctor agreed to a discussion by phone with the family and they were shocked and angry that they had not been contacted before as they thought their father would live for several months. I continued to support the family and the patient was transferred to a nursing home, where he died. I attended the funeral, where the anger of the family was expressed by pointed acknowledgement during the service of the care provided by the nursing home over a 24-hour period, but with no mention of the hospital where the patient had spent several months. From this dilemma, my belief in persisting with advocacy was reinforced. However, I was made aware that direct discussion with patients and families about outcomes can be difficult for other staff. The experience honed my vigilance and readiness to work proactively in the event of a similar future situation. I would seek in future to intervene earlier and not to assume that full communication will automatically occur.

(Jan Thomas)

■ Professional 'sea change'

Over the past few decades there has been an interesting and growing phenomenon of professionals making 'career shifts'. As people increasingly work together in multidisciplinary teams in the way described, it is not uncommon for many to leave their original profession and move to another related discipline. Professional shifts can and do take place when a person decides that there could be different ways of viewing the world, and that these ways may make more sense in terms of personal congruence. People are increasingly moving through a number of qualifications, using previous study and experience to leapfrog into different careers. Massive shifts towards online education appeal to mature-age workers, who aspire to new career paths that were previously not possible because of the difficulty of managing work and study together. The positive side to this professional sea-change movement is that the combinations of different disciplines add both breadth and depth to the professional workforce. Take, for example, the lawyer who turns to psychology after many years working with separating families; the police officer who decides to pursue social work after a career in child protection; the teacher who becomes a criminologist as a result of interest in juvenile offending behaviours; or the physiotherapist who decides to study natural therapies or become a chiropractor. These career shifts build on and extend practical and theoretical knowledge, and also offer new perspectives in terms of values and ethics. Moving from one discipline to another can provide excellent opportunities for sharing these different professional perspectives.

THROUGH THE EYES OF A PRACTITIONER

When I left school at the age of 17, I decided to go straight to university to study Speech Pathology. I completed the first year but then decided that I wanted to change across to Physiotherapy. I completed that degree and started working with young children with physical disabilities. I was very focused in my work on motor skills and improvement of coordination and muscular function, but the part of my work I ended up enjoying the most was the talking time that I had with the children's families and carers. Because they were usually in the room while I was doing my treatments with the children, we had a lot of time to talk. I realised that there was just so much to being a carer of a child with a disability, and how important it was for these carers to have someone listen to them. I decided, after working for 10 years as a physio and then having my own child, that I wanted to change my career path to counselling. I ended up doing this and now have a great job where I am paid to talk with people and help them to make decisions about the needs of their children. I still use my skills and knowledge from physiotherapy, but have added in the emotional dimension to the physical, which feels really well rounded.

(Susie Smith)

◾ Value clashes across the professions

In the ideal scenario, once we become a professional, we will have a strong sense of professional identity and will be able to hold professional views intact. We will be able to respect the views of others, engage well with interprofessional learning, and enrich a workplace by the cumulative bringing together of different perspectives and values. It is unfortunate, however, that many people do not have good knowledge of the value foundations of professional disciplines other than their own, and have little respect or tolerance for difference of opinion. Value clashes impact negatively on workplace morale and create toxic cultures that are stressful, which in turn impacts on staff turnover. This highlights the need for us to have more than a superficial understanding of other disciplines, and raises the question of how such learning should be attained. The premise of this book is that the interprofessional context is now a feature of contemporary workplaces and that, in order for professionals to work collaboratively in the best interests of clients and service users, knowledge of one's own discipline and also the discipline of co-workers is a basic requirement.

REFLECTION 1.2

1 Considering your response to Reflection 1.1, think about the value positions involved in each of the professional disciplines listed. What do doctors, journalists, or social workers value? Work through the list again, this time considering the value positions of each discipline.

2 Think about the other disciplines mentioned in this text so far. Imagine that you are working with a team of people from legal, psychology, human resource management, nursing and podiatry – or any others on the list. Of these, which would you say that you 'respect'?

3 Are there any disciplines that you would find harder to respect than others, and why do you think this is?

4 What are the impacts of lack of respect within a team on multidisciplinary practice? Can you think of what might happen to relationships and communication? Consider any times when you have witnessed this in a workplace.

THROUGH THE EYES OF A PRACTITIONER

When I studied my Social Work degree in the mid-1980s, I remember doing first-year Psychology and Sociology courses with hundreds of other students from disciplines that I knew nothing about. I became none the wiser through the rest of my education, but was very fortunate to complete two field placements in areas where I was working alongside people from different disciplines. One of these placements, in a community legal centre, was particularly instructive as I came to learn about the very different values that can be held between legal and social work professions. When asked to complete a pre-sentence report for a client who was facing court on multiple charges of sexual assault, my assessment was that this man had a significant history of abuse himself as a child, showed little remorse for serious offences or understanding of the impact of his actions on the women he had assaulted, and was resistant to taking any responsibility for his behaviour. The defence lawyer requested that the bulk of my assessment be deleted from the report, wanting the focus to be on the client's abuse history in the hope of obtaining a more lenient sentence. I refused to modify my assessment as requested by the lawyer in the interests of providing a full picture of this client, and the report was subsequently not tendered to the court. The evidence spoke for itself and the client did go to jail for a time, but the recommendations for intensive therapeutic interventions, as well as the social and family context, were lost to the court. In hindsight, I wish I had been able to have better communication with the lawyer about my position, but I felt dismissed by him as causing a problem. After many years of practice, I have a much better understanding of how to work with lawyers, and can hold my assessments strong even in the face of opposition.

(Donna McAuliffe)

■ Making the case for interprofessional education

Having established that we operate within an interprofessional context, and that there is some movement of people around different professions, we will explore two questions of great importance that set the foundations for exploration of interprofessional education (IPE) in this book. The first is how IPE is defined and what this means for how students can learn together before they graduate to enter the workforce. The second is where, in a professional curriculum, students can best come together to learn about important elements of the practice of others. It is the premise of this book that courses on ethical practice and professional conduct are among the most suitable locations for IPE because of the nature of the actual content and the capacity for dialogue and learning from others.

A commonly cited definition of IPE is that used by the Centre for the Advancement of Interprofessional Education (CAIPE, 2002) in the UK. This definition is as follows: 'Interprofessional education occurs when two or more professions learn with, from and about each other to improve collaboration and the quality of care.'

A number of principles underlie IPE, and these are important for us to consider as they preserve the unique place of each discipline within the collaborative learning environment. IPE is about acknowledging but setting aside difference in power and status of different professions; presenting each profession positively and distinctively; and agreeing on 'ground rules'. As part of the process of IPE, we need to explore dealing with difference while searching for common ground, focusing on evidence and drawing connections between theory and practice. The outcomes from IPE are:

- to enable each profession to improve its own practice to complement that of others
- to engender interprofessional capability and inform joint action to instigate change
- to engage with systematic knowledge generation and research with the ultimate aim of improving services to individuals, families and communities.

From this definition and the principles of IPE, we can see that there is great benefit in disciplines learning about each other so that we can better understand positions, while also learning to hold steady, distinct positions in our own discipline when seeking common ground.

■ Defining the interprofessional space

There is quite a lot of terminology in the interprofessional space, and some of these terms are used interchangeably in literature. Garner and Orelove (1994) wrote extensively about the differences between 'multidisciplinary', 'interdisciplinary' and 'transdisciplinary' teams, arguing that unless individuals are committed to working well together in the interests of patient/client care, discipline boundaries would always intrude on effective teamwork. Reel and Hutchings (2007) use the term 'interprofessional care' in their wirting about teams working together in the clinical context. Jessup (2007, p. 330) argues that there is a distinct difference between the terms 'multidisciplinary' and 'interdisciplinary', and defines these as follows:

> Multidisciplinary team approaches utilise the skills and experience of individuals from different disciplines, with each discipline approaching the patient from their own perspective. Most often, this approach involves separate individual consultations. These may occur in a 'one-stop-shop' fashion with all consultations occurring as a part of a single appointment on a single day. It is common for multidisciplinary teams to meet regularly, in the absence of the patient, to case conference findings and discuss future directions for the patient's care. Multidisciplinary teams provide more knowledge and experience than disciplines operating in isolation.
>
> Interdisciplinary team approaches, as the word itself suggests, integrate separate discipline approaches into a single consultation. That is, the patient-history taking, assessment, diagnosis, intervention and short- and long-term management goals are conducted by the team, together with the patient, at the one time. The patient is intimately involved in any discussions regarding their condition or prognosis and the plans about their care. A common understanding and holistic view of all aspects of the patient's care ensues, with the patient empowered to form part of the decision-making process, including the setting of long- and short-term goals. Individuals from different disciplines, as well as the patient them self, are encouraged to question each other and explore alternate avenues, stepping out of discipline silos to work toward the best outcome for the patient.

This distinction is important when exploring the ethical landscape in which we function. In order to promote an interdisciplinary approach to ethics, it is necessary to look for common ground in professional values, which are often enshrined in professional codes of ethics and statements such as the 'Hippocratic oath' (from medicine). An interdisciplinary or interprofessional approach to ethics provides an opportunity to search out those relationships and connections that will provide a more holistic outcome for our clients and service users. Bronstein (2003), writing more than a decade ago, suggested that the time was right to explore the development of new models and frameworks related to interdisciplinary work, recognising that the creation of cultures of collaboration does not happen without intentional discussion between and among professional groups.

REFLECTION 1.3

1 What terms are you aware of that explain the process of working with other professional groups?

2 At this stage in your professional development, what skills do you think you would need for working with those from other professional disciplines?

When we look at what defines different disciplines, we see a commonality of purpose – a commitment to optimal health and wellbeing, social justice, ongoing professional development and integrity in practice. Interprofessional ethics is about working together with others to reach a shared understanding of how we collectively maximise outcomes for people. Fortune and Fitzgerald (2009), in their exploration of the challenges of interdisciplinary collaboration in acute psychiatry between occupational therapy and nursing staff, concluded that interdisciplinary respect is the key to successful collaboration. Further, Sargent, Loney and Murphy (2008, p. 233) found, in their study of interprofessional work in primary health care, that 'lack of respect for other health professions and stereotypical views can interfere with teamwork and collaboration'. In the mental health field, Norman and Peck (1999) also found that tensions could happen between staff from different professional disciplines when roles are unclear, identities are perceived to be under threat, and different professional values are not well understood. Let's look at an example that explores this further.

A psychological perspective on responses to a person suffering acute anxiety as a result of post-traumatic stress may focus on interpersonal factors and look at cognitive behavioural responses to interventions; a social work perspective might also acknowledge these interpersonal factors but would take a broader perspective on social, cultural and structural factors that can impact on anxiety. A medical or pharmacological perspective may focus primarily on biochemical responses. While there may be quite significant common ground in the understanding of what causes people to suffer from anxiety following trauma, any points of difference in assessment may have implications for ethical standards, particularly if the person is resistant to using medication or does not, for cultural reasons, consider that particular interventions are appropriate. These professionals, working together in a multidisciplinary mental health team, will need to find ways to reach common ground and agreement about how best to proceed with a treatment regime. The bringing together of expertise from a number of perspectives will provide a much more comprehensive plan of action, but only as long as the points of common ground and shared understanding can be attained in a collaborative and collegial way. Medical staff therefore need to respect the work of their allied health colleagues, and the place and role of medical responses also need to be respected by non-medical practitioners.

THROUGH THE EYES OF A PRACTITIONER

In my former management role, I had a staff member who traded on her rather big personality, the dividend being personal popularity with the multidisciplinary team. This popularity managed to obscure the team's recognition of her poor professional practice. Despite endeavouring to address practice issues and develop clear performance expectations, no change was evident. I therefore made the decision not to extend her locum. At this point she recruited the nurse manager (with whom she had developed a personal relationship) who strenuously supported her in opposition to my decision. A formal appointment was made to discuss the issue with a senior team member. She sat in complete silence, maintaining constant, respectful eye contact and an open and attentive demeanour as I outlined my concerns in full. She heard me out completely, and I then did likewise for her. A calm and considered discussion ensued, though no agreement was reached. This example raises many issues regarding ethical practice: there was an absence of awareness of self; professional/personal boundaries were blurred; there was an unwillingness to engage in critical reflective practice, consider and respond to feedback; and finally there was collusion and inappropriate involvement of other staff in a professional issue. However, it was the meeting with the senior team manager that had the most profound effect on me. Through her willingness to set the scene by quietly listening, we joined together in the space to share the focus of our attention, and as a result our professional relationship remained intact and we continued to have a very positive working relationship. This is the ideal to aspire to in interdisciplinary conflict.

(Joanne Williams)

■ Interprofessional ethics education: providing a clear rationale

Developing an understanding of appropriate ethical responses and decision-making in clinical and community practice has long been a part of professional education. As we will see in later chapters, different disciplines have their own histories of documented codes of ethics and standards of practice, and these date back to the very beginnings of these disciplines as each sought to establish their ethical foundations. The professions have a somewhat chequered history in terms of regulation of their practice, with many now regulated by legislation and formal structures of accreditation and accountability, while others continue in a self-regulatory model without legislated or formal processes to afford protection to the public. Ethical principles – including a commitment to beneficence (doing good), non-maleficence (doing no harm), autonomy, justice, integrity, veracity, fidelity and truthfulness – will also be discussed later in this book.

The opening questions here are whether ethics is taught at tertiary level within the different disciplines that make up a growing number of professions and, if so, how it is taught. It is true to say that the more established professions, such as medicine, psychology, law, nursing, journalism, education and social work, have been teaching professional ethics for many years, but equally true to say that there is great variation in how this is done and where ethics is placed within the curriculum. Ethics has many homes, and can sit comfortably within courses on philosophy, human development and behaviour, human rights, research or law. You may have already touched on some study of ethics in these courses. In looking at the history of ethics education, there has been divided opinion about whether ethics should be infused through many courses within a program of study, or whether it should have a place as a discrete course in its own right. Ideally, a mix of infusion of values and ethics through all courses, combined with a stand-alone course explicitly about ethical responsibilities and professional practice, will give a well-rounded coverage of the important knowledge that is needed to ensure readiness for practice. Most professional programs have field education, internships, or field placement/work experience/practicums embedded within them, and the timing of the professional ethics course within a program's structure then becomes a point of debate. Should you be taught all about the ethical standards of your profession before you venture into the field so that you can be aware of what to look for and how to critically analyse practice that you then observe, or should you be given only the basics, then sent out to the field, and come back to reflect in more depth on your observations? It seems that the rule of thumb is that courses (or at the least content) on ethics and professional practice should sit within a defined curriculum; that students should not be sent blindly into the field with no knowledge at all of expected professional values and acceptable behaviours; and that continued reflection on issues of ethics should be a requirement throughout a course of study.

What then follows is that medical, nursing, psychology, social work, occupational therapy, education, law, media and communications, business and environmental practice, to name just a few, diligently develop their own courses, based on their own respective codes of ethics, and ensure that students have good grounding in the professional values of their discipline. What does not happen, however, or happens by default, is that teachers do not become familiar with what a social work code of ethics might dictate about privacy and confidentiality in relation to minors (relevant if a teacher and social worker are working together with a problematic family situation); an occupational therapist and a psychologist may not understand that they are on the same ground when working with a person with a disability around issues of capacity and consent; and a lawyer and a doctor may have different interpretations of the meaning of quality of life in respect of a patient they share. It could perhaps be argued that it is quite enough for us to know about our own disciplines, and that is quite sufficient, without there also being additional requirements to know too much about the disciplines of others. It is difficult to counter the argument, however, that also knowing the perspectives of others on points of ethical interest will give us a more rounded appreciation of the collaborative care environment into which vulnerable clients and service users step. For example, a nurse may not need to know how an occupational therapist measures up and arranges for bathroom aids to be installed into an older person's home to increase safety, but it may be worth knowing that the occupational therapist will have a commitment to duty of care in agreeing to send a frail person home where there is risk of a fall. While the nurse may need to clear a bed for another patient, the occupational therapist may request that the older person not be discharged until safety considerations have been addressed and family involved in any other decisions about the patient's ongoing care. The case for interprofessional ethics education has support from a logical perspective on this basis.

Professional education has traditionally taken place in disciplinary silos, and this continues to be the predominant model of training for the professions. Doctors train with doctors, psychologists with psychologists, and lawyers with lawyers. Allied health professions may at times study some courses together, for example physiotherapy, speech pathology and occupational therapy may all study anatomy and physiology together, but it would be rare for them to share courses in professional ethics. Journalists and business administration students may study marketing together, but not courses on professional conduct. It is curious that those issues that cause the greatest professional divides and differences of opinion, and which have capacity for causing greatest harm in terms of incompetence, professional negligence and misuse of power, are those that are neglected when it comes to IPE. The focus of this book is to bridge the divide by offering insight into the different worlds of disciplines that claim professional status in the helping and social care industries, and demonstrate the possibilities for collaborative learning that can come from gaining an appreciation of different value positions on some of the most controversial issues.

■ Ethical literacy: a prerequisite for professional practice

The concept of ethical literacy has steadily been gaining momentum in tertiary education and within practice across many of the professional disciplines. What this essentially means is that as practitioners, we need to have a sound working knowledge of the fundamental tenets of ethical decision-making so that our work can be grounded in ethical principles that are generally enshrined in the codes of ethics of professions. An ethically literate professional should have:

- a clear understanding of what constitutes professional integrity and appropriate conduct and behaviour consistent with socially acceptable standards
- a good knowledge of issues such as privacy, confidentiality, informed consent and capacity for consent
- clearly defined boundaries around practice that enable professional and personal congruence
- a willingness to have their practice scrutinised by others so that their justifications for decisions can be transparent and accountable.

A person who is ethically literate will also:

- have sound knowledge of ethical theory and be able to use this to provide justification for our actions and decisions
- seek wise counsel and use supervision and mentoring appropriately and in a timely manner
- be able to identify an ethical dilemma clearly and name the competing ethical principles, to enable their use in ethical decision-making
- be aware of cultural considerations, look for culturally discriminatory laws or policies and uphold respect for diversity and difference
- be very aware of their own value positions, acknowledge judgements and bias and seek to ensure that they do not impose their values on others
- keep ethics on their professional and personal agenda, and promote this to their colleagues.

A person who is not ethically literate, in contrast, may not:

- demonstrate sound judgement or firm boundaries in practice
- have good justifications for decisions
- be able to clearly relate actions to ethical foundations
- have a good awareness of ethical responsibilities as outlined in a respective code of ethics
- have sufficient knowledge of acceptable standards of conduct
- be prepared to take personal responsibility for decisions.

Practitioners with poor ethical literacy may also:

- attract complaints by colleagues or clients, leading to transient employment
- not be transparent in their practice
- not consult others when necessary
- become complacent with supervision
- generally not be overly concerned with ongoing professional development
- typically treat colleagues who raise ethical concerns with contempt or minimise important ethical issues in a workplace
- be blind to potential situations of ethical risk
- neglect to follow stipulated policies or procedures, giving preference to their own interpretations.

The risks of having an ethically illiterate team, or individuals within a team, in a workplace are high in terms of potential consequences for quality care of vulnerable people. If a group of people working together do not understand client rights, informed consent, implications of privacy and confidentiality, how to treat people with respect and encourage self-determination and autonomy, or if there are unclear boundaries around professional relationships, harm can be caused. Dysfunctional multidisciplinary teams can lead to impasses in decision-making, inconsistency in care plans, and poor outcomes for clients. Complaints are likely to be more common, tensions between staff higher and morale lower. Paying attention to how a team functions in terms of ethical literacy is an important job for managers and those in supervisory positions. The primary aim of this book is to ensure that ethical literacy is high on the agenda of all professional disciplines.

THROUGH THE EYES OF A PRACTITIONER

As operational management and professional management are increasingly separated in current health contexts, it is not unusual to be professionally responsible for a practitioner but not have line management responsibility for them. This can be difficult as professional management relies not only upon practitioners willingly engaging in the team or program goals but also upon their operational manager supporting these goals. So interprofessional working is like a good relationship. It takes time and effort to make it work well. It is vital to learn as much about all the different disciplines within the team, how they work, their ethical frameworks and other drivers. As a manager, I find that this knowledge allows me to scan the working relationships for potential issues as well as understanding points of difference when conflict happens. Most professions have one key goal: good patient care. It is just that achieving this may look different sometimes to different disciplines or even practitioners. That is why it is central to any good decision-making that the patient's voice is maintained in any decision-making as their rights and wishes should be either met or as closely supported as possible, despite or as well as health-care targets.

(Anne-Louise McCawley)

REFLECTION 1.5

Imagine that you are a member of an interprofessional team in a healthcare or human service setting. Read this scenario.

> You come into work one morning to find a number of members of your team engaged in heated debate in the tea-room about a patient who has just recovered from a heart attack, and who has asked one of the nurses to buy him a packet of cigarettes. One of the team is strongly advocating for patient autonomy, while others are adamant that the patient should be reprimanded about taking up a much-needed hospital bed while clearly having little regard for the consequences and health risks of continuing to smoke.

1 In the face of these opposing views, what would you be likely to do? For example, would you join the debate and take a position to argue through, or would you decline to offer your position for fear of alienating someone on the team? Would how you respond be influenced by whether you were a smoker or a non-smoker?
2 At this point, how would you describe your ability to work collaboratively with others and to respect their potentially different value positions?

■ Conclusion

This chapter has set the foundations for this book's exploration of the way we as professionals can work collaboratively together to provide optimal care for people in the social, health and human services. It is a premise of this book that we do not generally work in isolation from others, but even when we do, it is likely that clients and patients will be connected to other systems and services. IPE is a way of ensuring that you will enter the graduate workforce with an understanding that your colleagues may have different perspectives on some issues, and that common ground may need to be found in the interests of collaborative care. Working from a position of respect for others is important, allowing for preservation of unique discipline differences while maintaining a commitment to shared understandings. We propose that, while all disciplines cover many areas in their education, and while program structures have to canvass broad knowledge and skill development, there are appropriate spaces for interprofessional learning about ethical responsibilities and professional practice. The case has been made for ethical literacy to be high on your agenda as you move into the professional workforce.

The next chapter moves on to focus on moral philosophy and ethical theory. It is important that we learn to crawl before we walk, and this knowledge forms an important foundation for understanding how values are patterned, how social norms are constructed, and how cultural interpretations can influence our behaviours and decisions.

2

Moral philosophy and ethical theory: setting the foundations

■ Learning objectives

■ **TO EXPLORE** the history of moral philosophy and discuss its foundation in social, health and human service practice

....

■ **TO IDENTIFY** key ethical theories and explore how they inform social, health and human service practice

....

■ **TO ESTABLISH** connections between moral philosophy, ethical theory and interprofessional practice

....

■ **TO UNDERSTAND** the importance of knowing ourselves ethically in order to practice ethically

....

■ Introduction

THIS CHAPTER SETS out the history of development of moral philosophy and ethical theory and the contributions that these bodies of knowledge make to the professions. Western, Eastern, Indigenous and other philosophical traditions are explored, as are the main ethical theories, levels of ethical understanding, and concepts of relativism and absolutism. The starting point is to ask what relevance moral philosophy and ethical theory have for professional practice, and why we would spend time engaging with philosophy in this way. The answer is straightforward: it is about professions' need to understand the basis on which actions are taken and decisions made, and to provide justification for decisions made, in the interests of preserving integrity and accountability. It is also about understanding issues of structural power and oppression and the philosophical arguments that are used to support inequality, injustice and the unfair distribution of resources. A professional, or group of professionals acting in a collaborative way, should be able to have their individual and collective decisions placed under scrutiny by others. In order to stand up to this scrutiny, justifications need to be based on sound rationales. These rationales have been provided over many centuries by 'philosophers', who have given wisdom about ways to understand decision-making based on what have now been clustered into a vast array of ethical theories. As Socrates mused so long ago, 'The unexamined life is not worth living' (Johnson, 2011). This chapter provides the backdrop to the ethical issues that will be explored in detail in later chapters, and gives us a way to understand the positions that we, our colleagues and others might hold on particular issues.

Hugman (2005, p. 1) states that:

We can no more avoid facing moral issues than we can avoid breathing. It is impossible to think of human society without recognising the role that moral values and beliefs play in the way in which day-to-day life is conducted. Our ideas about what is good and what is right are woven into the fabric of thought and action so that, whether we are conscious of it or not, they affect our wishes and our choices.

(Reproduced with permission of Palgrave Macmillan)

Practising within the social, health and human services brings us into contact with people from diverse populations, experiencing the full spectrum of challenges and making decisions and choosing actions as a result of these challenges. As practitioners, we endeavour to walk alongside our clients as they struggle with life-changing events, attempting to guide, treat, advocate or intervene on their behalf. It is not possible to do this without being faced with questions about their experiences, the challenges they face and how we might feel and respond to them in these situations; and it is inevitable that at some point we will be confronted with some of life's 'bigger questions'. Why do we suffer? Why do we make the particular choices that we do when faced with suffering? Why do we have certain reactions to the suffering of others? How we respond to these questions depends on a variety of factors, such as early family of origin experiences, the worldviews we have (sometimes unconsciously) adopted as an adult, and our values and beliefs. Self-awareness is a critical part of professional development and a useful way to begin this journey is to gain a solid understanding of what others who have undertaken the road to self discovery have offered in terms of understanding morality.

Social, health and human service disciplines rest on a foundation that draws from the tradition and scholarship of moral philosophy. Understanding this foundation provides us with a way to navigate through challenges and to make difficult professional decisions. Practitioners need to grapple with challenging concepts such as why we as humans are the way we are and why we do the things we do. Why do some people limit the liberties of others? Why do some live selfless lives in service to others? Can people's behaviours change? Can values, beliefs and attitudes shift? This chapter enables an initial understanding of the importance of moral philosophy and ethical theory to the foundations of principled practice. Rather than delve into the highly complex literature about moral philosophy, the following sections will draw out some of the themes likely to be most useful for interprofessional practice.

■ Tracing the history of moral philosophy: influences on ethics education

Timelines of philosophy – defined as the study of the nature of existence, reality and knowledge – date back to the early classical Greek philosophers of 600 BCE. The earliest recorded philosopher was Thales, who believed that 'all was made of water', beginning a journey of discovery that saw well-known names such as Pythagoras, Socrates, Plato and Aristotle positing ideas about the pursuit and understanding of virtues and character, and setting up philosophy as a questioning discipline that encouraged dialogue and challenging discussion. The term 'Socratic dialogue' sometimes used in philosophical and ethics education, is a method of group decision-making relying on attainment of consensus on a philosophical question such as 'what is happiness?', or 'what is my responsibility to my community?' The emphasis is on questions rather than answers; slow exploration rather than rapid resolution; suspension of judgement rather than reliance on assumption; and listening to others rather than focusing on taking a standpoint. It is a collective rather than individualistic activity and the principles of Socratic dialogue are useful to bear in mind when thinking about ways to assist people from different disciplines to work together in the interprofessional space. In the teaching of medical ethics, for example, use of 'Socratic dialogue' techniques illustrates how educators/teachers work with students in a way that ensures that 'students are treated with empathy and respect, as this is the only way to foster students who will be empathetic and respectful' (Neitzke & Fehr, 2003, p. 93).

Following the classical philosophers were the 'Hellenistic philosophers' (300 BCE to 0 BCE) who were much more pessimistic than their predecessors and were largely concerned with how to live well in a world that was problematic and troubled. Four schools of thought emerged during this time: the Cynics (who rejected custom and convention); the Stoics (who believed that a good and virtuous life is one lived in accordance with nature and that a level of detachment from life will lead to a calmer and less turbulent experience); the Epicureans (who focused on pleasure and freedom from fear and the belief that it is human nature to seek out a pleasant life and that the most successful way to achieve this is to live a life of moderation); and the Skeptics (who believed that nothing can be known for certain).

The period following this was the era of Roman and Christian philosophy (up to 500 CE) where Seneca promoted the idea that human suffering was beneficial for the soul; Epictetus believed that humans are responsible for their own actions, but also have a duty to care for others; Plotinus espoused happiness as disconnected from material wealth and possessions; and Augustine developed the 'just war theory' (based on the idea of legitimate defence by force). These early Christian philosophers also pondered the role of religion and spirituality alongside the pursuit of truth. These philosophers explored ideas relating to justice, rights, divinity, morality and equality. During the rise of humanism and the period of renaissance (1300–1700 CE), thought focused on the power of reason and exploration of the influences of metaphysics (what composes the universe and what are the features of human nature?); on epistemology (what are the sources of knowledge?); and on ethics (by what measures do we judge human behaviour?). We can see that early modern philosophers such as René Descartes ('I think therefore I am') proposed rational thought and evidence as the foundation of problem-solving; Spinoza believed that all events are predetermined; and Thomas Hobbes, who was an absolutist, argued that the state is based on a social contract with members of society. The period of enlightenment (1600–1800 CE) saw philosophers such as David Hume, Adam Smith, John Locke and John Jacques Rousseau ('Man is born free, but is everywhere in chains') struggle with issues that were more political, such as the separation of powers and development of legal systems. Hume developed ideas about the need for an unequal distribution of property so that 'thrift and industry' could flourish, and Smith advocated for what would become known as free-market economics. One of the most influential philosophers of this time was Immanuel Kant, the German philosopher who formulated the categorical imperative known more commonly as 'do unto others as you would have them do unto you'. Kant's deontological philosophy is highly influential as a duty-based rational thought doctrine that essentially relies on people having 'goodwill' that motivates all actions.

The period of the industrial revolution (1750–1900 CE) saw the emergence of philosophers such as Jeremy Bentham, John Stuart Mill, Karl Marx and Friedrich Nietzsche. Utilitarian thought stands in opposition to Kantian ethics as it posits a 'greatest good for the greatest number' philosophy in which the primary considerations are what will generate the greatest happiness or pleasure over pain for the greatest number of people. The focus is therefore more on decisions made by weighing up consequences of actions than on the duty to perform actions because of goodwill or rationality. There were some differences between these influential philosophers: for example, Bentham and Mill were social reformists, while Marx was a social revolutionary dedicated to the destruction of oppressive capitalist societies.

Both Marx and Nietzsche were strong critics of Christianity, with Marx describing religion as 'the opiate of the masses' (Appiah, 1989; Scharfstein, 1998; Waller, 2005).

The extensive literature on modern philosophical thought that takes us up to the present day shows a complex interplay of ideas, hypotheses and absolutist or relativist debates, linked back to the philosophical commentaries of earlier times. John-Paul Sartre ('Man is nothing else but that which he makes of himself'), the French existentialist, argued for the primacy of choice, freedom and responsibility, and was sympathetic to communism and Marxist ideas. Michel Foucault, also a structuralist thinker on the radical left, contributed to understandings of cultural constructs, power and postmodern influences. Jacques Derrida, the father of 'deconstruction', was strongly political, positioning himself against apartheid, war, and the death penalty. Bertrand Russell, a British analytical philosopher, advocated for the scientific method and empirical evidence and was also a staunch atheist and pacifist ('War does not determine who is right – only who is left'). John Rawls was instrumental in putting forth a theory of justice, advocating for duties of civility, and positioning justice as fairness. Peter Singer, an Australian moral philosopher, has written extensively on animal welfare and liberation, and has adopted a controversial utilitarian perspective on many issues, such as world poverty, abortion, euthanasia, infanticide and surrogacy (LaFollette, 1997; Minch & Weigel, 2009).

A review of the literature and a scan of websites on the topic of classical through to contemporary moral philosophy and ethical theory clearly reveal that the voices of women have been silenced through history. Despite this, there have been women who have made invaluable contributions to philosophical thought and paved the way for many of the later developments in the feminist ethic of care literature. The wife of Pythagoras, Theano of Croton, is quoted as saying, 'Better to be on a runaway horse than to be a woman who does not reflect'; Mary Wollstonecraft, Hannah Arendt and Simone de Beauvoir (the partner of Sartre) challenged the social structures of inequality for women in work and education; and Jane Addams was a founder of social work. All of these women critiqued patriarchal systems and provided an alternate voice on social arrangements (Chenoweth & McAuliffe, 2014). Highly influential women in contemporary philosophy, such as Virginia Held, Joan Tronto, Alison Jagger, Carol Gilligan, Nel Noddings, Margaret Urban Walker, Martha Nussbaum, Rosalind Hursthouse and Nancy Snow, have contributed to the growing body of work on feminist ethics, virtue ethics, relational ethics and moral psychology. As with the male philosophers previously discussed, these women do not share common positions on issues of ethics or philosophy; they have been engaged in critical debates with philosophers of both genders; and they defend their positions with reference to philosophers from the classical, renaissance and industrial revolution periods. Some of the greatest and most thought-provoking debates of history have been those waged in the theatres of philosophy (Minch & Weigel, 2009).

■ Western philosophies

From looking back on the historical development of predominantly Western moral philosophy and ethical theory, we can clearly trace the arguments and counterarguments for rationality, logic, relativism, aesthetics, illusion, nature versus nurture, cultural socialisation and construction, power relations, and a critique of the social structures of class, race and gender. Notions of freedom and free will, character and virtues, determinism and justice are all concepts that we struggle with in contemporary workplaces as we engage with people and systems of service delivery, education and health care.

Beauchamp and Childress (1979) developed what has become known as the 'four principles approach' to bioethics, which has been extended to broader social and human services. These four principles have their roots in moral philosophy and are extensively cited in the medical, nursing and other health literature. The principles are:

- respect for autonomy – people are self-governing and have freedom from control of others
- non-maleficence – the obligation not to inflict intentional harm on others
- beneficence – the duty to do good and contribute to the welfare of others
- justice – the obligation to provide fair, equitable and appropriate treatment, in accordance with what people are due or owed.

In addition to these ethical principles, Beauchamp and Childress (1979) outline a set of ethical 'rules' designed to guide actions. These rules are categorised as 'substantive rules' such as confidentiality, privacy and fidelity; 'authority rules' that determine who should be responsible for actions; and 'procedural rules' that set a process for action. A corresponding set of virtues attach to rules: for example, 'truthfulness' corresponds to veracity, and 'faithfulness' to fidelity. These ethical principles and rules are clearly located in individualistic Western philosophical worldviews, which is why it is important to also explore alternate worldviews that will provide a more balanced understanding of moral philosophy. In the next sections, we will explore Eastern, Indigenous and global philosophical traditions.

■ Eastern philosophical traditions

In our multicultural world, sensitivity to cultural worldviews and beliefs is an important part of professional practice. Western moral philosophy is the dominant theme in literature in most ethics courses in Australia, yet many of the traditional values of Eastern philosophies are highly congruent with caring professions. Eastern philosophy is a much older tradition than Western philosophy, with key influences from China, India and Japan. It is based on a range of influential individuals, philosophical systems and 'religions'. As Hawley (2007, p. 132) points out, there are two main differences between Western and Eastern philosophies: 'The lack of distinction between philosophy and religion in the Eastern tradition compared with the separateness of philosophy and religion in the Western tradition; and the perception of God and gods'.

There is much crossover between Western and Eastern traditions, but also key areas of difference. Ethical concepts in the Western tradition are founded on goodwill, duty and individual excellence, whereas the Eastern tradition is focused on compassion, increasing individual awareness or insight and acting for the collective (Suzuki, 1959).

The core Eastern philosophical principles are:

- harmony (fitting well together), cooperation, goodwill and unity
- respect – politeness, kind regard and modesty
- hospitality – consideration, welcoming and sharing
- balance – equilibrium and protection of the environment.

The key objective underlying Eastern philosophical perspectives is to understand how our experiences, ideas and thoughts arise in conscious experience (Billington, 1997). To do this, Eastern philosophies demonstrate a cyclical rather than linear pattern of growth and understanding. Individual insight is attained through ethical behaviour and as insight grows, ethical behaviour leads to greater insight. In this way, individuals' understanding of themselves and the world has a direct impact on their ability to behave ethically, and the more ethical their behaviour, the more they learn about themselves. The cycle is repeated endlessly as individuals gain more and more insight. Acting unethically therefore results not only in affecting others negatively, but also has an impact on your own path to awareness. This puts individuals in an interdependent relationship with others and recognises that causing harm affects not only others, but also the individual who acts harmfully.

■ Hindu philosophy

The Hindu philosophical canon contains a complex and diverse set of ideas, schools and traditions based in India and Nepal. Common themes in Hindu moral philosophy include karma and liberation theories, the goal of freedom from rebirth, dharma theories and stages of life theories. Ethical concepts are founded on duty and virtue (Bernard, 1947). There are four aims of human life:

1 Material wellbeing
2 Pleasure and enjoyment
3 Morality and social responsibility
4 Liberation from repeated rebirth.

(Bernard, 1947)

One of the most influential contemporary Hindu philosophers was Mohandas Gandhi. His ideas on non-violent struggle (*ahimsa*), justice, harmony and the pursuit of truth have made a significant contribution to work within the health and human service fields in Eastern and Western countries alike (Ray, 1950). Gandhi spoke of the need to love your opponent and to see them not as your enemy, but as a fellow human being, stuck in the cycle of rebirth and delusion. He believed that extending kindness to them in the face of violence would help them to see the 'truth' of their behaviour and thus provide them with a chance to understand 'reality' and 'truth' (Streng, 1973). This would enable them to grow and develop as human beings. Gandhian ideas of ethical behaviour are therefore centred on extending compassion and wellbeing for the benefit of the collective human race. In the process, individual wellbeing is also achieved.

■ Ethics in Buddhist philosophy

Ethical ideas within the Buddhist canon hold many similarities with Hindu philosophical views, but are based on a non-religious applied system of strategies to develop psychological insights. It is a requirement for these insights to be used for compassionate, ethical action (Keown, 2005). Laypeople abide by five key precepts in order to develop insight and lead an ethical life:
1 Avoid killing (and promote life)
2 Avoid stealing (and practice generosity)
3 Avoid sexual misconduct (and promote love)
4 Avoid negative speech (and use your words for kindness)
5 Avoid intoxicants (and promote positive good).

(Hanh, 1998)

A foundational training with the Buddhist system is the 'Eightfold Path', which sets out eight behaviours to adhere to in order to reach insight. Four elements of the Eightfold Path are specifically related to ethical behaviour:
1 Skilful thought
2 Skilful speech
3 Skilful action
4 Skilful livelihood.

The most influential person associated with Buddhist philosophy is of course the historical Buddha, Siddhartha Gautama. Through his own reflective process of meditation, the Buddha developed a systematic method of mind training, with the ultimate goal of reaching enlightenment. A major component of this is the teaching that ethical behaviour assists the individual to reduce their suffering. Further, ethical behaviour towards others, based on the compassionate knowledge that all human beings suffer, fosters communal growth and acknowledges the 'inter-being' of all life (Dalai Lama, 2011).

■ Ethics in Chinese philosophy

Ethical teaching from within Chinese philosophy is based in the idea of harmony between the natural world and all organisms in it – including people. Taoism ('the way') concerns the interplay between opposites (yin and yang, male and female, negative and positive). The three 'jewels of the Tao' described in the foundation document the *Tao Te Ching* are compassion, moderation and humility. Key importance is placed on courtesy, ritual, ideal standards, reverence, generosity and benevolence (Carus, 2009). Chinese philosophy identifies the following ethical requirements:

> Seek constant adjustment in order to align human behaviour with natural rhythms.
> Relationship obligations guide behaviour between husband and wife, parents and children, ruler and subject.
> Fulfilling these obligations leads to a just and harmonious society.

> (Yu, 2007)

The most influential Chinese philosophy is that of Confucian ethics, which holds to three main principles:

1 *Li* – ideal of conduct (reverence, courtesy, ritual, propriety)
2 *Jen* – virtue of goodness and benevolence (concern for others regardless of class or rank)
3 *Chun-Tzu* – idea of the true 'gentleman' (displays the five virtues of self-respect, generosity, sincerity, persistence and benevolence).

> (Shun & Vong, 2004)

■ Middle Eastern philosophy

Persian, Babylonian, Arabic and Jewish philosophies fall into the category of Middle Eastern philosophies, and all are strongly linked to religious persuasions. There is much contested territory within these philosophies, and Lovat (2010), for example, sets out some of these issues in discussion of engagement with Muslim individuals and communities, within a context of struggle. As he says:

as each post-9/11 day passes, for those who understand the true beauty and positive contribution of Islam to civilising cultures, the sight of its essentially altruistic spirit and ethos of care being colonised by a culture that includes fanaticism and violence constitutes a sad truth.

(Lovat, 2010, p. 186)

The 'five pillars of Islam', which guide the life of a Muslim, are:

- *Shahadah* – recital of the basic statement of Islamic faith
- *Salat* – performing prayer rituals five times a day
- *Zakat* – paying money to aid the poor
- *Sawm* – fasting during the month of Ramadan
- *Hajj* – pilgrimage to the Mecca.

Islam contains a complete moral system that defines a universal standard of morality and ethics. Within this system, actions can be defined as moral or immoral. Central to defining ethical behaviour is *Al `Amal Assalih* (virtuous deeds). The Qur'an outlines that virtuous deeds include character traits such as piety, humility and accountability to God. With regards to ethical behaviour, patience, charity, gratitude and courage are considered foundational to both individual morality and contributing to the moral health of society (Ali, 1998). To lead an ethical life, Islam teaches that an individual must undertake a process of purification, exercising moral behaviours in much the same way as one exercises the body for fitness (Rafiee, 2004).

■ Ethics in Judaism

Morality and ethical behaviour in Judaism are defined by God in the primary texts of Judaism, the Torah and Talmud. In these texts, God sets out a moral law for all humanity. Many of the ethical requirements that Christians follow originated in the Torah, outlined in the 10 Commandments:

1 I am the Lord thy god, who brought thee out of the land of Egypt, out of the house of bondage.
2 Thou shalt have no other gods before Me.
3 Thou shalt not take the name of the Lord thy God in vain.
4 Remember the Sabbath day to keep it holy.
5 Honor thy father and thy mother.
6 Thou shalt not murder.
7 Thou shalt not commit adultery.
8 Thou shalt not steal.

9 Thou shalt not bear false witness against thy neighbor.

10 Thou shalt not covet anything that belongs to thy neighbor.

(Sicker, 2008)

Judaism also sets out a range of ethical behaviours relating to social justice, with commands to take action to ensure that equity and fairness for all are considered (Sherwin, 2000).

In determining what actions are ethical, Judaism holds that the human mind alone is not equipped to decide on the right path. The word of God and religious literature must also be explored to determine the moral course of action. This process differs from secular ethical decision-making, in that it moves beyond a reliance on the human mind, to include a system of 'checks and balances' by considering what the Jewish Canon has to contribute on a matter (Sherwin, 2000).

THROUGH THE EYES OF A PRACTITIONER

When I was a student studying ethics as part of my Social Work degree, I can remember wondering what other cultural traditions might have to contribute to my learning. I noticed that only Western ethical traditions were represented in the material we studied and, as someone with an interest in Buddhism, I noticed the differences between what I was learning about at university and my own philosophical leanings towards an Eastern approach. Western philosophy provided me with a solid foundation but it seemed very strongly associated with the individual and external growth or outward good deeds. I thought the lack of information on non-Western philosophies was a serious omission in our ethics training, especially when many of the future clients we may be working with will be from non-Western traditions.

I decided to explore the issue of how other worldviews and philosophical traditions understood ethics and I've made this an area of learning in my life. This has proved very beneficial as I have had many clients from non-Western traditions and having at least a basic understanding of what ethics might mean from within their cultures has enabled me to work with them more closely. In particular, I had a lot of clients from India and I believe my knowledge of the key differences between Western and Eastern philosophical worldviews made me a better social worker for these clients.

I'm now in the very fortunate position of teaching ethics to undergraduate and postgraduate social work students and I've been able to contribute some of this knowledge on Eastern philosophical systems to their courses. Every time we cover the material, I've had at least one student come up to me and share how valuable they felt it was to learn about philosophical traditions outside of their own. I've also had many students from Eastern backgrounds tell me how wonderful it was to see their own traditions included. As an educator, I've also benefited from greater understanding of the backgrounds of my students. For example, when working through ethical dilemmas, students from Eastern, African or Indigenous traditions might include a focus on the best outcome for the client's family and community when working through a dilemma. If there are issues pertaining to confidentiality, students from non-Western traditions sometimes demonstrate the belief that the client's family has a right to know certain information or that a client has a duty to their family to share this information. This of course isn't always the case but it's been important for me to learn that the lens that we view ethical issues through can be different depending on our traditions. I plan to expand my search to include learning about Islamic and African philosophical traditions, as I can see that this knowledge also needs to be included in ethics education.

I believe that one of the great benefits of globalisation has been the growth in opportunity to learn from all of the world's traditions. I think this can only enrich our experiences as learners, practitioners and global citizens.

(Lyndal Greenslade)

Although it is helpful to learn about the ethical requirements of different religions, it is important to remember that individuals can rarely be categorised neatly under one umbrella. People might identify with a particular religion, but interpret the teachings of that religion differently. Others might broadly follow a religion more as a cultural heritage than as a practiced set of behaviours. As a social, health or human service practitioner, you might find yourself with the need to learn more about a particular religion if you have clients from that tradition. Keeping an open mind and a willingness to learn more about a client's ethical views and where they come from is essential if you are to practice ethically yourself.

■ Indigenous worldviews

The inclusion of Indigenous worldviews in philosophical and ethics literature is very recent and discussion of these concepts rarely takes a place in ethics education beyond an often tokenistic inclusion of case examples. Indigenous scholarship, according to Coates (2013), has historically been constrained and discouraged. Indigenous worldviews provide a rich tapestry of interrelated concepts, incorporating 'respectful individualism', 'communalism' and 'spirituality' and bringing together ideas of wholeness, harmony, balance, nurturing, growth and healing. The concept of 'mino-pimatisiwin' refers to 'the good life' – an Aboriginal approach to helping that brings together individual, family and community (Hart in Gray, Coates & Yellow Bird, 2008).

Leanne Simpson, as cited in an article by Hart (2010), has outlined seven principles of Indigenous worldviews. Hart (2010, p. 3) quotes Simpson as follows:

> First, knowledge is holistic, cyclic, and dependent upon relationships and connections to living and non-living beings and entities. Second, there are many truths and these truths are dependent upon individual experiences. Third, everything is alive.

Fourth, all things are equal. Fifth, the land is sacred. Sixth, the relationship between people and the spiritual world is important. Seventh, human beings are least important in the world.

To extend these principles further, Baskin (2007) refers to the importance of relatedness and reciprocity in Aboriginal ethics, and explains how some of the tenets of Western ethics, such as the construction of boundaries to distance relationships, can be highly problematic in this context because of the intrinsic connection between the helper and individual, family or community. Fejo-King (in How Kee, Martin & Ow, 2014), who speaks of the importance of connectivity, kinship systems and the passing down of knowledge through generations, explains how the dominant Western worldview relegates Indigenous worldviews to lesser status, creating a negative impact on the way that services are delivered to Aboriginal and Torres Strait Islander peoples. It is therefore important that Indigenous worldviews take their place in interprofessional education (IPE) so that practitioners who work with Indigenous peoples and communities can have a more informed understanding of differences in approaches and perspectives.

■ Ethical codes within non-geographical groups

In addition to philosophical traditions located by geographical groupings or religions, the rise in flows of communication across borders has enhanced the growth of other groups that contribute philosophical ideas that contain ethical components. For example, the 'New Age' movement is a collection of Eastern-influenced metaphysical thought systems that emerged during the 1970s, concerned with the pursuit of harmony and enlightenment. The movement's focus on personal growth has contributed to the publication of many 'self-help' guides on how to live an ethical life. Borrowing from Eastern philosophical systems, many in the New Age movement believe in karma – the idea that your thoughts and actions have a direct effect on your experience in this life and the next. As a result, New Age moral principles stress the ideals of love, holism and self-improvement as the best means of ensuring positive karma. A key concept in New Age ethics is self-spirituality and 'getting in touch with this "spiritual self" is a moral imperative in the New Age milieu since it is the only avenue towards spiritual growth, the good life, and basically, salvation from modern alienation' (Houtman & Aupers, 2010, p. 211).

Ethical codes are also seen in groups that share common ideologies. For example, vegans hold the belief that it is unethical to consume or use an animal for any purpose. This may include receiving medications or vaccinations that contain animal products. Considering this information may help a doctor or other health professional to better understand the choices that a vegan patient may make. Environmentalists believe that polluting the water and air is unethical and as a result seek to reduce actions that contribute to the destruction of the natural world.

With the growth of online technologies and social networking, it can be expected that philosophical ideas that were once separate and isolated may be given the opportunity to grow and develop into significant contributors to the ongoing development of philosophy and the discussion on what it means to act ethically.

REFLECTION 2.2
1 What do you think are the major points of difference between Western, Eastern and Indigenous worldviews and philosophies?
2 How might different foundations of moral philosophy cause conflict in practice contexts with clients from non-Western backgrounds?

■ Towards a global ethics

Traditions from the East (including Middle East) have been mixing and influencing Western traditions increasingly since the 1970s and, as a result, have arguably influenced the growth of the newer ethical theories, such as virtue ethics and ethic of care. In addition, unfamiliar ideas from Eastern philosophies are beginning to influence the West and this can be seen in the growth of new interventions such as mindfulness therapy, which emerged from the Buddhist tradition. Western science has been used to explore physiology and positive effects of meditation and this has led to a growth in knowledge in the fields of neuroscience and psychology. There is a growing belief that ethical behaviour can be a central factor in building more peaceful human relationships around the globe and that drawing on the commonalities between all humans can foster a collective ethical project of compassionate action.

For social, health and human service practitioners, knowledge of non-Western traditions allows us to draw from a wider source of wisdom to better understand what is meant by ethical behaviour, what our ethical obligations might be, what the impact of our own behaviour may be on us both professionally and personally, and how the client's tradition may impact on their worldview.

THROUGH THE EYES OF A PRACTITIONER

The diversity that characterises minority groups in Australia can be enriching and daunting for practitioners, and it can be confusing to know what the 'right' approach is with service users from backgrounds that are relatively unfamiliar. What has helped me to work in this dynamic field is the understanding that it is not about being condescending or knowing absolutely everything there is to know about someone's background. Anyone who identifies as being part of a minority group outside the normative white, middle or upper class, urban, English-speaking, Christian, middle-aged, heterosexual, healthy, male standards carries a unique set of intersecting identities. So the 'right' approach is about being respectful and acknowledging multiple realities, and learning enough about someone before making significant decisions that will affect their circumstances.

As practitioners come across people with vastly different worldviews and cultural norms – among service users, colleagues and students on placement – a culturally safe approach becomes important because it acknowledges unique explanatory frameworks. Cultural safety is about an environment in which there is mutual respect, openness and willingness to listen, and shared understanding. It has helped me a lot to embrace this approach and try to understand each person's story, their narrative about their issues, and their hopes for the future, to allow him or her to feel safe within the relationship. Since a culturally safe approach shifts the attention back on how the other person experiences the relationship, I am more likely to work in a way that will lead to positive outcomes for us both.

(Caroline Lenette)

■ Exploring ethical theories

The literature on moral philosophy and ethical theory can be challenging to grasp as it attempts to contemplate questions that have no solid certainties.

Chenoweth and McAuliffe (2014, p. 63) state that:

> Ethical theory is a way of applying moral philosophy to contemporary situations. There is a broad range of perspectives on human nature and the relationship between individual freedoms and the role of the state, the law and public good ... Theories offer us many ways of viewing the world; ethical theory gives us ways of articulating decisions that have a moral or value base to them.

Moral philosophy and ethics have their own language and, to complicate matters, not everyone agrees on the definitions of key terms. It is helpful to read through a number of different definitions and decide which ones provide the most clarity. Preston (2007, p. 16) provides one such definition of ethics: 'In general, ethics is concerned about what is right, fair, just and good, about what we ought to do, and not just about what is the case or what is most acceptable or expedient.' He goes on to define values as: 'those principles or attitudes to which we attribute worth. They become for us guidelines with moral significance.' McAuliffe (2010, p. 42) argues that the moral realm involves anything to do with 'questions about rights, duties, responsibilities and obligations'. The terms 'moralist' and 'ethicist' are also referred to in literature. The difference between the two is that a moralist is concerned with behaviour and offers guidance on what is right, whilst an ethicist is concerned with the underlying assumptions and principles of what is considered right and wrong.

In addition to these terms, it is useful to have an understanding of the three levels into which ethics is sometimes divided. Metaethics is a concern with broad philosophical concepts and whether these truly exist. For example, when we ponder the 'big questions', such as truth, duty and morality, we are thinking at the metaethical level. Normative ethics is concerned with application of moral concepts to daily problems, such as using a theory or idea to help us to make a practical decision. Applied ethics refers to particular areas of interest, such as environment issues, animal rights or euthanasia. It is likely that we will deal with ethics on all three levels in much of our practice. Take, for example, the situation of a person who is homeless. At the metaethical level, we might ask questions about poverty and why it is that a planet so rich in resources cannot ensure that all people have safe, secure and affordable housing. Normative ethics might focus more explicitly on the dilemmas of housing, tenure, stock and eligibility for subsidised housing. Applied ethics would focus on homelessness as a social problem, and might also ask questions about whether people have the right to choose to be homeless.

In addition to these three levels of ethics, the terms 'relativism' and 'absolutism' are key concepts in most ethics literature. Ethical relativism denies the existence of absolute moral standards, rejects fixed moral rules, and sees ethical decisions justified on the basis of context and consequences. Ethical absolutism holds that moral standards are universal and objective and that ethical rules can be formulated and held under all circumstances. These two ways of looking at ethical issues become very important for contemporary social, health and human service workers who practise in a global context, where the actions of different cultures may be very different. For example, a nurse who works with refugee families may be confronted by a situation where a daughter has undergone female genital cutting. From a perspective of ethical relativism, it may be possible to argue that there is no firm rule that this practice is wrong as it is part of an ancient cultural tradition that is complex and intrinsically linked to roles and identities within that culture. However, an absolutist perspective would hold that female genital cutting is always wrong and that it is inappropriate to make allowances for the practice due to cultural considerations.

Understanding key ethical theories provides us with the knowledge to begin to locate ideas and issues within their ethical 'home'. Being able to do so provides a way to unpack complex ethical issues and dilemmas so that we can better navigate through them (Reamer, 1993). Once we have knowledge of ethical theory, we are more able to identify and critically reflect on competing ethical viewpoints. Having a clear understanding of the many ways that people make decisions also helps to clarify justifications when people rely on following rules, weighing up consequences, considering relationship and context, and focusing on the public good. This will become clear when exploring ethical decision-making processes in Chapter 5.

Working out how to write a chapter or book on ethical theory that will not completely overwhelm students with the complexity of moral philosophy is no easy task. There is a tendency in the human service literature towards keeping the educational aims straightforward, as seen in the social work ethics text by Bowles et al. (2006), which sets out a clear framework of virtue-based ethics, deontological or duty-based ethics, and consequentialism. A very useful construct for categorising the approaches to ethics is provided by Banks and Nohr (2012), who clearly set out the main ethical theories, theoretical approaches and methodologies as follows:

1   Principle-based ethics include 'Kantian' principles and 'utilitarian' principles.
2   Character and relationship-based ethics include virtue ethics; ethic of care; and communitarian ethics.
3   Narrative and case-based ethics include narrative ethics and casuistry.

Dickens (2013) follows suit and sets out four ethical approaches in a table that includes:

1   Kantian (duty)
2   utilitarian (utility)
3   virtue (character)
4   care (relationships).

We will focus here on some of the more commonly explained ethical theories, in the knowledge, however, that there are many more that could be explored if this were a full text on moral philosophy.

Deontology (duty-based Kantian ethics or non-consequentialism)

Deontological theory, also known as 'non-consequentialism', establishes that the rightness or wrongness of an action depends on duty and is based on the premise (as espoused by Kant) that humans are rational with capacity for reason. Categorical imperatives are unconditional universal commands, such as 'thou shall not kill' or 'do not lie'. The Golden Rule, 'do unto others as you would have them do unto you', highlights reciprocity, and the principle of respect for persons is summed up in the maxim 'act so that you treat humanity, whether in your own person or in that of another, always as an end and never as a means only' (Preston, 2007, p. 31). A deontological position can be demonstrated if we have a firm belief in a rule that can never be broken, such as 'pregnancy termination is always wrong', or 'children have a duty to obey their parents'. As a social, health or human service practitioner, holding deontological views can prove both useful and challenging, depending on which of these views our society supports. For example, if you work in the field of child protection and believe that there is an unbreakable rule that children should never be physically or emotionally abused, then this should not prove too problematic as our society endorses this view. However, if you work in the same field and believe that parents who are drug users should forfeit the right to raising their own children, this might prove problematic as this view is not necessarily endorsed by current thinking or shared by all who work in child protection. Deontology is critiqued for an over-reliance on rationality, and the difficulty of resolving dilemmas between absolute moral rules when context does become an important factor.

Utilitarianism (teleological theory or consequentialism)

Utilitarianism is home to the phrase 'the greatest good for the greatest number' and is a theory often used in the political realm to justify decisions on the basis of the common good. One of its problems, however, is that such rationales often neglect the interests of the more marginalised and vulnerable members of the community – those who do not have a strong voice. Going back to the previous example, if a policy was developed that dictated that the newborn baby of a mother who has a substance misuse problem should be automatically removed from her care, this could be justified on the grounds of economics and therefore overall benefit to the community who do not have to foot a bill for ongoing child protection interventions, efforts at family support, or potential treatment for the child down the track. This justification and focus on the societal implications does not take the position of the child into account, or that of the child's parents for that matter, in considering 'greater good'. Consequences for the child might be identified as physical and emotional safety, improved opportunities for health and wellbeing and psychological stability. Alternately, those arguing a counter-position (that newborns should not be automatically removed) might rely on evidence about attachment, parental and sibling bonds, and mental health impacts for parents whose child is removed from their care at birth.

Utilitarianism aims to minimise pain and maximise pleasure. It relies on a weighing up of alternatives and exploration of what should happen for an individual to determine his or her own path. There are strong connections to liberalism, yet the claim is that 'utilitarianism can justify the violation of human rights' (Preston, 2007, p. 38). Within this theory sits 'act utilitarianism', which weighs the consequences of actions, and 'rule utilitarianism', which nominates rules or a hierarchy for considering options. Most laws are examples of rule utilitarianism; for example, we might say that stealing from people will result in a society where there is more mistrust and unhappiness, and therefore rule that stealing is against the law. Act utilitarianism relates more to individual actions; so, if a person does not break into a house and steal from another person, he or she will prevent unhappiness for that person's family and children.

Virtue ethics

This ethical theory originated with the work of Plato and Aristotle and concerns the central question 'What is the good life?' This includes exploring what actions may contribute to making us better people and whether our decisions can be justified in terms of virtues such as loyalty, compassion and honesty. This theory is also particularly useful for social, health and human service professionals, who are often motivated by the desire to make compassionate and virtuous choices and to undertake a journey of self-betterment. For example, when asked why they undertook covert actions at the risk of losing their jobs, participants in Greenslade's (2013) study responded that 'it was the right thing to do' and 'it's who I am'. Virtue ethics has been critiqued for focusing on character rather than action but, despite this, its implications for professional practice are clear when we consider the question of what qualities we might want to see in our colleagues and managers, and what attributes of character we might want to develop for ourselves.

Ethic of care

This theory stems from the feminist perspective and focuses on social relationships rather than abstract rules. It was developed in the 1970s and 1980s as a means of questioning some of the underlying assumptions in existing ethical theories. An ethic of care asks 'What does a caring response require in this situation?' Like virtue ethics, it focuses on compassion, kindness and love. A clear definition of the ethic of care is provided by Featherstone (2010, p. 73): 'While consequentialist and deontological theories emphasize universal standards of impartiality, the ethic of care emphasizes the importance of relationships, and, particularly, the interdependence between individuals in achieving mutually beneficial outcomes.' For example, going back to the earlier example of a hospital's newborn policy, a social worker employed in a hospital may be faced with an ethical dilemma about whether or not to uphold the policy if a baby's mother divulges her intermittent drug use to the social worker in confidence. An ethic of care response would consider the relationships and connections between the mother and child, extended family and siblings, and potential ongoing relationships with service providers and healthcare staff. A response coming from this perspective would acknowledge issues of gender and power, and would bring to awareness the political impetus for devising a policy that is more focused on curtailing future child protection costs than supporting family relationships.

Communitarianism

Finally, communitarianism sees an emphasis on the community or the public good and holds that individuality only makes sense in the context of community. This ethical theory is particularly useful when working with non-Western cultural groups who may believe that decisions necessarily involve the whole family or community. In looking at the example we have been following, a communitarian response might be to engage a broader kinship or extended family and community in a supportive way with a focus on developing communities that are free from substance misuse and have strong, stable parenting practices. The focus would therefore be at the level of the community, not necessarily at the level of the individual or family unit except as this is part of community.

■ Ethical pluralism

When considering which ethical theory best explains a decision we might need to make, or one made by others, we might find that no single theory perfectly explains the actions undertaken. Ethical or moral pluralism is the belief that there are multiple perspectives on an issue, each of which contains part of the truth but none of which contains the whole truth (Hinman, 2008). This theory is highly compatible with postmodern perspectives. In the interprofessional context, ethical pluralism provides a space for asking questions about how we work together when there are possible competing value positions. Hugman (2013) presents a way of thinking about pluralist practice that focuses on four key ideas. The first is *clarity*, which is the attention given to ethics as a professional skill and the awareness of what constitutes good practice. The second is *persistence*, which is the acknowledgement that working with values takes time and that there is often a need for developmental space. The third is *humility*, which is the understanding that other points of view exist and that various positions are not 'wrong' because they differ. The final key idea is *reflexivity*, described as 'the capacity to reflect on one's own contribution to shaping ethical considerations; listening to others while maintaining a sense of one's own ethical self' (Hugman, 2013, p. 89).

REFLECTION 2.3

1. What new terms have you encountered so far in this chapter? You might find it helpful to create a glossary that lists these new terms. You can add to the glossary as your knowledge increases.
2. Which ethical theories are you initially drawn to? Can you identify the concepts and themes within the theory that resonate with you? Why do you think this might be?
3. Which ethical theories do you find challenging? Can you identify the concepts and themes within the theory that you struggle with? Why do you think this might be?

■ Knowing oneself ethically

The values that we hold dear develop over time as we make contact with a variety of people, ideas and experiences. Our parents, culture, spiritual traditions, life events, the books we read and movies we watch all contribute to helping define our value base. As we think back to the values we held as children and compare them to the values we hold now, we will no doubt find that some of them have stayed the same and some may be very different. This highlights the fact that our values change as we do. Understanding that values change over time allows us to appreciate that even people with a very different value base to us may not hold those values forever – and values that we believe define us may seem less of a priority further down the track.

REFLECTION 2.4
Reflect on your values and beliefs, and consider these questions.
1 What or who has influenced your moral development?
2 Can you identify those who hold different moral views from your own? Who are these people and what relationship do you have with them? It may help to think about figures in public life who take particular stances on social issues – these often become political.
3 Are your values dynamic or static? Why do you think this?
4 Do your values change depending on the situation? Think of a scenario from your life or work when you thought your value position was firm but it changed when confronted by a situation.
5 What 'value messages' govern your life now? How have these messages changed over time?

■ Why it matters

Work in the social, health and human services requires that practitioners attempt to approach their practice in a non-judgmental way. After working our way through this chapter, we should be able to see that it is impossible to be 'value-free'. If we are to live up to the requirement of non-judgemental practice, then the starting point is to identify and understand our own value judgements, so that we can be aware of how they might potentially impact on our practice (Corey, Corey & Callanan, 2007). We may find that when we work with individuals who share common values, the process feels easier and the fit more natural, and conversely that when we work with those who hold very different values, we are less comfortable. As you continue to work on identifying your value base, list the values or attributes that you would ascribe first to someone you consider to be good or worthy and then to someone you consider not to have a good moral character.

■ Conclusion

This chapter has identified some of the primary moral philosophies that serve as a foundation for work in the social, health and human services. Understanding moral philosophy and the ethical theories that provide justifications for action is important if we are to delve deeply into our own beliefs and the actions that they inform. Work in the social, health and human services inevitably involves confronting complex situations, and we will need to make decisions that have an ethical dimension. It is therefore essential that we develop a good knowledge of ethical theory, as this will help us to explain our actions and consider possible motivations for the actions of others. Using this knowledge to develop an intimate view of who you are and how your values and beliefs impact on your work is the cornerstone of solid ethical practice.

The next chapter extends the exploration of key principles to explore social justice and human rights approaches, and sets out a discussion of resource allocation and the activist endeavours that attempt to uphold these principles. The content we have explored in this chapter provides a foundation for what follows in the book, as we refer to ethical theories and ethical principles throughout the rest of the text.

3

Ethical activism: exploring human rights and social justice in the interprofessional space

■ Learning objectives

- **TO DEFINE** rights-based frameworks and explore the history of a human rights–based approach
- **TO IDENTIFY** how a human rights–based approach can be implemented in interprofessional practice
- **TO EXPLORE** activism in practice, identifying traditional and new forms of taking action against injustices
- **TO IDENTIFY** ethical issues relating to resource allocation and explore navigating these issues in practice

■ Introduction

WE HAVE ESTABLISHED in the first two chapters of this book that much of the work that we do as professionals in the social, health and human services has a distinctly moral dimension, clearly founded upon the acknowledgement that we work in a space defined by duties, obligations, responsibilities and rights. We have seen the importance of understanding principles that are universal about respecting people and doing no harm, as well as the more contested principles such as upholding autonomy, cultural relativism, privacy and justice. The growth of what are known as 'rights-based frameworks' has been a natural progression over time, and the dual concepts of human rights and social justice have been the subject of many excellent books. Any text on interprofessional or applied ethics would be neglecting an important body of knowledge were human rights to be omitted as a core conceptual perspective. As Connolly and Ward (2008, p. 17) state: 'The concept of human rights provides a way of reaching across the deep divisions of country, ethnicity, gender, class and conduct in a search for what is common to all people of the world.' Human rights–based perspectives provide an additional method of approaching the professional role, by placing the rights of the individual and/or group as central to any intervention. Adhering to a human rights framework in practice therefore requires that professionals have both a sound knowledge of what rights individuals are entitled to and a willingness to take action to assist individuals to achieve them. Sometimes, the knowledge base of a different professional discipline – the law for example – is needed to clarify these rights in a particular context of practice.

In Chapter 2, we saw how the influences of moral philosophy give us cause to consider what people are entitled to in life; how virtues and character shape actions; and how rules and consequences, means and ends are weighed up in decision-making. We also saw that the principle of justice, one of the foundational ethical principles that sits alongside respect for autonomy, beneficence and non-maleficence, is closely linked to notions of equity and equality and is an important defining principle in the allocation and distribution of resources. When we consider the work we are called to do in schools, hospitals, prisons, rehabilitation services, disaster relief or aged care, the common theme of service provision and management is how to ensure that people get what they need in a way that is not only in their best interests, but also does not place in jeopardy the common good and best interests of society as a whole. We need to consider both the individual and the collective.

The ethical theories discussed in Chapter 2 give us a way of understanding some of the rationales for why human rights of more disadvantaged or marginalised people are often overlooked or deliberately thwarted in the interests of political and economic imperatives, which are often utilitarian. The ethics of care and relational responses move us away from justice approaches that are more deontological, and towards consideration of humanness, connectedness, reciprocity and mutuality.

While it is important to explore the concepts of human rights and social justice, the primary focus of this chapter is on the ways in which these concepts can be operationalised through activist practice in the interprofessional space. This exploration acknowledges the breadth and depth of the human rights literature and argues that collaborative partnerships between professional groups can promote strong advocacy and purposeful practice. If human rights are truly to be recognised, then the potential for activism through people combining knowledge and skills to combat injustice is a very real and exciting possibility. We will explore examples later in this chapter.

■ Exploring the history of human rights

Notions of human rights date back thousands of years, with historians citing early documents of the ancient Persians and Indians as including references to the rights of individuals by nature of their humanity. Key documents such as the English Magna Carta (1215), British Bill of Rights (1689), the French Declaration of the Rights of Man and of the Citizen (1789) and the United States Declaration of Rights (1776) are cited as influential in informing the human rights position. The 18th and 19th centuries saw philosophers such as Thomas Paine, Georg Wilhelm Friedrich Hegel and John Stuart Mill adding to the human rights discourse through discussion and debate on the nature of rights. Contemporary human rights discourse became a preoccupation after the First World War, through the establishment of a number of key bodies, including the League of Nations and later the United Nations, which began to enshrine human rights in their key documents. Made in 1948, the Universal Declaration of Human Rights, a founding document of the United Nations, has become a central document in framing the human rights agenda.

■ A matter of definition

Defining human rights is problematic, as notions of what constitutes rights frequently change. Even so, Nipperess & Briskman (2009, p. 58) argue that 'human rights are a contemporary global discourse'. Ife (2012) suggests that a discursive approach to human rights should be adopted, whereby it is recognised that no fixed, objective definition can adequately express ideas about rights. Instead, a discursive approach holds that rights are constructed through human interaction and are informed by ongoing dialogue as to what constitutes a common humanity. This approach allows for changes in ideas about rights to be incorporated as they emerge, and avoids the pitfalls of locking our understanding of rights into a fixed social, cultural or political context. That said, defining the parameters of what is meant by a human rights discourse is necessary to arrive at some common understanding of what is a human right and what is not.

So popular are discussions and demands on rights that it seems that almost every experience can and has been framed as a right. Smokers cite the right to smoke, shooters the right to bear arms, and some parents the right to physically discipline their children. Adopting a rights stance has been a powerful way to enshrine behaviour so that challenging the behaviour is to suggest seriously damaging the humanity of the person. It is clear that some parameters around what can logically be claimed as human rights are useful, particularly in terms of being able to defend those rights.

Ife defines what we mean by human rights as 'those rights which we claim belong to all people, regardless of national origin, race, culture, age, sex or any other characteristic. Such rights are therefore universal and apply to everyone, everywhere, while more specific and circumscribed rights will only apply to certain people in certain circumstances' (Ife, 2012, p. 19). Another definition provided by Connolly (2013, p. 54) is that human rights are 'guaranteed entitlements that we hold because we are human'. She goes on to argue that there is an essential difference between *human* rights and *moral* rights, the latter being more what we deal with on a day-to-day basis. Moral rights are defined as lesser than human rights as there is a lesser degree of harm if they are not met. There is also the question of *civil liberties*, the legal rights afforded to people to carry out lawful activities without restriction. There have been many examples of claims that civil liberties have been violated by governments intent on exerting control over particular groups of people. A recent example in Queensland is the 'anti-bikie laws', which have outraged civil libertarians (and a significant percentage of the general population) in efforts to curtail association between outlaw motorcycle gang members. Civil Liberties Australia (n.d.), the peak body for civil liberties groups in each state and territory, has a website that tells a concerning story about intimidation, harassment and intrusion by those in positions of authority and power into people's private lives. The CLA website asks whether CCTV cameras in movie theatre toilets are appropriate; whether imposing school detention on a weekend is fair and just; whether people have the right to not vaccinate their children; and whether a person who is an 'innocent bystander' should be arrested for 'hindering police'. These sorts of issues demonstrate the everyday situations faced by people as they go about their lives and work in a context where 'rights' (human, moral or civil) are continually questioned and in many cases overridden. These are also the sorts of situations that are routinely dealt with by professionals in the areas of law and justice, social work and human services, and education and health. Given this, it is clear that we need to have a good understanding of what rights people claim they have and under what rationale, what rights are upheld in law, and what rights are perhaps culturally determined. Integrating a human rights perspective into a professional identity will help us focus on potential abuses of rights and exploitation of positions of power, and raise awareness of the silencing of marginalised voices.

REFLECTION 3.1

1   Can you make a list of all the 'rights' to which you as an individual consider yourself entitled?

2   Which other 'rights' do you consider part of the community to which you are connected (a neighbourhood, or a group/club/association)?

3   Have any of the rights you hold to be important been violated, and on what grounds was this violation justified?

4   Have you ever been in a position where you had to curtail or impede the rights of another person? What impact did this experience have on you later?

■ Three generations of human rights

The history of human rights discourse has been identified as having developed in 'three waves' (Wronka, 1992). First-generation rights are understood to encompass civil and political rights and are concerned with fundamental freedoms such as rights to vote, freedom of speech, free assembly, fair trial, citizenship, privacy, freedom of religion and freedom from discrimination and intimidation. These rights are also referred to as 'negative rights', as they relate to rights that need to be protected rather than those that need to be realised. Ife (2012) argues convincingly that first-generation rights dominate public perceptions of what people are entitled to, and are often used by politicians as examples of government that is taking care of individuals.

We have all been part of, or witnessed, organised non-violent protest rallies where police are deployed to 'assist' people who are marching by controlling traffic. Government sets up situations that publicly demonstrate a commitment to human rights, yet the operationalisation of policies that sit at the next level can often mean that these rights are not fully realised. An example is people's right to access their medical, employment or psychiatric records under 'right to information' (RTI) legislation. Legislation of this nature sends a message to the public that they have the right to know what has been written about them and what information has been stored and shared with others. This right to information, however, comes with many restrictions, such as time limits, fees and charges (at times exorbitant) and exclusions or denials, which are all dictated by the same laws that make the promise of access in the interests of justice.

Second-generation rights refer to economic, social and cultural rights. These rights relate to social provisions or services that individuals require to meet their full human potential. These include the right to employment, adequate food and clothing, adequate wages, housing, education, health care and right to income security. These rights are known as 'positive rights', as they require the state or territory to take a more active provision role. While the first-generation rights previously discussed had their origins firmly in liberalism, second-generation rights are based mainly on a socialist foundation since there is a need for government interventions to secure them as part of a societal system (Ife, 2012). While these rights go hand in hand with first-generation rights, they are less able to be guaranteed by law except in situations where minimum standards need to be established.

Third-generation rights are those that belong to a collective or group, such as a community, society or nation, and include the rights to economic development, to benefit from world trade, and to live in a harmonious society and a clean environment. This generation of rights is very much a product of the late 20th century, in recognition of the inequality nations experienced as a result of colonialism, free trade agendas and environmental destruction. It could be argued that these third-generation rights are likely to increase in importance as the world becomes more interconnected through globalisation, and collective international efforts to focus on environmental impacts bring more disciplines together to find ways to address climate change and ecological management.

■ Human rights contested

Although most people would support the idea of human rights, critiques of a human rights discourse cite a lack of cultural diversity in framing understandings of human rights. Debate on the applicability of notions of human rights to non-Western cultures advances the idea that contemporary notions of human rights are informed by Western preoccupation with individualism and fail to fully incorporate more collective worldviews. This debate captures the conflicts sometimes arising when trying to apply a human rights discourse to cultures that give primacy to the collective over the individual. For example, advancing the individual rights of a particular person may jeopardise the collective rights of a community (Ife, 2012; Hugman, 2013).

Although the debate on the cultural appropriateness of human rights discourse is an important one, some caution needs to be exercised to assure that it is not used to justify practices that cause clear suffering, such as female genital cutting (FGC). For example, defenders of FGC argue that it is a cultural practice that plays an essential role in strengthening the community and gender roles for women (cultural relativism), whereas human rights advocates see it as a violation of women's rights (ethical absolutism). In a globalised world, ensuring that all cultures have input into defining the human rights discourse will allow contemporary notions to continue to unfold.

■ A human rights practice approach

Now that we understand what is meant by a human rights discourse, and what falls within the realm of human rights, identifying how it can be used to inform practice in the social, health and human services will allow us to consider the implications of a human rights practice framework. According to Ife (2012), human rights practice frameworks rest on a foundation that includes several key elements:

- Praxis (the notion that theory and practice are interwoven and draw on both knowledge and action): 'Knowledge without action would be ungrounded, sterile and irrelevant; and action without knowledge would be anti-intellectual, uninformed and usually dangerous' (p. 216).
- Morality (an understanding of practice as a moral endeavour and a willingness to engage with others in the pursuit of moral actions).

- Passion (a commitment to maintaining rage against oppression and injustice and a vision for a better world).
- Ideology (the notion that human rights–based practice is inherently political and is congruent with a collectivist and socialist approach).
- History (the importance of acknowledging patterns of oppressive structures and behaviours through history so that context can be created).
- Structural disadvantage (the idea that 'the personal is political' – human rights practice recognises the need to incorporate an analysis of the impacts of class, race, gender, sexuality, nationality, disability, culture and age on oppressed individuals and groups).
- Holism (an emphasis on interconnectedness and ecological understandings of sustainability and wholeness).
- Postmodernism and poststructuralism (an acceptance of ambiguity and celebration of diversity, and an understanding of power, deconstruction and blurring of boundaries).

In looking at these foundations of human rights–based practice, it is instructive to note that there are some areas that may set up immediate challenges for interprofessional practice. The issue of ideology, as one example, raises the question of how people can work constructively together when they may come from quite different ideological positions. What happens when one person is apathetic in an area about which another feels passionately? How do colleagues working together reconcile differences when one sees a client's behavior as resulting from individual choice and conscious pathological intent, while another sees the same person through the eyes of structural disadvantage, poverty and racism? The concept of empowerment, also a fundamental premise of human rights practice, can be another issue for professional disciplines that are more educated and socialised to 'treat' problems and impose solutions on the basis of expertise rather than assist people to manage life concerns more autonomously. These are just some of the challenges for interprofessional practice when working with issues of human rights.

■ Understanding power and the role of advocacy

The term 'empowerment' was previously mentioned as being a central way of working within a human rights approach. Empowerment is defined by Ife (2013, p. 277) as 'providing people with the resources, opportunities, vocabulary, knowledge and skills to increase their capacity to determine their own future, and to participate in and affect the life of their community'. The concept of 'power with' is an important conceptual shift for many who work in professions that traditionally exercise power in a way that sets expertise and knowledge up as a barrier to collaborative relationships that would encourage autonomy (Chenoweth & McAuliffe, 2014). We can look at an example of how an empowerment approach that uses advocacy as a strategy might work in practice. A person goes into hospital following a cardiac incident and, following treatment, is given information about what changes to lifestyle, diet and stress need to happen to avoid further health troubles. An approach that is more in line with the concept of 'power with' will acknowledge the person's capacity to make important changes in line with their own understanding of the health-related impacts of lifestyle, diet and stress, and will encourage them to harness the important supports that need to be in place in the person's life to gain maximum benefit from the changes. An authoritarian approach from an 'expert knows best' position will often impede development of a relationship that may be important for ongoing health reviews. At a more structural level, an empowerment approach will explore all the factors that might be present in a person's life that are impacting on optimal health and wellbeing. It might be that stress is the result of financial pressures brought about by unemployment, brought about by economic downturns in a particular industry. It could be that poor dietary choices are linked to lack of education and knowledge, or limited resources for freshly available, affordable and healthy produce. This could be related to drought and decreased government assistance to farmers who supply that produce, or it may be that the person lives in a remote area with little access to preventative healthcare services.

The concept of advocacy, then, is closely related to empowerment approaches and involves strategy and intervention that are often required once an assessment has been made about lack of access to resources or an inequitable distribution of services. In the example provided here, any member of a healthcare team could become involved in an advocacy role to lobby for resources to educate people about heart disease, ensure that people have access to affordable medical care, or become involved in intergenerational programs to address general health issues at all stages of the life cycle. An interprofessional approach might see a medical doctor working closely with a nursing team to assist allied health staff to provide education programs in the community, in local schools and in workplaces. A dietician and an exercise physiologist might work together to develop a community-based nutrition and exercise program. A community development worker might lobby for funds to employ a project worker to run a healthy ageing program and network with the local healthcare providers to reduce costs. This project worker might then advocate on behalf of group members to obtain reduced rates at the local gym so that financial impediments to engaging in regular exercise can be minimised. As stated by McDonald et al. (2011, p. 184): 'Advocacy is often the process that can guide us to challenge and negotiate inequitable power arrangements, whether it be on behalf of an individual service user, a group, or an entire community.'

■ Connecting human rights to social justice

The concepts of human rights and social justice are commonly intertwined in the literature, yet the meaning of social justice is often not as clear as there are no charters, declarations or laws that set out exactly what the term means. One of the clearest distinctions between the two concepts is that put forward by Eileen Baldry, as cited by Hugman (2012), in a keynote address to a Community Legal Centres Conference in 2010. Hugman acknowledges Baldry's contribution to the development of a clear way to bring human rights and social justice together. Her central premises are:

1 Human rights are concerned with access to those things necessary for a truly human life;

2 Social justice is concerned with the way society distributes social and material resources to meet human needs in a finite world.

(Hugman 2012, p. 382)

When conceptualised in this way, it is clear that human needs, and the way resources are distributed to meet those needs, are the core concerns of those working in professions that focus on people. Social justice is the way that human rights are realised. In the interprofessional context, it is possible that people working together from different disciplines may have divergent understandings of how resources should be distributed to meet needs, and individuals may have various definitions of what social justice, fairness and equity mean. Going back to Chapter 2, we can see the significant influences of philosophical worldviews, cultural considerations and ways of viewing human nature and behaviour, and understand that these influences will shape views on who is 'deserving' or 'undeserving' of services. How resources are distributed, and according to what criteria, within human rights and social justice frameworks or neoliberal perspectives, will be explored in a later section of this chapter.

Human rights and social justice are two values that are inextricably linked in the social work literature. This is probably not surprising given that the international Definition of Social Work takes the position that the principles of human rights and social justice are fundamental to social work. This definition clearly and unequivocally declares the central place of both human rights and social justice in social work. While the two concepts are clearly important to the profession, they are often discussed as though they are one concept. Indeed, one of the findings of my PhD research into human rights and its relationship with critical social work was that social workers, both practitioners and academics, found the distinction between human rights and social justice difficult to identify and often used the two concepts interchangeably. This is reflected in the literature more widely, which also often conflates the two concepts. A clear recommendation arising from my research is the imperative for social work education to move beyond rhetorical commitments of human rights to in-depth explorations of human rights and its relationship with social work practice. I would argue that this means explicitly exploring the connection between both human rights and social justice, consciously deliberating on the differences between the two concepts and examining the ways in which they integrate with each other.

(Sharlene Nipperess)

■ Towards a socially just allocation of resources

As professionals working in the complex world of social, health and human services, we have an often onerous responsibility for finding ways to equitably distribute goods and services to people who require assistance. Resources are finite and competition and demand for necessities of life mean that systems need to be developed to share around what is available among those most in need. The resources that we are referring to might range from financial assistance in the form of emergency relief payments to those in poverty, through to allocation of organs for those in need of transplant. The media is full of stories about fairness in distribution of resources, often within the domain of social, health and human services. Should a person who smokes be allowed access to a heart–lung transplant? Should a premature baby who has little chance of survival be kept alive at the expense of others who have a better chance? Should a newly arrived refugee family be given priority housing over a family who have been on a public housing wait list for years? Should governments commit money to foreign aid, or keep resources within their own countries? Resource allocation can have major ethical implications, and social policies are largely developed from the competing demands of many key stakeholders. One of the key ethical concerns is how power can be used and abused in the allocation of resources, and political, economic, cultural, gender-based and social imperatives may drive forward the agendas at play. In the interprofessional context, those professional groups that have higher status, expertise and influence may often have greater control over resource allocation.

■ The complexity of resource allocation

The way that we decide 'who should get what' dates back historically to the era when decisions were based on notions of 'deserving' and 'undeserving'. In England, the Poor Law of 1601 was designed to assist those unable to work, or those who were ill, orphaned, or had a disability. A clear distinction was drawn between these 'worthy poor' and those assumed to be malingerers or fraudsters, referred to as the 'able-bodied poor' (Chenoweth & McAuliffe, 2014). Although we are referring to a time more than 400 years ago, there is still evidence of the 'deserving/undeserving' mentality inherent in social attitudes towards people who are seen as 'dole bludgers', or 'welfare cheats'. Mutual obligation requirements fuel potential for discrimination in situations where people with mental health issues or other disabilities are expected to look for work, and parents are required to re-enter work when their children reach a certain age. The political imperatives of reducing the welfare debt are clear.

When we think about ways of dividing up resources, we need to consider on what basis the allocation should be made. It is important to draw the distinction between the terms 'inequality' (the differences that exist between individuals) and 'inequity' (the response to the way that inequality is managed). The ethical principle of justice is the primary determiner of allocation, and considerations are generally based around two factors. These are, according to Beauchamp & Childress (1979), either utilitarian strategies (social efficiency and the greatest good) or egalitarian strategies (fair opportunity and the equal worth of individuals). These strategies underpin distributive justice, and resources can be allocated to each person in the following ways (p. 330):

- an equal share
- according to need
- according to effort
- according to contribution
- according to merit
- according to free-market exchanges.

Rowson (2006) defines a number of ways that decisions can be made about what people *deserve*, what they are *entitled* to, what they *need* and what their *capacities* are. These ways of making decisions about distribution also include strategies that are based on 'lottery' approaches (luck of the draw), first-in-first-served and triage (priority of need).

REFLECTION 3.3

1 Can you think of a time when you needed to decide where to direct personal resources (e.g. money or material possessions)? On what basis did you make your decision?

2 Can you identify which of the distributive strategies you would be most likely to place at the top of your list? Think about why this might be the case.

■ The politics of sharing

Decisions made at the policy level by government concerning the allocation of resources are inherently political in nature. Governments must weigh up the competing interests of a variety of stakeholders, often with intense pressure from lobby groups. Added to this is the knowledge of how decisions they make will be perceived by the voting public. Political ideologies also play a part in determining who gets what. In Australia, conservative governments have traditionally allocated resources away from lower socio-economic groups in favour of the wealthier segments of society, while Labor governments have tended to increase public spending and welfare entitlements (Jamrozik, 2009). As a result of the political nature of resource allocation, the experience of allocating resources as a professional working within the social, health or human service sectors will be inevitably linked to the political ideologies of the day. Employees in government organisations often need to follow directions from those in higher authority, even if they do not necessarily agree with decisions that have been made. In the interprofessional context, it may be difficult to understand why a colleague for whom you have great respect suddenly cuts funding from a service for vulnerable young people. Tension and conflict within a team may be caused by a decision to provide resources to one form of intervention over another, or by a direction to change eligibility criteria for a service. It is not uncommon for resource-driven ethical dilemmas to create divisions, which is why it is so important that interprofessional collaboration and information sharing remain high on the agenda. Although professionals will be guided by the policies and procedures of their employer, this will not make it any less difficult to watch as those in need go without. Regardless of directives on how resources are to be allocated, practitioners will still need to make difficult choices that lead to some people receiving assistance and others being turned away. Doing more with less has become a reality for social, health and human service professionals in economic climates of austerity.

REFLECTION 3.4

Think about these scenarios:

1 The deadly tsunami that hit parts of Indonesia and Thailand in 2004, killing thousands of people and leaving thousands more homeless, happened in the same week that bushfires claimed the lives and homes of hundreds of people in rural Victoria. Charitable organisations were calling for donations from the public. You decide to donate. Where do you put your money? On what basis do you decide?

2 You have enough emergency relief money left in your community centre budget for the month to assist one more family in need. Two families arrive at the centre at the same time. One is a refugee family with four small children who have no money for food. The other is an elderly couple with their grandson who are well known for spending a lot of time at the local gaming lounge. They are active volunteers in the community. They also have no money for food. Who do you help and why?

3 You are the organ transplant coordinator for a major hospital. A kidney is donated from a young man who died in a car accident. There are two potential recipients. One is a 15-year-old-boy with Down Syndrome. The other is a 37-year-old woman with a serious heroin addiction. What do you decide and why?

4 You are deciding on the award of a major grant to a community group for proposed work to benefit a local community. The decision is between a group that is working to capture and kill crocodiles that have been threatening fishermen. The other is a group that wants to paint a mural on the side of a local pub. Who gets the money?

As you thought through these decisions, what did you notice about where you placed your own personal priorities?

What were the factors that mattered most? Why?

■ Ethical activism

Historically, social, health and human service practice has been divided into those interventions that seek to bring about broad systemic change, such as policy, educational or advocacy work, and those that are centred on the individual casework or patient treatment approach. This separation has often resulted in practitioners who work primarily in the domain of individual practice justifying a lack of attention to the broader human rights context. As we have seen, a human rights framework challenges this view to suggest that all practice in the social, health and human services must incorporate action that seeks to advance the rights of individuals and groups towards social justice objectives. This approach dictates that practitioners do not shy away from conflict where this is necessary to promote a human rights and social justice agenda.

Political activist Saul Alinsky (1971, p. 22) believed that 'change means movement. Movement means friction. Only in the frictionless vacuum of a non-existent abstract world can movement or change occur without that abrasive friction of conflict'. Central to this is the belief that practitioners must be prepared to seek out opportunities for activism. It is difficult to comprehend at times the generic complacency evident across all sectors of society when so many social issues remain highly problematic. Treatment of asylum seekers and children in detention centres; the tragic consequences of alcohol-fuelled violence; health epidemics such as obesity, heart disease and diabetes; the abuse of children in the care of the state; homeless families and children; and appalling standards of care in aged-care facilities and residential homes for people with disabilities. These are all issues that demand moral outrage.

THROUGH THE EYES OF A PRACTITIONER

In the current political environment, it seems harder to protest or advocate a view that diverges from mainstream conservative thought. This is a great challenge for social work. We have long struggled with the internal dichotomy of the 'care and control' aspects of our role, and have many instances in our history of adding to the misery and oppression of different groups. Examples include the forced adoption of babies of young single mothers and the forced removal of Aboriginal children from their families. Despite our focus on social justice and human rights, I am deeply concerned that we are at great risk of letting ourselves be used to provide care to vulnerable, traumatised people, such as asylum seekers and refugees, that is grossly inadequate in meeting their basic needs, but which allows authorities to say that services are being provided. If we are not careful, we will again become enablers of oppression, rather than champions of human dignity and justice.

(Teresa Scott)

Social, health and human service practice has a long history of activism, and many codes of ethics of different professional disciplines include statements about the need to promote social justice and equality. From the early nurse activists, to the pioneering women of social work, to the anti-psychiatry movement, many practitioners have chosen an active path to challenging theories, practices and beliefs that they identified as unjust or inaccurate. In the contemporary context, activism continues as a strategy for challenging inequity, but the reality is that it is not as prominent as it perhaps should be given the many structural and systemic barriers that clients continue to experience. Many workplaces prohibit staff from speaking out about internal problems, and organisational cultures can often promote a sense that 'rocking the boat' is not worth the trouble that might follow. Despite this, there are many intervention strategies utilised by practitioners who engage in activist practice and these include networking, campaigning and lobbying for change, mobilisation of resources to effect redistribution to those in greater need, and policy and law reform activities. Activism, in all its forms, seeks to give power to disadvantaged individuals and groups, by assisting people to gain more power over their personal choices and life chances, their ideas, resources and economic choices. As well, engagement in activist activities is often a very rewarding part of practice as it allows workers to experience an important level of congruence with their values and beliefs, and enables them to deliver on professional responsibilities. McAuliffe (2012) encourages practitioners to develop courage in their professional lives so that this congruence can be fully realised.

REFLECTION 3.5

1 Make a list of the top five social issues that you consider are worthy of moral outrage.
2 What opportunities can you identify for taking action on these issues?
3 If you were to engage an advocacy approach to lobby for change on one of these issues, what would this look like?

■ Micro forms of activism

Activism takes many forms and has a philosophical grounding at the more radical and non-conservative end of the political spectrum. Those who undertake activist practice generally do so from a very strong value position firmly rooted in a concern for justice. In later chapters, we will explore conflicts that can arise in workplaces, and look at what can happen when employees decide to take action against observed injustices or harm to others as a result of negligence, malicious intent or impaired practice. Practitioners who engage in overt activism generally feel confident to stand up to challenging workplace practices, will openly make their views known, and do so with confidence that they are backed by a professional code of ethics or standard of conduct, using existing policies and laws to substantiate claims. Many will ensure that they have the support of an industrial union before taking action on an issue that is likely to be contested or place their employment at risk.

Contemporary human service and health organisations, particularly government and statutory agencies, are typically organised within a framework of risk management, which means that those in positions of authority often attempt to exert control over employees by closing down opportunities to publically protest or raise concerns overtly within workplaces (Briskman & Uriz Peman, 2012). As a result, a new method of activism is beginning to be documented. This method sees social, health and human service professionals involved in a range of micro forms of activism, undertaken in daily practice. Recent research conducted by Greenslade (2013), who interviewed a number of practitioners employed in statutory contexts, suggests that micro forms of activism may be increasingly covert, such as:

- acting in opposition to organisational directives
- looking the other way when clients do not comply with service rules
- 'creatively' filling out forms to overstate a client's problem so that they may receive a service
- being 'flexible' with rules and laws
- 'turning a blind eye' when colleagues evade directives from management
- breaking the law to optimise clients' opportunities or protect them from punitive practices.

Greenslade's (2013) research supports findings from other empirical studies on covert workplace activism in the social, health and human services which suggests that the central reason behind the choice to undertake these actions covertly is that it is the most achievable method of meeting clients' needs (Abramovitz, 2005; Aronson & Smith, 2009; Baines, 2001; McDonald & Chenoweth, 2009). Additionally, a common theme across these research studies identified that the current welfare delivery model is not amenable to overt methods of activism, with workers expressing high levels of fear of reprisal should they openly challenge policies and procedures which prove problematic in meeting client need. Participants in these studies therefore made the decision that the best method of meeting client need was to take action without the knowledge of their managers or co-workers. There are many implications for practitioners who engage in covert activism in situations where there is conflict between organisational and professional values. Difficult decisions about whether to stay or leave are common, and many succumb to stress and experience mental health issues, mechanistic completion of work tasks devoid of interest or commitment, and become cynical and negative about practice (Greenslade, 2013; McAuliffe, 2005b). Ultimately, this is not constructive for the social, health and human service workforce. Issues of the impacts of organisational and professional conflict are explored further in Chapter 8.

Covert activism carries with it some very real potential harm. Not only is the worker putting themselves at substantial risk of reprisal which could include job loss, a negative impact on professional reputation, and possibly prosecution if they have broken any laws, but clients may also be at increased risk if it is discovered that they received a service to which they were not entitled. Regardless, the existence of covert activism attests to the strong motivation that social, health and human service workers have to deliver on their professional requirements to work towards social justice.

In the interprofessional context, practitioners who engage in covert activism can place colleagues in a difficult position if these colleagues become aware of activities that management has not sanctioned. Say, for example, that a youth worker has decided to spend time with a group of at-risk young people on weekends to support and work with them on a music project to raise money for an orphanage in Mumbai, to which they all have a deep commitment. The agency policy is clear that staff will only work with young people during the hours that they are paid to do so; hours that are increasingly restricted by funding cuts and that do not take account of weekend work. Colleagues of the youth worker are made aware that contact is happening outside of stipulated work hours, and that there is an ongoing breach of agency policy. Yet the fact that these young people have maintained their commitment to the project, and have pursued an activity that will make a difference to the lives of others, makes everyone reluctant to bring the youth worker's covert strategy to the attention of management. Covert activism in this case may well be seen to be in the interests of the young people involved, but does create a situation where secretive activities place a number of people in a difficult position.

REFLECTION 3.6
1 What are your views on the ethics of covert activism?
2 What actions would you be prepared to undertake covertly for the benefit of your clients, and what would you not be prepared to do?
3 Have you ever witnessed, been engaged in, or heard about covert activist practices? What were some of the risks, and what were the ultimate benefits?

■ Activism in practice: examples from the field
Social workers organise a 'people's inquiry'

In response to the Australian Government's mandatory detention legislation and the impact of this legislation on a group of asylum seekers aboard the *Tampa*, seeking refuge in Australia, the Australian Council of Heads of Schools of Social Work undertook an inquiry into mandatory detention when it became clear that the government would not. The People's Inquiry into Detention sought to change asylum-seeker policy and to provide a public forum for the stories of asylum seekers to be heard. Identifying this policy as a breach of the human rights of the individuals involved, the People's Inquiry saw social work academics, students and practitioners join with other professional groups and individuals involved in the asylum issue to hold 10 public hearings across Australia. Soon after it had released a report in 2006, the People's Inquiry called on the incoming Labor government to remove racism, restore human rights and reinstate accountability, demands that have led to changes in asylum policy. Support for the People's Inquiry was strong and resulted in the publication of a book about the process, *Human Rights Overboard* (Briskman, Latham & Goddard, 2008).

Professor Linda Briskman, a social worker who played a central role in the People's Inquiry, believes that activism is a professional duty of human service practice, citing the principles enshrined in the Australian Social Work Code of Ethics of 1999. Aware of the risks involved in participating in activism, Briskman (2008) suggests that practitioners need moral courage to speak out and challenge inequity and that choosing not to act when faced with situations that clearly diminish the rights of individuals or groups is to be a collaborator in such practices.

Psychologists take a stand against torture

Activists from within the American Psychological Association (APA) joined forced with concerned groups and individuals to address the issue of psychologists' involvement in torture and human rights abuses within American detention centres. Beginning with the drafting of an online petition calling for the APA to speak out against the use of psychologists in torture, the group followed up with demands for a written statement that clearly stated the inappropriateness of psychologists' involvement in these practices. In 2008, a membership referendum campaign was run by the APA to explore the stance of APA members on this issue, resulting in a new, clear policy barring psychologists from working within US detention centres that violate the American Constitution or international law, unless they are working directly for the detainees themselves or for a human rights group advocating for the detainees (Olson, Aalbers & Fallenbaum, 2009).

In recognition of the need to explicitly detail what would occur should APA members disobey the new policy, member activists continued to work with interested groups to pressure the APA to further state the ramifications for practising in detention centres. In response, the APA established a 'Presidential Advisory Group on implementation of the petition resolution'. The report of this group outlined the policy and included actions to be taken against APA members who practised in contradiction to the policy.

■ Interprofessional activism: strength in numbers

Collective action and collaborative partnerships between people of different professional disciplines provide excellent opportunities for strong advocacy and activism through the pooling of intellectual and skills resources. There are many examples across different workplaces of people coming together to work on projects, community action initiatives, research studies and therapeutic interventions with the explicit aim of joining with others and connecting knowledge and know-how. Part of interprofessional education (IPE) is learning how to find out about what others can offer, and how others position themselves in terms of their value base, ontology and epistemology. When practitioners from different disciplines come together to take action on a social issue that may require advocacy and lobbying at the political level, such associations are generally developed with conscious thought about what expertise is needed and who has the credibility and reputation to advance the cause. So, as an example, if a community development worker is working with a community group that decides to take action on an environmental issue impacting their community, it would be wise to network with people with this expertise such as an environmental planner or ecologist. If a group of concerned citizens at risk of losing their homes under a proposed bridge or tunnel development contacts a community association for assistance, they might need the specialist services of lawyers to safeguard their property and tenancy rights. Lawyers and housing workers could collaborate on strategies to ensure people's rights are protected.

THROUGH THE EYES OF A PRACTITIONER

I have participated in animal rights activism for about 25 years but looking back over the actions I've taken, I can see that my activism became much more focused when I gained a professional qualification as a social worker and when I teamed up with a group of friends from different professional backgrounds. In my teens, my activism involved attending events organised by groups like Animal Liberation, wearing slogan T-shirts and handing out brochures. Now, as a social worker, I can see that I bring the knowledge and skills of my profession to the activism I plan and participate in outside of my day-to-day job. I have a fairly clear idea of what social justice means to me now and I've gained professional skills in advocacy and group work. I've also honed my research and communication skills and these are proving very useful in my activism. What has really helped though is working alongside a small group of friends who are lawyers, planners, teachers and artists. When we bring our professional skills to the table, we can plan and execute activities very efficiently and effectively. For example, teachers have a good working knowledge of how to present a message so that it's likely to be absorbed well. Lawyers can explore the boundaries between what might be legal and illegal and have knowledge on the likely penalties involved in undertaking illegal action. They can also advise on what to do if arrested. I've found artists to be invaluable sources of creative ideas as well as highly skilled in producing visual materials that catch the eye. Typically, we will all meet up and plan an action. This will involve lots of passionate discussion before we begin to focus on how best to undertake the action. It's at this point that we will use our professional skills by dividing up tasks into our areas of expertise. We all have professional identities to consider and different comfort levels over our names being associated with some of the activities we undertake. So we plan very carefully giving full consideration to ethical issues relating to our actions. We have a solid understanding and interest in matters relating to ethics from our professional training, and really enjoying nutting out our thoughts and feelings relating to the ethics of our work. All of our animal rights activism is done outside of our day-to-day work at this point. This is because it doesn't really fit neatly into our day jobs. My experiences of taking action alongside people from different professional disciplines have taught me the value of utilising skill sets across professions. Even though there seem to be limited opportunities in the current work climate to devote to activism, it's interesting to imagine what could be accomplished if we could join together to fight a common cause.

(Diana Prince)

■ Conclusion

This chapter has explored the history of human rights–based approaches and how these can be, and have been, implemented into professional practice in the social, health and human services. Given that all social, health and human service practice operates within a political framework which directly dictates policy and practice realities, a human rights practice framework provides practitioners with the knowledge and skills to identify inequality and take action to improve the rights of those with whom we work. To focus exclusively on the individual and their individual problem is to do only half the job. A number of important concepts have been introduced in this chapter that will become relevant to the discussions in chapters to follow. Concepts of empowerment and advocacy and the notion of ethical activism are commonly cited in the literature in many professional disciplines, and the calls for practitioners who are in a position to make significant changes to unjust and inequitable social policies and laws are part of the professional legacy. If we are in a position to influence change, uphold human rights and advocate for more socially just practices in the interests of better outcomes for vulnerable, disadvantaged and marginalised people, then we have an ethical responsibility to do so. The next chapter will move on to discuss the regulatory context of professional practice, aiming to ensure that practitioners who choose to engage in activist and other interventions with individuals, groups and communities do so in a way that upholds the ethical and value base set out in earlier chapters.

4

Regulation of the professions: codes of ethics and standards of practice

■ Learning objectives

- **TO IDENTIFY** the nature of professions and explore the role of professional associations
- **TO EXPLORE** the history and function of codes of ethics and standards of conduct and practice
- **TO IDENTIFY** how professional practice is regulated and what regulation bodies exist in the Australian context

■ Introduction

WE HAVE WORKED our way so far in this exploration of interprofessional ethics to a position where we can appreciate the need to identify the similarities and differences between groups of people who claim 'professional status'. In Chapter 1, we gave a definition of the term 'profession' and looked at some of the tensions that can prove difficult for interprofessional collaboration in the workplace. We then moved on to explore ways that moral philosophy and ethical theory can be used to form a foundation on which justifications for actions are given, and ways that different worldviews can support either relativist or absolutist positions. One of the important themes of previous chapters has been an emphasis on professions 'doing no harm', which entails an understanding and acknowledgement of power and potential abuses of it. The focus of this chapter is on the regulatory context that has developed over many decades to provide protection for members of the public who receive services from others in a contractual arrangement. Services in the social, health and human services can be sought and received voluntarily, but there is a large section of the industry that is charged with responsibility for ensuring that people who may be at risk are not harmed by either themselves or others. Children and minors, people with mental health or disability issues, vulnerable older people, and people traumatised by violence and abuse, are some examples of those who may need protection from delegated authorities. When people lose capacity for other reasons, such as an accident or illness, protections also need to be in place to ensure that they are not disadvantaged or harmed by those caring for them. For example, if a person has a serious car accident and ends up in a coma in hospital, it is important that protections exist so that, while he or she is unable to look after their affairs, others do not come in and sell his or her assets, leaving the person homeless. If a person goes to a chiropractor for treatment of a sore shoulder, he or she needs to be confident that the chiropractor has the required qualifications, competence, and insurance cover to do that therapy. People also need to be assured that if a service they receive does not meet requirements, or harm of some sort is experienced, they have recourse to a complaint system that will bring the practitioner to account, and result in some form of restitution. There have been significant advances in quality assurance in health care and legal systems over recent decades, which have seen moves towards increased openness and encouragement of a cultural shift towards a 'no blame' system in the management of 'adverse events' and 'clinical incidents' (Atkins, Britton & de Lacey, 2011; Kerridge, Lowe & McPhee, 2005).

As we will see in this chapter, the regulatory context of professional practice is quite complex, and different professions have taken quite different pathways towards self-regulation or regulation by an external authority. There is a political and economic imperative at work that clearly favours professions to be self-regulating, except in cases where potential harm to the public can be very clearly specified and has been demonstrated through evidence. Writing in the late 1950s, Ernest Greenwood (1957), a sociologist, identified the ideal attributes of a profession as including systematic theory, recognised authority, community sanction and approval, professional culture and a code of ethics. Ethical codes and practice standards are therefore typically developed as a group of practice specialists seeks professional status. As we will see, ethical codes and practice standards serve multiple functions in professions, and discussion on the appropriateness and usefulness of such codes to prevent harm is prevalent in the literature. To make informed decisions on the utility of codes and standards in professional social, health and human service practice, it is necessary to develop an understanding of the functions they perform, and to look at these in the context of a broader regulatory framework.

■ The nature of professions: a recap

To begin with, it is important to establish what we mean when we use the word 'profession'. If we were to ask a group of people to describe what a profession is, they would most likely have the traditional occupations, such as doctor or lawyer, in mind when they answered. What do these occupations tell us about what a professional is? A doctor or lawyer has specialist knowledge and skills and uses them to perform a service for a patient or client. As a result, we afford them a certain level of respect and even deference. They may have specialist 'tools' and a uniform of sorts, which further separate them from the general public. We may know that they have trained for many years to gain their skills. This traditional view of what constitutes a professional still influences us today, even though many more occupations are now seen as professional and these occupations may be quite different from the early professions.

REFLECTION 4.1
1 What occupations do you think of when you think of a profession?
2 What is it about these occupations that you think makes them professional?
3 What occupations would you classify as non-professional and why?

When examining the nature of professions, Chenoweth and McAuliffe (2014) identify two key views: the Functionalist view, which is concerned primarily with maintaining the status quo and protecting the public; and the Critical view, which asserts that professions are self-serving and largely concerned with protecting their elite members. If we subscribe to the Functionalist view, we might believe that professions serve an important role in assisting people to function well within the boundaries of socially acceptable behaviour and that, as a result, we will be afforded a level of protection. For example, a lawyer prosecutes people who break the law and the legal system may decide to incarcerate criminals in an effort to protect the rest of us from harm. Likewise, doctors can ensure that patients with communicable diseases are treated and the public is protected as a result. The Critical view of professions argues that they promote greater distance between the professional 'expert' and the clients they engage with, which implies that professionals have more power than those with whom they work. This view suggests that, in establishing a professional 'elite', the belief that clients can be experts in their own lives is threatened.

Debates about what constitutes a profession have been going on for a very long time. Some contemporary writers suggest that the concept of a profession is not as important as it once was, given that people with a variety of qualifications can now undertake the same role. Think of a case manager in the field of mental health, who may have trained as a nurse, a counsellor, an occupational therapist or a social worker. In some jobs, an individual with no formal qualifications but many years' experience may be employed to do the same job as someone with formal qualifications and little practical experience. Undoubtedly, the question of what makes a profession will continue to be asked, and the answers may change as work environments continue to evolve.

■ Professional associations: developing professional culture and identity

If we go back to the Greenwood definition of what constitutes a profession, we see that development of professional culture is an important part of people coming together to form an identity that can then be conveyed in some way to others. Millsteed (2006) states that there are essentially four ways to promote accountability in the professions. These are through professional associations, regulatory bodies, civil laws and criminal courts. The first of these is worth exploring in some detail. Professional associations have arisen in many different disciplines as people with leadership aspirations have emerged to form connections with others who share a common purpose and belief in the necessity of promotion of professional identity. In many situations, professional associations have become important in giving legitimacy to a discipline as it takes its place in the competitive industrial and employment arena. These are generally peak bodies representing the interests of members at a national level, and they also provide students of the discipline with a way to connect to an established entity that holds firm the profession's vision, mission statement, ethical practices, and accountability for educational standards. Professional associations are also generally very active in the public sphere, commenting on issues of importance to the discipline and engaging with political processes where relevant to promote positions that are representative of the values of the discipline. The more members belong to a professional association, the greater its potential political leverage.

Examples of the development of some of the better known professional associations, and the issues that they have promoted in recent times, are as follows.

The Australian Medical Association (AMA) was formally established in 1962 (although there were state/territory branches dating back to the 1880s) following the lead of the British Medical Association, and through its history it has been clearly connected to the need for protection of professional interest. As stated in an account of the AMA history, there was 'a need to unite and represent the physicians, surgeons and other medical practitioners and defend their interests from those of the apothecaries, barbers, blood-letters and all the other disparate groups who had attached themselves to medicine in those days' (AMA, 2012). The AMA has been a strongly influential body in terms of health policy and provision in this country, and despite a somewhat turbulent history of state/territory and federal collaborations, has a key seat at the government table on issues including public health, therapeutics, healthy ageing, Indigenous health, and medical research. The motto of the AMA is 'pro genere human concordes', which means 'united for humanity'. The AMA has a history of advocacy and makes regular public comment on issues of social importance. A current issue that provides an example of how a professional association can shape government health initiatives is the call for a national summit on alcohol misuse and resultant harms (AMA, 2014).

The Australian Psychological Society (APS), like the AMA, was formed as an offshoot of the British Psychological Society in 1966. It has a Board of Directors, a number of Colleges (for example, Clinical, Forensic, Organisational, Health) and 44 Interest Groups (for example, ePsychology, Psychologists in Schools, Deafness and Psychology, Psychologists for Peace, Trauma and Psychology). It has more than 21 000 members. The APS has a very active public profile: it engages with public policy submissions, continuing professional education and development, and provides assistance to the workforce on issues of professional and ethical practice through the APS Professional Advisory Service (Ask APS). Issues that the APS has been vocal about in recent years include gambling-related harms, the mental health of refugee and asylum seekers, and the impacts of natural disasters (APS, 2014).

The Australian Association of Social Workers (AASW) has approximately 7000 members and was formed in 1947 following the development of similar associations in the US and UK. Social work is an example of a self-regulating professional discipline in Australia (as will be explained more later in this chapter) and, as a result, it has a robust National Ethics and Professional Practice Standards Committee that manages serious ethics complaints, and provides advice to members through the National Ethics and Practice Standards Consultation Service. The AASW has a Board of Directors, nine Branch Committees of Management, a number of practice groups in various locations, and a staff team that lead initiatives on social policy, research, education and accreditation of social work programs, and assessment of international qualifications. The Australian College of Social Work (ACSW) promotes advanced practice, and the AASW has an active voice on issues including submissions to the Royal Commission on Institutional Responses to Child Sexual Abuse, and responses to the National Disability Insurance Scheme (NDIS). Membership of the AASW is voluntary, but many employers require social workers to hold eligibility for the AASW (AASW, 2014).

Occupational Therapy Australia (OT Australia) had its origins in state- or territory-based branches, much like many of the other professional associations, and formed a federal peak body in 1951. The membership of OT Australia is approximately 5000, and this profession has recently been included in the National Registration and Accreditation Scheme (NRAS). Occupational therapy has, like social work, contributed to the NDIS negotiations, and has also been active in promoting OT services in schools (OT Australia, 2014).

The Australian Professional Teachers Association (APTA) represents 120 000 teachers across all levels of education (government and non-government) and is committed to promoting quality education and learning practices. Education is a very complex structure in Australia, as there are quite significant differences across state or territory jurisdictions. There are a multitude of quite specific educational associations in each state or territory, focusing on areas such as gifted and talented, early childhood, middle years, outdoor education, drama, guidance counselling, library support, learning difficulties, and information technology. Unlike other professional associations, the teaching and education body does not appear to have a significant advocacy role on areas of more general public interest. One exception is the National Framework for Values Education, which is supported by the Australian Agency for International Development (AusAID) and aims to introduce students to global values around health, environment and international issues (APTA, 2010).

The Law Council of Australia was formed in 1933, and is representative of the many legal councils and judicial bodies across the country. It acts on behalf of approximately 60 000 lawyers. The Law Council of Australia has been particularly vocal on the issue of immigration detention and asylum seekers, and has been highly critical of detention policies. It has also played a major role in reconciliation strategies with Aboriginal and Torres Strait Islander peoples, providing guidance on issues such as land rights, native title, and criminal justice responses to over-representation in the criminal justice system. The Law Council's many divisions focus on a range of civil and criminal law areas, such as Alternate Dispute Resolution, Elder Law, Legal Aid, Privacy Law, Human Rights, and Anti-Terror Law (Law Council of Australia, n.d.).

The Australian Nursing and Midwifery Federation was established in 1924 (as the Australian Nursing Federation) and represents more than 220 000 nurses. Midwifery was included in 2013 to represent the growth in this part of the discipline. This is a very politically active association that advertises as both a professional association and an industrial union, and its campaigns are closely connected to industrial issues that affect patient care and the quality of nursing practice. Areas of activity have included aged care and quality of services, rural and remote palliative and cancer care, veterans' affairs, shortages of hospital beds, and opposition to up-front GP costs (Australian Nursing and Midwifery Federation, 2014).

The Australian Community Workers Association (ACWA) started in 1970 and was formed to represent the interests of the 500 000 workers who are employed or working voluntarily in the social and community services sector but do not have a qualification that gives them eligibility for one of the other professional associations (such as APS or AASW). These workers include aged-care professionals, youth workers, rape crisis counsellors, child protection workers, housing officers, disability care officers and welfare officers. ACWA has established standards for accreditation of community welfare programs, has a code of ethics, and has spent significant effort on lobbying for pay increases for the community workforce, which is traditionally female-dominated, with lower rates of pay. While ACWA is not an industrial union, members are covered by the Social, Community, Home Care and Disability Services Award 2010 (SACS Modern Award) (ACWA, 2012).

THROUGH THE EYES OF A PRACTITIONER

I joined the AASW soon after graduation initially. In the 1970s, I let it lapse for a few years, like many practitioners caught up in the debates about the 'elitism' of professions. I suppose now I would be regarded as a traditionalist as far as social work professional bodies go. I am 100 per cent in favour and think they are even more critical for social work at this time. Many people nowadays want to evaluate the value proposition before paying money to join any kind of body, be it a postgraduate course or a gym. I think as social workers we need to examine the value proposition for the perspective of our own professional values as well as the money. I would join AASW for the same reasons I became a social worker. An important reason for me is that membership provides a sense of belonging and solidarity with my fellow social workers. This goes beyond local and national spheres to the whole international community. Being part of the AASW immediately links us to social workers from New York to Nigeria. This is enormously helpful in advocacy efforts, in promoting values of social justice and human rights in often hostile political or workplace environments. A professional body also has a key role in maintaining standards and quality in education, in human service provision as well as the conduct of individual practitioners. We all need to get behind efforts to safeguard vulnerable people and promote excellence in our work. The AASW, despite any shortcomings it may have, can be a powerful vehicle to do just that.

(Lesley Chenoweth)

Some common themes emerge from this short synopsis and snapshot of a small number of professional associations. The role of advocacy and the connection with political processes are important parts of the professional association agenda. It has clearly been recognised that national leadership and an amalgamated effort, by way of federation, is essential to having a strong voice, but one of the ongoing sources of tension for many professional associations is the balance between representation on local issues and commitment to working on larger issues at the national level. There is a role for both state- and territory-based representation and connection with members at that level, and the more strategic and policy responses that need to come from a more centralised authority. We have discussed the ethical responsibilities of human rights responses and the need for advocacy strategies at the macro level in the previous chapter. From an overview of the types of issues that a selection of professional associations are addressing, it does seem that collectively pressure is exerted on government to develop policies and laws that are humane and in accordance with anti-discriminatory practices.

The interesting question from the perspective of interprofessional ethics is what sort of collaboration happens *between* professional associations. For example, would the AMA contact the AASW to co-author a submission on refugee and asylum seeker interventions? Would the APS and the OT association form an alliance on practice in mental health? An example of an important strategic alliance that has formed in allied health is Allied Health Professions Australia (AHPA). This body represents more than 50 000 allied health workers, including dieticians, speech pathologists, audiologists, social workers, psychologists, chiropractors, genetic counsellors and pharmacists. AHPA's vision is 'the right person in the right place at the right time', and major projects funded in the past few years have included 'Helping Children with Autism', the 'Indigenous Allied Health Network', and 'Shared Care in Chronic Disease Management'. The aim of a body such as AHPA is to promote multidisciplinary and interprofessional collaboration at a strategic level, to improve health outcomes. Another body that has become quite important is the National Alliance of Self-Regulating Health Professionals (NASRHP), which represents people in some disciplines that have not yet achieved regulatory status, such as speech pathologists, dieticians, sonographers and audiologists. Another example of a peak body, which was founded in 1981, is the Secretariat of National Aboriginal and Islander Child Care (SNAICC). This body focuses on the policy and advocacy areas of child protection, early childhood, social justice and human rights, and family and community support. It represents many different disciplines working across the child and family welfare, education, child protection and legal systems, and its influence with government is well recognised.

The common factor in all of these peak bodies and professional associations is their recognition that, to make a difference, they need a united voice and a consistency of purpose. While there will always be tensions between federal/national and state/territory agendas, there are many good examples of practitioners working collaboratively with others, and moves towards interprofessional initiatives are encouraged.

REFLECTION 4.2

1 What are your views on professional associations and their benefits to members? Are there also benefits to the public?

2 What would a professional association have to offer you as an incentive to join?

3 What differences do you perceive between professional associations and industrial unions? Do you think one organisation can play both roles, or should these remain separate?

■ The development of ethical codes and practice standards

As groups of qualified individuals began to group together to pursue a professional identity, often through the types of professional associations discussed, codes of ethics and practice standards also developed, to formalise what 'acceptable practice' means. It is not uncommon for disciplines to have a number of sets of documents that form the integrity and accountability framework for practice. These have many names, including codes of ethics, codes of conduct, and practice standards.

Although there is no agreement on what can be cited as the very first code of ethics, contenders include the Hippocratic Oath (4th century BCE), Percival's Medical Ethics (1803) and the Code of Ethics of the American Medical Association (1847) (Davis, 2003). The Nightingale Pledge of 1893, on which nursing was founded, reads as follows:

> I solemnly pledge myself before God and in the presence of this assembly, to pass my life in purity and to practice my profession faithfully. I will abstain from whatever is deleterious and mischievous, and will not take or knowingly administer any harmful drug. I will do all in my power to maintain and elevate the standard of my profession, and will hold in confidence all personal matters committed to my keeping and all family affairs coming to my knowledge in the practice of my calling. With loyalty will I endeavour to aid the physician, in his work, and devote myself to the welfare of those committed to my care.

> (Gretter, 1893/2014)

Banks (2004) highlights the types of inclusions that codes of ethics generally contain, which are:

- statements about the core purpose or service ideal of the profession
- statements about the character/attributes of the professional
- ethical principles
- ethical rules
- principles of professional practice
- rules of professional practice.

While codes of ethics generally set out to establish what is expected of a person who is qualified to perform a certain professional role, practice standards documents and codes of conduct accompany codes of ethics, to provide greater guidance on implementing the broader value statements embodied in the codes. Webster (2010) has drawn a clear distinction between codes of ethics and codes of conduct. He says that the difference 'lies in the locus of surveillance and control. The former is professionally based and seeks to create a self-reflective "insider" space for ethical deliberation, while the latter is statutorily driven and privileges "outsider" scrutiny and external regulation and control' (p. 32). One of the difficulties that we often face, particularly in large government departments, is the overwhelming number of documents that exist to govern practice. Not only must we be familiar with societal laws and agency policies, but we must also be aware of professional requirements. What happens when organisational mandates and professional responsibilities conflict, as they sometimes do, is discussed in Chapter 8.

Reamer (2013) argues that codes of ethics are essentially designed to address the following: problems of moral hazard (conflicts of self-interest); issues of professional courtesy (rules of behaviour); and issues around duty to serve the public interest (provision of pro bono services). Reamer further sets out the multiple functions of codes of ethics as:

- articulating a principal mission, values and ethical principles
- offering guidance to both workers and employers in addressing ethical issues
- providing protection for clients from incompetent practice and delineation of standards for practice
- providing a mechanism for self-regulation
- protecting workers from litigation.

From this list, we can see that codes of ethics serve both 'care' and 'control' functions, attempting to optimise protection for clients at the same time as protecting the role of the professional. How well they perform on either function has been a subject of debate. Critics point to the difficulty of utilising codes of ethics and practice standards in complex ethical territory, suggesting that it is simply not possible to take the 'rules' outlined in codes and easily apply them, when many situations professionals face in practice depend on a variety of competing interests and agendas (Downie & Calman, 1987). Codes have also faced criticism for lacking clarity, being unrepresentative of diverse views, and being overly located in one (Western) cultural tradition (Corey, Corey & Callanan, 2007). However, it would be fair to say that many professional codes of ethics have made significant advances in cultural inclusivity, which is being highlighted as an area of importance when codes of ethics are subject to revision. In the review process of the AASW Code of Ethics that took place across 2008–2009, for example, one of the significant issues was active engagement with the AASW National Ethics Group with a number of Aboriginal and Torres Strait Islander social workers, who wrote the sections of the revised code of ethics that covered culturally competent, safe and respectful practice. One of the review panel members made the following comment about this process:

> Vital to the progression of the Code of Ethics into current and future practice was the key connection of the new document with the original owners of this land, the first Australians. Of all the wise and successful decisions throughout the revision process were the conversations with the Indigenous social work group. The history of social work and Aboriginal rights is one of the embarrassments. The work undertaken with this Code has been essential. Sadly not a step taken in an earlier time.

> (Ros Giles)

Despite criticisms of the utility of codes of ethics and the relevance of practice standards across diverse fields, professions have continued to develop and revise these documents, countering the criticisms by suggesting that codes and standards can provide general guides as opposed to giving definitive answers relevant to all contexts (Chenoweth & McAuliffe, 2014). If we embrace the ideal that professionals have the skills and practice wisdom to interpret and apply codes and standards to difficult practice situations, we can avoid being overly prescriptive, and promote the autonomy of professionals (Freeman, 2000).

REFLECTION 4.3

1 Thinking about your profession or field of practice (e.g. mental health, public health, research, or clinical practice), can you identify the benefits of codes of ethics and practice standards?
2 What do you consider are the important elements that should be included in a code of ethics? How detailed do you think a code of ethics should be, and how specific should its directions be on appropriate conduct?
3 What sanctions or penalties do you believe should be placed on professionals who violate ethical codes or who engage in malpractice in your discipline?
4 How large or small a role should government play in regulating practice?

■ Exploring and using professional codes of ethics

As social, health and human service practitioners, we need to be aware of the codes of ethics and practice standards documents endorsed by our professions. As we have seen, these documents provide guidelines about professional behaviour and as such, are the 'go to' documents to help us navigate difficult ethical territory. Additionally, codes of ethics help strengthen our professional identity, and being able to refer regularly to these documents helps remind us of the value base of our disciplines. As well as having a good working knowledge of the code of ethics that governs one's own discipline, it is also obviously beneficial to know about the codes of ethics that offer ethical guidance to our colleagues. Say that a practitioner finds him or herself attracted to a client, and decides to terminate the relatively short-term therapeutic relationship when he or she finds out that the feelings are mutual. It is entirely possible that different ethical codes might give different guidance on a situation like this, particularly when the focus is placed on the nature and length of the therapeutic relationship and exploration of potential for harm. If the practitioner were a psychotherapist, the situation might be viewed differently than if he or she were a financial counsellor. If there had been a counselling relationship that had been ongoing for three months, this would perhaps be viewed differently to a financial problem-solving relationship of only two weeks.

While it is important to have ready access to the code of ethics that governs the discipline in which we work, it is more important to know how to use it well as a proactive tool for ethical practice. McAuliffe (1999), in her doctoral research on ethical dilemmas in front-line social work practice, found that social workers did not use the AASW Code of Ethics in any systematic or reflective way while they were entrenched in a dilemma. Only three out of 30 research participants used the Code of Ethics when they were thinking through what they might have done differently after (in some cases quite a long time after) being involved in a complex ethical dilemma. The others did not think that the Code would have been helpful, and many admitted that they did not know that there was a code of ethics for the profession. A similar study conducted in psychology to explore ethical decision-making also found that knowledge of the APS ethical principles and standards was lower than expected. This study used a number of hypothetical vignettes to explore familiarity with the APS Code of Ethics, and while the psychologists had no problems identifying ethical dilemmas and recognising breaches, their ability to recognise the relevant code sections was inconsistent (Morrison, Morrissey & Goodman, 2006). To place these findings in an educational context, it has really only been since the mid-1990s that professional ethics courses (in both Psychology and Social Work programs) have been taught as discrete units in universities. The emergence of ethics advice services run through professional associations and other organisations, and increased attention to continuing professional education that focuses explicitly on ethical decision-making and application of codes of ethics, are welcome initiatives that appear to be well used by members of the AASW and the APS, according to statistics provided in the annual reports of both associations.

REFLECTION 4.4

1 How easy or difficult is it to find the code of ethics relevant to your discipline on the internet? How can you be sure you have found the most recent version of the code, and when was it last updated?

■ Regulating professional practice

One of the most contested debates taking place in the contemporary social, health and human service environment is the question of the extent to which government should, or should not, regulate or licence members of specified professional disciplines. There is a broad position in the Australian Government that self-regulation is the preferred model unless a professional group is likely to cause harm and place the public at risk. In other countries, this position has changed back and forth over many decades, but in Australia the list of licensed or registered professional groups has remained reasonably stable.

The complaint mechanisms which play a part in regulating professions and services in the social, health and human service industry in Australia are governed by:

•   health complaint commissions in each state and territory

•   federal and state/territory fair-trading complaint management organisations

•   national and state/territory health practitioner registration boards for licensed professions

•   self-regulating professional associations with voluntary membership.

Practitioners in licensed and unlicensed occupations are subject to codes of conduct, codes of ethics, practice standards and complaint management systems within the jurisdiction of various organisations. The codes and jurisdictions applicable to each practitioner differ significantly depending on which state or territory they practice in, and whether their occupation is subject to mandatory regulation (in which case practitioners need a licence before they can use that occupation's title). McAuliffe, Sauvage and Morrissey (2012, p. 57) set out a comparison of how a number of professional bodies in Australia would deal with a hypothetical case of a sexual-boundary violation. After exploring the responses by six professional bodies, they stated that:

> The most notable and alarming difference between the various occupations is that despite similar potential for exploitation and harm to the client in this scenario,

the law ensures that only psychiatrists and psychologists must be registered and accountable to a statutory board. Counsellors, psychotherapists, and social workers in private practice who choose not to be a member of any professional association are not subject to any regulatory provisions whatsoever.

Systems for the regulation of health professions have changed rapidly in Australia since 2010. As of 2014, the 14 occupations requiring statutory registration and licensing by the Australian Health Practitioner Regulation Agency (AHPRA) under the National Registration and Accreditation Scheme (NRAS) are:

- Chinese medicine
- chiropractic
- dentistry
- health work with Aboriginal and Torres Strait Islander people
- medical radiation
- medicine
- midwifery
- nursing
- occupational therapy
- optometry
- osteopathy
- pharmacy
- physiotherapy
- psychology.

Regulation is governed by the Health Practitioner Regulation National Law (the National Law) and each professional discipline has a National Board charged with responsibility for protecting the public. Complaints are made through a systematic process and AHPRA manages registration of members and accreditation of students, and maintains consistency of standards across the National Boards.

The occupations of social worker, psychotherapist, counsellor, welfare worker, case worker and a range of alternative healthcare occupations are self-regulating; that is, federal or state/territory legislation does not require practitioners in these fields to register, nor are they subject to an ethical code or formal complaints mechanism in law. However, many practitioners in these disciplines voluntarily join one of a range of professional associations, which are governed by by-laws under incorporation acts. These self-regulating professional associations only have jurisdiction to regulate those who choose to become members, and they are only able to investigate complaints in relation to their members. This is a widely recognised problem for clients who may experience harm at the hands of practitioners in the private sector, as they do not fall under any regulatory system. Some professional groups believe that occupational regulation is critical for protection of the public and have lobbied strongly for a number of years for its introduction; and while some disciplines have been brought into the jurisdiction of AHPRA (for example, occupational therapy), others have not (for example, social work).

Note that intense lobbying by many of the unregulated professions has led the federal government to conduct a recent investigation into how this sector of the workforce can best be managed without incurring the cost of bringing it under the banner of the NRAS. The Australian Health Ministers' Advisory Council released a comprehensive report in 2013 on 'Options for Regulation of Unregulated Health Practitioners'. Following consultation around the country, a Decision Regulatory Impact Statement (RIS) was released with the conclusion that a national code of conduct with enforcement powers for breach of the code should be developed as the best option for those professions that continue to self-regulate. This option will not set minimum standards for entry into practice, but will focus on enforcement action, which is a form of negative licensing.

■ The case of social work: a 'self-regulated' profession

Social work, despite efforts dating back to the 1960s, remains an unregulated and unregistered profession. The Australian Association of Social Workers (AASW) is the professional association that accredits educational programs, and students who graduate from an approved institution are then 'eligible for membership' of the AASW. Many employers make this eligibility a prerequisite for candidates applying for social work positions. Membership of the AASW is voluntary and there are currently approximately 7000 members in Australia. The AASW has a Code of Ethics (2010), and a number of sets of Practice Standards for mental health, supervision and general practice (2013a). The AASW employs staff, who work as part of the National Ethics and Professional Practice portfolio and who are responsible for managing complaints about alleged unethical conduct of social workers, and for providing information about ethical issues in practice on request to members. If the AASW receives a complaint about a social worker, this can only be investigated if that practitioner is a member; although it cannot manage complaints about non-members, it does help complainants to access other avenues.

The AASW Ethics Complaint Management Process is governed by a set of by-laws (2013b), and is administered by a National Ethics Panel, which refers complaints for hearing by a three-member panel. The Hearing Panel interviews all concerned parties, reaches a decision on whether the complaint can be substantiated in relation to a breach of a section of the AASW Code of Ethics, and determines penalty. Options for penalty range from a reprimand letter, to periods of supervised practice, through to termination of membership resulting in ineligibility. Employers can be notified, and names can be made public in serious cases. Decisions can be appealed on specified grounds. While the AASW has engaged in significant political lobbying to be considered eligible for AHPRA, and has been successful in providing evidence of harms that social workers can cause to vulnerable clients, registration is still elusive. In 2014, the AASW was successful in obtaining a registered trademark that enables its members to demonstrate that they have completed a qualification that makes them eligible for the AASW. While government has moved towards introduction of a national code of conduct for unregistered professions, which could include social work, the AASW maintains its position that NRAS is the most relevant body to regulate a profession that works with people who are potentially at risk of harm by social work services. The AASW is opposed to a negative licensing scheme, on the basis that such schemes do nothing to proactively prevent unethical conduct. The AASW position paper, setting out its opposition to the National Code of Conduct, includes compelling evidence for social work to be included in NRAS (AASW, n.d.).

When we consider what sorts of harms can potentially be done to people who receive services in the areas of counselling, psychotherapy and casework, it is important to understand that these are broad-ranging and can have traumatic impacts that can affect people for life. As an important contribution to the evidence on impacts of harm, Sauvage (2014) has completed doctoral research on the impacts of complaint processes on people who have experienced harm, and as part of this research developed a list of the types of harmful practices from a comprehensive review of the literature:

- Illegal activity that harms a client (including assault, paedophilia).
- Boundary transgressions, violations and abuse of trust including sexual involvement; verbally sexualising or romanticising therapy; financial dealings; dual relationships; use of inappropriate touch; personal disclosure issues.
- Psychological exploitation, including cult-like techniques and 'mind control', or those involving pseudo-spiritual ideas and 'magical thinking', where the therapist imposes a distorted view of reality from an expert position; psychological grooming for dependency and exploitation financially, psychologically, emotionally, spiritually or sexually; use of expert position to invade clients capacity for boundary setting, to use authority to unreasonably direct clients' major life decisions.
- Unclear or non-existent contracting about limits of service or unexpected outcomes; over-servicing or under-servicing; failure to provide grievance or restitution procedures.

- Lack of thorough assessment, effective intervention, or referral.
- Contravention of clients' rights to confidentiality, poor or inaccurate reporting or note-taking.
- Practitioner impairment, workload stressors, burnout, moral distress.
- Dominance of therapists' values, beliefs, advice or method of therapy in a manner that is disempowering or harmful for the client.
- 'Empirically' unproven or questionable methods without a clear evidence base, lack of knowledge of neuroscience, trauma and mental health–specific issues.
- Problematic approaches to transference and counter-transference.
- Mismanagement of 'therapeutic alliance ruptures' and 'termination'.
- Distant, cold, unengaged manner, lacking in human quality.

THROUGH THE EYES OF A PRACTITIONER

Importance of occupational regulation

Through the process of doing doctoral research about cases where a service went wrong, or where a practitioner's conduct was considered unethical or exploitative of clients, I discovered just how powerful we are in roles in the health and helping professions. It is for this reason that I strongly advocate for robust regulation and supervision of all occupations in the health and helping industries. There must be avenues for setting practice standards and accountability.

Before doing the research I never had the opportunity to see just how tragic and complex the impacts can be in these cases. It was not something I was exposed to in my undergraduate degree. In fact, when power was mentioned it was always in a positive way, focused on the 'empowerment' of clients. Yet one of the strongest themes voiced by research participants (including those who had been involved in complaints either as clients, practitioners or complaint managers) was that power wielded in cases that went wrong was largely 'un-owned', 'underestimated' and 'unmanaged'. There was also a strong critique of the notion that clients have capacity for self-determination when interacting in the context of professional influence.

One way of owning power is to reflect now, as you read this, on whether you have a robust awareness of the myriad ways that harm can occur. Are you aware of cases? Have you spoken to colleagues about them? Most people think that the main way to harm a client is to breach sexual boundaries (this significant exploitation of trust may lead the client to suicide, and in many high-profile cases the practitioner involved has also committed suicide). The power to impact a person psychologically is also enormously powerful and complex. How we make assumptions about clients and formally assess, diagnose and report about them are powerful. Whether we do this with strong supervision is important. Our words, tone, consistency of interactions, regularity of follow up, and how we assist clients to manage their expectations of our role, can be helpful, or potentially lead to risks of harm. We may consciously or unconsciously promote an unhealthy dependence in our clients, which has complex psychological, relational and financial impacts for them. We may choose to overlook evidence-informed practice principles and promote specific healing ideologies and methods of practice without comprehending the risks. The dynamics in these cases only become apparent when you read the human stories, hear people's voices and understand their lived experience, perspectives and circumstances. So, take whatever opportunities you can to learn, not in a morbid but in a constructive way, from cases which went wrong. Search the internet, read transcripts of cases that went before ethics and registration boards. This information can then inform your position regarding the value of occupational regulation.

(Deborah Sauvage)

REFLECTION 4.5

1 Do you believe that government has a role to play in regulating members of professions, and if so, to what extent should it be involved?
2 Do you consider that professions like social work and counselling or psychotherapy should be regulated by the Australian Health Practitioner Regulation Agency? What differences do you see between these and the other listed professions, such as nursing, medicine or psychology?
3 How do you think the unregulated disciplines should best be managed to prevent potential harms to the public?

■ Responding to complaints: a framework of natural justice

It is clear from the preceding discussion that the regulatory system is complex and there are many entry and exit points for clients and practitioners. Rather than explore any of the individual systems that manage complaints made about the conduct and practice of people who work in the social, health and human service industry, it is perhaps better to provide an overview of what factors should be considered in the event of a complaint being made about practice, and the need to respond to such a complaint.

As a starting point, we need to understand that complaint processes are built on the acknowledgement that people who are recipients of services have a right to complain about those services, and that the respondents to complaints have a right to put their case forward to explain circumstances that may have influenced a particular course of action or decision. The important principle of natural justice (or procedural fairness) underpins our legal and regulatory systems, meaning that matters should be dealt with fairly and impartially; that all parties have the right and opportunity to be heard; and that processes will be transparent and not subject to bias. The concept of 'therapeutic jurisprudence' is also important, as it represents the move towards education and mentoring in complaint processes, reducing the emphasis on punitive measures. An example of a response that might result from a substantiated complaint, in accordance with this principle, would be the imposition of a period of supervised practice, or a requirement that a respondent engage in a period of counselling or therapy. When a complaint is made about a practitioner, it is reasonable that the respondent should have a clear understanding of the grounds on which that complaint has been made; access to all relevant documents; and the opportunity to receive support and advice about their response to the complaint. Matters should be dealt with in a confidential and non-discriminatory way, and any limitations to confidentiality clearly explained; time frames for responses should be clear and complaints managed expediently; and avenues for appeal of decisions should be made available. Respondents should be clear about what might happen as a result of a complaint being substantiated, what penalties might be imposed, whether employers will be notified, and whether outcomes of an investigation may be made public.

There is no doubt that being involved in a complaint process can be a difficult experience for both clients and respondents. Organisations that have responsibility for management of complaints need to ensure that their actions are transparent, fair, and clear in terms of processes and expectations, and that they afford all parties to the complaint a timely resolution that will result in outcomes to validate substantiated allegations, provide restitution where appropriate, and respectfully acknowledge the emotional impacts of the process in the longer term.

■ Conclusion

This chapter has explored issues in the regulatory context of professional practice, and has highlighted a number of important points. First and foremost, we need to understand that, despite all proclamations about 'doing no harm', the reality is that potential for harm does exist and vulnerable people need to be offered a level of protection from potential harms. It is not difficult to see how an incompetent medical practitioner who has been inadequately trained could cause physical harm in an operating theatre; or a dentist who does not observe hygiene practices could place patients at risk. Chiropractors, podiatrists and practitioners of Chinese medicine could cause harm through wrongful treatment, or through lack of knowledge of proper techniques. It is more difficult to see harms that are caused by psychological traumas, breaches of privacy, unorthodox rituals and group therapies, and insufficient attention to psychological needs.

We need to understand the implications of the unregulated professions, and the role of professional associations in setting standards of practice in a self-regulated environment. This chapter has set out the role of professional associations, and the place of codes of ethics and standards of practice, leading into the next chapter, which explores ethical decision-making processes and models. As we will explore in Chapter 5, ethical decision-making involves using our knowledge of our ethical responsibilities, as set out in codes of ethics, to respond within acceptable professional standards to ethical dilemmas when they arise. Later chapters will also set out the usefulness of codes of ethics to explorations of a range of ethical issues that regularly confront practitioners in the social, health and human services.

5

Ethical decision-making

■ Learning objectives

- **OUTLINE THE** history and development of ethical decision-making models and approaches in different professional disciplines

- **EXPLORE CRITICAL** components of ethical decision-making and the impact of conflict on functioning of interprofessional teams

- **IDENTIFY THE** skills needed for sound ethical decision-making in the context of interprofessional practice

■ Introduction

MAKING DECISIONS IS something that we all have to do every day in our lives, both personally and professionally. While some quickly and confidently make choices between available options, others tend towards caution and indecisiveness. Many factors affect the way we make decisions, including structural factors that lie outside individual control, but patterns of decision-making and responses to managing complex situations can become learned and entrenched over time. Some of these patterns are set in early childhood, based on parental and authoritarian responses to actions and behaviours, and may be consolidated in adolescence through risk-taking and experimentation, becoming subject to changeability in adulthood as we become more aware of the impacts of consequences through experience and retrospective wisdom. Klaczynski, Byrnes & Jacobs (2001, p. 225) offer a clinical definition of decision-making as

> a multicomponent process that begins with a recognised discrepancy between one's current state and one's goal state, involves identifying and evaluating the potential for various options to reduce the discrepancy, selecting and planning a course of action, implementing the required actions, evaluating the consequences of those actions, and processing and storing feedback regarding an action's efficacy.

The important part of this definition is the focus on decision-making as a 'multicomponent process', which requires attention to a number of steps in sequence, using conscious action and information to make a final determination of what action to take.

In the social, health and human services, the implications of decisions made can have far reaching effects on many people, groups and communities. We have seen in earlier chapters that ethical theories, such as deontology, utilitarianism, communitarian, relational and feminist ethics of care, can offer clarity around reasons for decisions and can help us understand why people make one decision rather than another, when both are potentially viable choices. For some, decisions are straightforward and there is a clear direction to follow, because there are laws, guidelines, policies or protocols that dictate which action is right or wrong, acceptable or inappropriate. For others, the laws and policies may be clear enough, but personal values dictate a different course of action in line with morality or conscience, making decisions much more difficult. 'Sitting on the fence' is a position that most professionals prefer to avoid for fear that others may judge them as indecisive or uncertain. Yet often we find that 'fence sitting' provides a unique vantage point from which the values and behaviours of others can be observed at a respectable distance. There is a great deal to be said for 'buying time' in decision-making, so that we can weigh up all possible courses of action and give due consideration to all foreseeable consequences. The cognitive process of predicting potential implications arising from decisions has been defined as 'forecasting' (Stenmark, 2013), and research indicates that people can be trained to improve their ability to forecast by expanding the number of consequences they are prepared to explore, including implications for themselves and others.

When practitioners enter the ethical dimension of work, however, and their decisions involve issues to do with rights, duties, responsibilities or obligations, there is often pressure to act quickly and decisively, and often, a number of other people are also engaged in the same situation, who may need to be included in a process of consultation. We have explored the role of interdisciplinary professional ethics in earlier chapters, and perhaps nowhere do these important dynamics play out more than in the *ethical* decision-making process. This chapter will scrutinise the field of ethical decision-making within the professions, exploring the plethora of models and approaches that have developed over time to help people work through difficult and complex choices in order to move towards an integrated development of a professional framework for authentic and useful ethical decision-making.

■ Exploring personal decision-making styles

How we make decisions is often closely linked to how we operate in the world generally. If we live and work at a fast pace, juggling many balls in the air, we are likely to make quick decisions to keep moving things forward. If we live life more slowly and methodically, we are more likely to take time to consider options before launching into impulsive actions. Decision-making is defined as 'the process of *making* a choice, where the emphasis is on making, that is constructing, a choice. Decision-making occurs when there is some degree of recognition of a need or desire to make a choice' (O'Sullivan, 1999, p. 10).

We can take a number of decision attributes into account when we look at what constitutes an important consideration in the context of the decision, including:

- how urgent the matter is and whether there is any room for delaying a decision
- how familiar the situation is and whether this familiarity helps us ground previous knowledge
- how unique the situation is and how many variables need to be weighed up
- how much risk there might be surrounding the decision
- how stable the external environment is and how likely the goalposts are to shift.

The more unknowns and uncertainty there are about facts, and the more information is missing, the more difficult the decision becomes; the higher the risk factors and conflict, the more cautious the approaches required. It takes practice to make decisions with confidence, and it takes time to accumulate experiences that can shape methods of justification. See 'Through the eyes of a practitioner' for an illustration of how some of these factors are balanced, in the context of work in paediatric health practice.

THROUGH THE EYES OF A PRACTITIONER

Ethical decision-making and guidance bear a huge responsibility and are not something that I take lightly. Ethically, I see myself as the interface between the parents who are trying to make a decision in a crisis, surrounded by emotions, driven by love and the enormous fear of loss and what they think they want and can cope with in the future *and* medical teams who are trying to act in the best interest of the child based on their own ideas of quality of life and aggressive interventions. I am a strong advocate of time and information as power, in the middle of ethical decision-making. I like to gently remind both parties that with regards to ethics and beliefs there is rarely one truth but a series of truths and my job is often to assist people to find the most ethical truth for them or the decision which feels most 'survivable long term'. Ethical decision-making is a combination of processes for me: an accumulation of 20 years' practice, experience and knowledge; a strong awareness of my own values with extreme care that these do not impose on practice; an acknowledgement of the strength of parental love and the way this will influence the parents I work with; and a sense of the spiritual nature and environment I work within. I take all of these facts and find a safe space to sit and work it through with all parties.

(Liz Crowe)

There are many definitions of ethical decision-making, but essentially it refers to the process of critical reflection, evaluation and judgement through which a practitioner resolves ethical issues, problems and dilemmas. McAuliffe (2012b, p. 41) further defines ethical decision-making as engagement in an exploration of values 'that may be evident in the personal, professional, social and organizational spheres – in order to establish where an ethical dilemma might lie according to what competing principles, and what factors take priority in the weighing up of alternatives'. Some literature also refers to the term 'moral decision-making', defined as 'that which is fundamentally concerned with reconciling moral disagreements between disputing parties, each of whom may hold equally valid moral viewpoints and may reach different yet reasonable conclusions on what constitutes "right" and "wrong" conduct in a given context' (Johnstone, 2009, p. 114). There are clear differences between decisions that have an ethical or moral dimension, and those that are more aesthetic or clinical or that concern problems that do not involve competing values. Having said this, it is difficult to think of many situations in our work with people that do not involve ethics or values at some level, particularly when we are talking about issues that have an impact on people's access to resources, quality of life, or human rights.

REFLECTION 5.1

1   If you were to ask someone who knows you well to describe what you are like as a 'decision-maker', what words would they use?
2   Do you think you have an established pattern or process for making decisions? Describe this.

Dolgoff, Loewenberg & Harrington (2009, pp. 48–52) discuss various approaches to ethical decision-making that highlight differences in philosophical positions, similar to those discussed in Chapter 2. The first of these, 'clinical pragmatism', is a conservative approach that supports maintenance of the status quo and focuses primarily on preserving social order. Decisions will be made in the interests of social stability and the harmony of social relations, without much of a challenge to unjust systems or discrimination. 'Humanistic ethics' emphasises individualism, freedom of choice and support for opportunities that will preserve equality. This approach, based on existential philosophy, with a strong emphasis on self-actualisation, shifts the responsibility from practitioner to client and encourages self-expression, although this is sometimes at the expense of the best interests of others. 'Religious ethics' focuses on a merging of law and ethics, and does not consider them separate. The belief is that right and wrong is divinely determined and authority lies with God. The 'ethics of caring' places emphasis on relationships and connection to others, while 'feminist ethics' locates private troubles in the context of public issues and critiques domination and power. 'Virtue ethics' focuses on the development of moral character over time and relies on people having the guidance and moral training to learn how to be of good character. When we look closely at our own ways of making decisions, and at what we give precedence to when we do so, we can see elements of these philosophical foundations inherent in our values and resultant actions. An awareness of what drives our decisions, in accordance with understanding of what we hold as most important, helps us justify them and is an important part of critical reflection.

■ Structural influences on ethical decision-making: understanding defensive practice

The context in which many social, health and human service practitioners go about their daily work is one governed by regulatory and legal processes and employer policies and protocols. Many organisations devote considerable time and resources to induction processes for new staff to ensure they comply with standards and clearly understand their statutory responsibilities. The dominance of risk management frameworks is a cumulative result over many decades of gradual erosion of professional autonomy, as the complexity of social problems has pushed duty-of-care obligations to the surface and subjected them to mandatory controls. The term 'risk society' has been used to describe the changes over time that have resulted in risk being formally predicted and 'managed' rather than accepted as part of the uncertainty that comes with social development (Beck, 1992; Giddens, 1990). According to Eileen Munro, who has written extensively on risk in relation to child protection, the implications of this shift are that practice has become 'defensive' and the focus has shifted from the protection of vulnerable clients to the protection of workers and agencies. As Munro says: 'defensive practice gives preference to avoiding the risks where the worker might be blamed over minimising the risks to the service user overall' (2012, p. 232). Examples of defensive practice in this context might include a child protection worker taking children into care prematurely, or a person being hospitalised on the basis of poetry that might indicate suicidal intent, which they published on a blog.

The question often asked is not 'what is best for the client?' but 'what do I need to do to avoid getting into trouble if something goes wrong here?' The equivalent in health care is known as 'defensive medicine'; essentially, attempting to reduce the risk of malpractice litigation by ordering excessive tests or referring for further consultations. Defensive practice can increase costs with little real benefit to clients or users of services (Kerridge, Lowe & McPhee, 2005).

More than a decade ago, Frederic Reamer, an American social work academic, developed the 'Social Work Ethics Audit Risk Management Tool' (Reamer, 2001a) which identified a total of seventeen areas of ethical risk. These risks included documentation and client records; boundaries and conflicts of interest; the giving and receiving of gifts; dual and multiple relationships; and terminating relationships with clients. This tool guided practitioners and employers to audit both policies and procedures systematically in an organisation, in order to establish the degree of risk through a ranking process. This risk related to users of services, practitioners within services, and the services themselves as employing bodies. The US ethics audit tool was taken by McAuliffe (2005a) and used as the basis for a research project with 10 Australian organisations, including hospitals, domestic-violence services, and small agencies based in the community, to trial its usefulness and determine the degree to which ethical risk was recognised in a different cultural context. This research found that there was significantly heightened awareness of the need for ethical decision-making frameworks in the agencies that were part of the research, and acknowledged issues that often increased ethical risk, including:

- lack of attention to open communication about sensitive issues, such as boundaries around both intimate relationships and friendships
- the giving and receiving of gifts
- privacy in documentation and client records
- termination of relationships
- issues to do with the death of a client or a worker.

There were often differences between what organisational policies dictated should happen, and what employees or volunteers actually did in their work practices. For example, while an agency might have a written policy about the receiving of gifts from clients, what staff actually did was sometimes different depending on a range of contextual factors. One of the partner organisations, a major hospital social work department, extended this research, going on to examine documentation in more depth, and making a number of important changes to its social work recording practices in medical records as a result (Cumming et al., 2007). This is a good example of an organisation turning a concern with risk, which as we have seen can lead to defensive practice, into proactive initiatives to identify potential problem areas and manage them by modifying practices to enable better attention to issues of ethical importance.

When exploring the aetiology of risk, and connecting this to ethical decision-making, we need to examine those structural factors that contribute to making some decisions more contentious than they may otherwise have been in different political or economic circumstances. For example, many ethical decisions come down to allocation of resources, as seen in previous chapters, which then means that some people will miss out on much needed assistance because they are not in a 'priority group' or are seen as less 'deserving' than others. This then becomes an issue of people's right to receive assistance, which should not always depend on their means or what they have contributed. Structural factors mean that many people are born into and live in poverty, many are and will remain unemployed, and many more have restricted access to education, health services and affordable housing. Marston, McDonald and Bryson (2014, p. 125) have offered an at-times scathing critique on the neoliberalist construction of welfare, highlighting how 'the dominant discourse about welfare is often conducted in terms of a behavioural and moral focus on the deficits of, for example, the homeless, the unemployed and the uneducated'. Such critique is important when seeking to understand the basis on which policymakers develop eligibility criteria for service delivery. The premise of many policies is based on the concept of mutual obligation – if you give, you will receive; if you work hard, you will reap financial reward; if you take care of others, you will be taken care of. This premise only holds if everyone starts from an 'equal position', which of course is simply not the case in societies that have socio-economic, cultural and political differences.

Ethical decision-making can be tied up with law and policies, codes of ethics and social mores, and can be dictated by the government of the day, with the expectation that employees of government will observe the 'party line'. Part of good ethical decision-making is being aware of structural influences and taking them into account in forming rationales and justifications. If a solution to a problem is restricted by budget because resources have been channelled into more 'worthy causes', this needs to be clearly stated. If a decision to provide or restrict a service is made on the basis of financial eligibility, age, gender, life choices, or health status, this should be transparent. As we move on to look at different models of ethical decision-making, it will become apparent that consideration of structural factors is embedded in models that take a broader view of ethics than is possible if we focus predominantly on the individual and the choices that people make. A comprehensive and inclusive model of ethical decision-making will acknowledge history, culture, different forms of disempowerment, discrimination and oppression, and will seek wide engagement with many people and levels of connection.

◼ Ethical decision-making in the professions: a plethora of models

An investigation of the historical development of ethics and models of ethical decision-making within the professions shows a reasonably common trajectory. Professions typically start with the articulation of a purpose and carving out of territory and claims of distinctiveness, moving into the development of an epistemology and ontology based on theoretical foundations, and then into the definition of skills and evidence for interventions. The development of a value base generally accompanies the clarification of purpose, and this then lays the basis for specification of how individuals who belong to that profession should behave in terms of conduct. Most of the professions we have mentioned so far in this book developed their formal codes of ethics early in their development, and have revised them many times as issues have emerged and further clarification has been required about what constitutes appropriate and effective practice. We have already seen in Chapter 4 that regulation of many professions has meant that decision-making sits within a controlled context, and the space for autonomous action has been eroded. Many of the ethical decision-making models that have developed within fields such as business, public policy and marketing, are designed to protect the bottom line – the financial imperative – and are often rigid and formulaic as a result. In other professions, such as education, nursing, psychology and social work, there is much more scope for autonomous flexibility, and this is reflected in the common ethical decision-making models in these fields. Next, we will examine the different models.

Many writers have attempted to categorise and describe ways in which ethical decision-making models have been developed and the premises on which they are based. For example, Chenoweth and McAuliffe, writing in the context of Australian human services, first set out a schema in 2005 that classified the ethical decision-making models available in the literature across professions, which contained three categories. In looking at the strengths of each of these groups of models, they then went on to develop an 'inclusive model of ethical decision-making' (McAuliffe & Chenoweth, 2008; Chenoweth & McAuliffe, 2014). This model, which has had broad application across other disciplines, will be explored further in the following section.

This first set of models relies on a structured formula – what Chenoweth and McAuliffe (2014) have identified as the 'process models'. These models set out a number of steps designed to assist a practitioner in the rigorous thinking through of an ethical dilemma, with a view to reaching a resolution that can be justified according to ethical theory, law and rules of conduct. A checklist often accompanies such models, and they are favoured by those who seek structure and prefer to adhere primarily to law or policy. The models are predominantly deontological in that they focus on rules and order, but they also allow for ranking of ethical principles in a hierarchy to assist professionals in weighing up alternative options according to possible consequences. For example, the ethical principles screen proposed by Dolgoff, Lowenberg and Harrington (2009) sets up a hierarchy of principles, in this order:

1 protection of life
2 equality and inequality
3 autonomy and freedom
4 least harm; quality of life
5 privacy and confidentiality
6 truthfulness and full disclosure.

In the case of a practitioner or a team dealing with an ethical dilemma in which the competing principles are protection of life versus quality of life, this prioritisation of principles would dictate that they act to uphold the first principle, the protection of life. Looking critically at this process, however, it is not easy to see why autonomy and freedom should rank higher than privacy and confidentiality, or why least harm should be a lower priority than equality and inequality; people will rank order principles differently according to context, beliefs and many other factors. The authors themselves have stated in an article exploring different ways of constructing value hierarchies, that 'we are not suggesting that there is one "right" hierarchy of ethical principles, or even that there should be agreement on a hierarchy; rather, that it may be useful to consider the implications of different priorities' (Harrington & Dolgoff, 2008, p. 195). Other examples of process models include the ETHIC model of decision-making developed by Congress (1999); the Robison and Reeser (2000) 'tracking of harms' model; and the Comprehensive Model of EDM from psychology (Miner, 2006).

The second set of ethical decision-making models comprises those that are more critically reflective in their orientation, and that focus attention on the relational nature of ethical deliberations and explorations of power. These 'reflective models' rest on feminist foundations, posing questions about uncovering value premises, challenging assumptions about right and wrong, and focusing on the decision-maker and his or her own experiences, intuitions and insights. Reflective models, again in keeping with feminist traditions, aim towards inclusivity and encourage active engagement with clients and others who have a stake in the outcomes in the decision-making process (Mattison, 2000). While the 'process models' tend to distance the decision-maker from the subject of the decision in order to maintain a more objective stance, the reflective models value the subjective and support broad consultation with others, particularly those with lived experience, who may be able to make valuable contributions from that experience. While it is true that reflective models also provide a structured process, the key difference is that there is a constant looping back to previous stages as new information comes to light, or reflections provide new ways of viewing a situation. Reflective models take laws, ethical codes and policies into account as part of information gathering, but making decisions in accordance with these rules is not a foregone conclusion if other contextual factors are more important. An example of an ethical decision-making model based on feminist philosophy is that developed by Hill, Glaser and Harden (1995), which drew both the rational–evaluative and the feeling–intuitive processes together, in a reflective process that emphasised the identification of power dynamics and imbalances.

The third set of ethical decision-making models contains those that place cultural considerations at the forefront, and that ask at each stage whether there is evidence of cultural discrimination within any part of the decision-making process. These 'cultural models' are much less common in the literature than the process and reflective models, but they still provide an important additional lens through which to view ethical dilemmas that have cultural dimensions. A model from psychology, which focuses on racial and ethnic culture, is the Transcultural Integrative Model for Ethical Decision-making (Garcia et al., 2003). This is a complex but highly relevant model for consideration of cultural factors, and it highlights the importance of seeking cultural expertise and consulting appropriately.

In a similar vein, other literature has addressed the issue of the need for a specialist ethical decision-making framework for dealing with issues of spirituality and religion in psychotherapy. This model, developed by Barnett and Johnson (2011), is a combination of process and reflection, with a series of very specific questions designed to assist psychotherapists in deciding whether to continue therapy, or refer to another practitioner, a client whose case involves spiritual or religious issues. This model requires the therapist to disclose any of their own religious or spiritual views that might have a positive or negative impact on a therapeutic relationship, and supports the practitioner's withdrawal from a relationship if there are indications that the practitioner has, or is likely to have, strong emotional reactions to spiritual or religious discussions. This model is firmly grounded in literature and research and is an example of a decision-making model that has been developed for a very specific purpose.

THROUGH THE EYES OF A PRACTITIONER

Occasionally I have faced genuine ethical dilemmas in my work, in which duties and obligations have clashed. Last year, I was unexpectedly confronted with a dilemma in which I had to make the 'best' decision for practice, but I knew that both outcomes I could choose had serious and negative implications for a mother. Even after much critical reflection, I felt 'stuck' and did not know what to do. I had no idea what was 'best practice' in that particular situation. So I decided that I needed to apply an ethical decision-making model to help with the process of analysing and considering what was really causing tension, and what I would feel most comfortable with. I had learned about these models at university, although I had no idea that I would really need or value it in practice. As I sat down and applied each step of the model to my case, I was then able to reach an outcome that I could justify, could be accountable for, and could live with. I believed it was 'best practice outcome' in the context, even though I knew it would still have implications for my client. In the heat of the moment, when you are faced with a serious ethical decision, as well as the other agency pressures, it is important that you have an effective tool, like an ethical decision-making model, that you can apply to assist with making difficult choices, to ensure best practice outcomes and processes for clients.

(Michelle Kemp)

■ The inclusive model of ethical decision-making: moving to the interprofessional context

As stated, the inclusive model of ethical decision-making (Chenoweth & McAuliffe, 2014) is an attempt to draw together the threads of what is important when a need arises to make a decision in a matter involving rights, duties, obligations or responsibilities. The original inclusive model was developed following a systematic overview of a number of models from other disciplines – a process that resulted in the categorisation of models we have explored in this chapter. The first step in development of the inclusive model was to clearly define the important dimensions on which such a model could rest. The four dimensions are:

- accountability
- consultation
- cultural sensitivity
- critical reflection.

While these are in no particular order, it is perhaps important to consider accountability to be of paramount interest because of the connection to transparency, openness, and justification. When we think about who we are 'accountable' to in our work lives, the first thought is generally to the employing organisation that funds us and to which

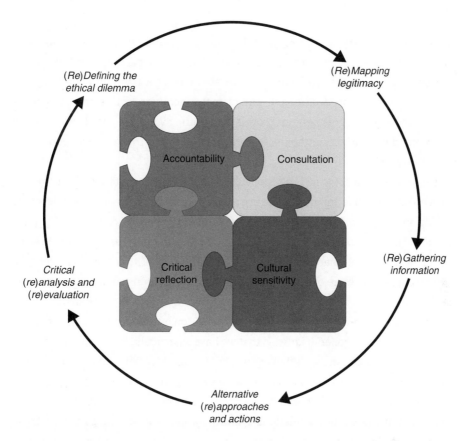

Figure 5.1 An inclusive model of ethical decision-making (*The Road to Social Work and Human Service Practice*, Chenoweth & McAuliffe 2014, p. 123. Reprinted with the permission of Cengage Learning Australia Pty Ltd.)

we are (supposedly and ideally) loyal. When we look at this more carefully, we can see that there are much broader societal implications and that employees are really accountable to the general public at large who pay taxes to support the existence of agencies and their staff. To be accountable essentially means being able to give an objective and unbiased account of oneself, acknowledging conflicts of interest, and following the line as far as it stretches. A person who is not accountable will shun any efforts to provide information, will postpone and defer appointments, and will generally not allow scrutiny of actions. In the context of ethical decision-making, there may be multiple lines of accountability, and part of the model is to painstakingly map these out. Accountability to self is a part of this process, which requires the capacity for self-awareness and critical reflection. In the interprofessional context, however, many other dynamics also come into play, not least the maintenance of good working relationships with colleagues and managers, meaning that accountability has to extend to peer relationships as well as employers and the public. When we work in a multidisciplinary team, it may be that the team as a whole is accountable to higher authorities such as health boards, an education department or a volunteer committee of management. Shared accountability gives a team an added impetus to reach consensus on decisions. If one or more members of a team opt out of a decision through disagreement, or provide a dissenting voice, this needs to be clearly documented so that accountability is rightly attributed to those who, in good faith, made the decision.

The second dimension is that of consultation. It is important to draw a distinction between talking to like-minded others in a reasonably informal way, and more formally seeking out people who have knowledge, wisdom and 'expertise' on a particular topic or issue. This type of more formal consultation is different from support. Seeking support is something that can be done as a natural part of friendship or a collegial relationship, and is more oriented to the emotional level than inquiry or information seeking. The person seeking support generally does not need or want advice – what they want and need is someone to listen to them. Consultation, on the other hand, is more deliberate and generally means that we have a particular question that requires an answer from someone with higher level knowledge. McAuliffe and Sudbery (2005) explored the range of reasons that social workers gave for either engaging or not connecting with others while trying to resolve an ethical dilemma. The key, of course, is to determine the nature of relationships with a view to determining issues of trust. Not surprisingly, this research showed that many of the participants were uneasy about consulting with colleagues who did not share their value base, and there was open hostility towards the practice of line management supervision, which was generally linked to performance appraisal. Social workers in this study were more likely to discuss ethical dilemmas with colleagues from the same discipline, and were quite principled in their reluctance to burden family and friends with work-related stress. They understood the implications of vicarious trauma, were cognisant of privacy and confidentiality, and were aware of the psychological and physical manifestations of stress caused by management of complex ethical dilemmas. The strong messages from this research were that social workers who did not consult appropriately, and who did not seek support, were more at risk of developing stress-related conditions, were more likely to leave jobs, and were often unable to separate their own needs from those of clients (McAuliffe, 2005b).

The third dimension in the inclusive model of ethical decision-making is that of cultural sensitivity. This is more than looking to identify ethnic or racial considerations, but is also about exploring culture in the more sociological definition of that term. This could include consideration of youth culture, drug-taking culture, or the culture of homelessness. When we are considering cultural sensitivity, we are actively looking to all dimensions of a situation that could in any way have cultural implications. These might relate to language, land, kinship, customs, rituals, religion or spirituality. Failure to look at cultural worldviews can blinker decision-making and result in discriminatory actions to the neglect of important information. In linking back to the principle of consultation, it is critical that cultural expertise is sought in situations that call for specific knowledge outside the general. Take, for example, a situation that involves need for knowledge of cultural protocols in moving into an indigenous community. A practitioner who is not experienced in working with First Peoples may easily neglect the necessity for prior engagement with elders, and can walk into a situation with limited knowledge about how to connect with key community members. A practitioner not accustomed to working with young refugee women may unintentionally neglect many of the important cultural rituals that go with rites of passage into adulthood. Lack of understanding of older people and the process of ageing can result in failure to promote autonomy and self-determination in decisions about end-of-life care. Urban-centric views and failure to acknowledge the culture of rurality and distinct differences of living and working in rural communities, can have a negative impact on decision-making about resource allocations and prioritisation of resources. From these examples, we can clearly see that attention to culture is an important platform of ethical consideration.

The final dimension is critical reflection. This is the ability to take a step back and look with as much objectivity as possible at experiences, previous knowledge, and learned understandings of new situations. Critical reflection is linked to critical thinking, which is the ability to think about thinking while thinking. To be able to subject oneself not only to self-scrutiny but also to the scrutiny of colleagues, peers and others, can be difficult. To be critically reflective is to be prepared to look more deeply than the surface, moving into a space of self-awareness that allows access to previously experienced subjectivities. Critical reflection is closely linked to accountability in that the primary aim of such reflection is to reach a justifiable position on an issue so that there is a degree of transparency, authenticity, genuineness and congruence between personal and professional values. Being able to engage in critical reflective practice is a hallmark of a professional person who can explore with honesty those value positions and moral standpoints that hold secure in any given situation. As previously mentioned, the feminist and reflective models of ethical decision-making rely on capacity for self-evaluative processes, with the aim being to make practice better rather than maintaining an even keel. Critical reflection, in these models, questions the use of power, socialisation processes, and structural impediments to people achieving their best potential. Using consultation wisely can ensure that we subject practice to the scrutiny of others, gaining valuable feedback about:

- moral blind spots
- areas in which our judgement is perhaps impaired
- issues that trigger emotional responses, standing in the way of objective logic.

There is now an impressive body of literature across many professional disciplines on critical reflection, critical thinking and the benefits to interprofessional teams of adopting a reflexive approach to practice.

REFLECTION 5.3

Consider the four dimensions of accountability, cultural sensitivity, consultation and critical reflection. Give rationales for your responses to the following questions.

1 To which of the four dimensions do you find that you naturally pay attention when making decisions?

2 On which of the four do you think you might need to make a more conscious effort to focus?

■ The process of ethical decision-making in the inclusive model: five stages

The four dimensions of ethical decision-making are intertwined and provide a solid basis from which to ask a range of questions that will lead an individual practitioner or a multidisciplinary team through a structured process to resolution of an ethical dilemma. The inclusive model of ethical decision-making has five stages, the first being identifying the actual problem and defining the ethical dilemma. In this initial stage, a practitioner needs to ask questions about the identification of competing ethical principles, including an exploration of which principles may be in conflict, for example:

- the best interests of the client versus the interests of a third party
- duty of care versus confidentiality
- collegial relationships versus loyalty to employer
- disclosure versus privacy.

This first stage is critical in deciding whether there is any ethical dilemma to deal with. Sometimes the process of working through this first step can bring about the realisation that while there may have been an ethical problem, the choices were always clear, and so there was never really an ethical dilemma as such. Having determined that there is a conflict between principles, the next question is to ask who has the authority to move forward and engage with the ethical dilemma – it is a question of accountability. It is often common for newer graduates to feel that they have to take responsibility for things that are not really their ambit or concern. Addressing this question at the first step helps a practitioner clarify whether an ethical decision-making model is needed and appropriate, and whether he or she should manage it or hand it to a higher authority.

The second step of the inclusive model is the step of mapping legitimacy. This is the important process of engagement with all identified stakeholders to ascertain who has a place in the decision-making process or outcome, and who should be held back at arm's length or, perhaps, disconnected altogether. In this step, cultural considerations often come to the fore and we should ask whether it is appropriate for certain people to be privy to information while others are denied such access. During this mapping, we identify people with whom we might consult about potential outcomes or consequences, ensuring that we have accounted for all significant people and their relevance and contributions. It is important to include cultural expertise in this process. If, for example, there is no Aboriginal or Torres Strait Islander worker in a team, and an issue arises about engagement with an Indigenous community, we may need to hold off a decision until we have sought such cultural expertise.

The third step is gathering information. While this might sound simple, it is rarely the case. We have discussed in earlier chapters the overload of materials, documents, laws and policies that dominate many proceedings. Organisations of varying sizes and complexity will have guidelines on many issues, setting out the policies, laws or mandates that employees are expected to follow. While law and policy may be reasonably straightforward, codes of professional ethics are generally open to interpretation. Also challenging is the search for literature, research or other evidence base that could provide the magic answer. Cultural knowledge is important here, and consultation with others to gain more information is a part of this step. In the interprofessional context, it can be difficult to bring together all the information required, so it is critical to complete the previous step to understand who has a legitimate place to work with the identified ethical dilemma.

THROUGH THE EYES OF A PRACTITIONER

In teaching, you have policies that guide practice. They give you a set of boundaries and within those boundaries you have discretion as to the path you will take. If it is a child-safety issue, it is black and white. If it is a social dilemma, then you look at what is available to you within those boundaries. You might go and speak to a whole range of people who have expertise. At the end of the day you document everything. Before you get to that, there has to be a process of data gathering ... it comes with experience.

(Paula Jervis-Tracey)

The fourth step in the inclusive model is the development of alternative approaches and action. If the previous step has been completed thoroughly, it should be no surprise to see how a list of possible decisions can be drawn up and the pros and cons developed. This step is often one that is moved through with haste, and there is general reluctance to do the hard work of thinking outside the box so that all possible outcomes can be rehearsed. By the time we are ready to consider alternatives, we may already have a sense of which option we prefer, and this is where the strength of interprofessional relationships are tested. Robust decision-making processes will allow for differences of professional opinion and will highlight the agendas that members of teams might have to push forward a particular outcome. It is important in this step that consultation continue and that people be sought for their willingness to play 'devil's advocate'. It is generally the case that we run ideas past people at this stage that we know are likely to agree with us. This is all the more reason to not fall into this trap, and in the interests of critical reflection and accountability, it is important that we thoroughly explore implications and consequences.

The final step in the inclusive model is critical analysis and evaluation. We cannot overlook this step if we are to fully engage with a process that is accountable and transparent. Most ethical decision-making happens quickly, and there is often little time for systematic reflection. Supervision is sometimes used as a way of going back over events to reconcile any lingering doubts and seek peer or superior validation of actions. One of the benefits of interprofessional practice is that it makes reflection and evaluation more likely to happen, as the stakes are higher should any member of a team be singled out for criticism down the track. There is almost a sense of self-preservation in making sure that we have acted in accordance with generalised best practice, and that we have the support of a number of others also tied up with a situation. In terms of potential external scrutiny of a decision, it is clearly more beneficial for a practitioner to be able to show that others supported their actions. The 'Through the eyes of a practitioner' insert gives an example of this.

THROUGH THE EYES OF A PRACTITIONER

I recall a very difficult ethical dilemma that I found myself in many years back when I was working in community development. I was working within a large government department that funded a number of community-based programs, and I became aware that funding was about to be cut to a number of the programs that I had responsibility for. The volunteer community members who had been the lifeblood of this particular program had no idea and were busy making plans for the next 12 months and were investing a great deal of time and effort in making those plans. I had to decide whether to inform these volunteers that decisions were being made to axe the program so that they could lobby their own politicians and do all they could to advocate for continued funding. The dilemma was the disclosing of what was pre-election confidential information. I decided to consult with a small group of colleagues that included the finance manager, the manager of another related program, and a local government advisor, all of whom supported me in disclosing the information in a way that did not directly breach the confidence of the employing organisation, but did give sufficient information to the volunteers to motivate them to raise their public profile and seek additional support for ongoing funding. In that case, it was very reassuring to know that I had the support of others should I find myself accused of leaking sensitive information.

(Donna McAuliffe)

■ Ethical decision-making: watching out for traps

The inclusive model of ethical decision-making outlined in this chapter is only one among many that you will come across in the literature, but you will find certain common underlying principles across models. Practitioners who fail to make sound ethical decisions (decisions that they have difficulty justifying) have generally fallen into one of the traps identified here.

Lack of attention to definition of the core ethical dilemma. Insufficient time is taken to unravelling the situation to clarify exactly what the competing ethical principles are. It is not uncommon for a situation to have a number of ethical dilemmas, some primary and some secondary. Sound decision-making relies on clarity of what dilemma is actually being dealt with.

Failure to consult. The primary reason that practitioners fail to consult is fear of the judgement of others. It can be difficult to admit that you don't know what to do or what the right course of action might be. In reality, chances are that if you are not sure, others may not be sure either. This is why you have an ethical dilemma to deal with. Accepting that consultation is a part of what has to happen will make this a more natural process and take away the concerns for reputation that can impede valuable collegial discussions.

Rigid thinking and complacency. It is common to retreat to a position of personal comfort when faced with a difficult situation. Staying with what has worked previously, going on knowledge that you have from past experiences, and perhaps staying with the relative safety of rules and policies, can provide security. Staying within a rigid framework can limit options and possibilities for thinking outside the box, and can blind you to new knowledge and different ways of seeing a situation. Doing something simply because this is the way you have always done it can lead to complacent and uninformed responses that may serve you well, but may not always be in the interests of others.

Lack of ethical literacy. A limited awareness of what ethics is, what values are, and where the limits and boundaries around acceptable and unacceptable conduct lie, can result in decisions that are uninformed and potentially cause harm. We have seen in earlier chapters the implications of ethical illiteracy and the dangers that come from lack of knowledge about ethics as core content for practice. A practitioner who does not operate from a position of ethical awareness and sound ethical knowledge can neglect the moral dimension of situations and make decisions that ignore the rights of others.

REFLECTION 5.4
In this chapter, you have read about the inclusive model of ethical decision-making. Now, reflect on the following questions.
1 Which components of this model stand out for you as important to incorporate into your own process of decision-making for future practice?
2 How might you make decisions in a different way in the future?

■ Conclusion

Ethical decision-making models – while useful in providing a structure for our practice decisions, reminders to cover all bases, and a platform for the justification process – cannot replace principled reasoning and confidence that decisions align with our personal and professional values. The examples of ethical decision-making models and processes provided in this chapter give a set of instructions of how to dissect a situation and subject it to rigorous scrutiny so that we can base our decisions on relevant information, sound knowledge, and reflective analysis. We have placed ethical decision-making within some contextual parameters, based around the need to acknowledge that today's neoliberal 'risk society' is a structurally inequitable landscape that can lead to defensive practice; and that individualistic frameworks are often antithetical to more socially just collectivist responses. In moving an ethical decision-making model such as the inclusive model (McAuliffe & Chenoweth, 2014) into an interprofessional context, the place of collegial relationships, dialogue and understanding of professional differences becomes increasingly important. In this chapter, we have focused on the importance of consultation with others, and emphasised the need to develop cultural sensitivity so that we do not make culturally discriminatory decisions. We need to avoid the tendency to make unilateral decisions, working instead from a more collaborative base that engages many others as legitimate co-decision-makers.

So far, this text has laid out the theoretical, conceptual and regulatory foundations for common practice issues, and set out processes for ethical decision-making. Now, we will turn our attention to how ethics is operationalised in different fields of practice, as the next three chapters move on to an investigation of ethical principles in practice.

6 ||||||||||||||||||||||||||||||

Ethical principles in practice

■ Learning objectives

- **TO DEFINE** the important ethical principles that underpin professional practice, including autonomy, informed consent, and confidentiality and privacy

- **TO CLARIFY** concepts of the 'duty of care' and 'duty to warn', and to explain the legal parameters around these obligations

- **TO EXPLORE** ethical writing, documentation and the keeping of records in a context of interprofessional collaboration

■ Introduction

THIS CHAPTER EXPLORES ethical principles that are founded on the growth of rights based agendas that grew in strength in the latter part of the 20th century. Alongside discussions on women's rights, gay and lesbian rights, children's rights, civil rights, and the rights of people living with disabilities, emerged a strong general consumer and patient rights movement that has consolidated the professional position of service on the basis of the duty both 'to do good' and 'to do no harm'. These rights movements have been characterised by an understanding of the power imbalances that exist between vulnerable people and those helping them, and also highlight the risks for professionals should clients feel mistreated (Connolly & Ward, 2008). In this context, documentation of the rights of clients and patients has become an important part of practice (Reamer, 2006). There is ample evidence in the social, health and human services of charters of patient rights, consumer complaint mechanisms, and professional codes of ethics that place primary importance on client rights. The consumer-led movements that promote peer mentoring and advocacy are powerful reminders that the recipients and beneficiaries of services are those who are best placed to comment on their efficacy, responsiveness, worth and integrity. An awareness of the rights of clients is therefore an essential component of ensuring that we are ethical practitioners. This chapter will develop and expand knowledge of client rights to autonomy or self-determination, informed consent, privacy and confidentiality, while also exploring concepts of the 'duty of care' and 'duty to warn'. In the interprofessional space, there is sometimes disagreement about interpretation and definition of some of these rights, particularly where ethical principles might conflict around perceptions of competence to make decisions, concerns about potential harms, and legal obligations to report or hold information confidential. The more that we as practitioners, coming from various disciplines, can know and understand about the perspectives of our colleagues, the better chance there is for cooperative planning and consensus on appropriate interventions.

■ Understanding autonomy: maximising liberty and agency

We feel better about ourselves when we feel that we have control over our lives and situations that are happening to us. This is the basic premise underlying empowerment and strengths-based approaches to practice. A sense of powerlessness when others are in control, or when control is slipping away from us, can erode confidence and lead to a feeling of futility and a loss of purpose. Helping people to maximise their opportunities for positive engagement and be actively involved in decisions affecting them, whether these relate to health, finances, housing, education or relationships, are core goals of person-centred practice. Teachers want children to embrace learning and make positive decisions about their educational aspirations. Healthcare professionals want people to consider preventative health measures, comply with treatment regimes, and take control of lifestyle factors that can lead to illness, chronic disease and premature death. Dieticians, rehabilitation counsellors, physiotherapists and chiropractors want people to make choices about their nutrition and physical activities that will not exacerbate existing conditions or injuries and that will prevent further problems that can have a negative impact on capacity to work, exercise or engage in recreation. Social workers, counsellors and psychologists want people to make good decisions about those they form relationships with and how they interact with significant others, how they parent their children, and what they do to create positive homes and workplaces. The language of choice, the ownership of responsibility for our own decisions, and the encouragement of independence are emphasised through professional education and form a foundation for working to maximise potential for growth and change. The theme of support for personal mastery is also woven through the many psychological, sociological and educational theories that form the knowledge base of the helping professions.

■ Autonomy: making our own choices

As we have seen in Chapter 2, bioethics, or the 'ethics of life' refer to ethics in the healthcare field where a primary principle is respect for autonomy (Lewins, 1996). Having its roots in liberal Western traditions of individual freedom and choice, autonomy preferences the notion that moral and ethical behaviour must involve the individual's own choice over their actions. As Reamer (2006, p. 32) says: 'the concept of autonomy ... implies self-rule that is free from both controlling interference by others and from limitations, such as inadequate understanding, that prevent meaningful choice. The autonomous individual acts freely in accordance with a self-chosen plan'. One of the prerequisites for autonomy is that a person must have rationality, which is the capacity to act intentionally and to reason through the consequences of actions.

In the social, health and human services, the term 'self-determination' is more often used to denote the requirement for clients to determine their own choices. Two conditions must be satisfied for autonomy or self-determination to be possible: *liberty* and *agency*. Liberty involves independence from controlling influences while agency refers to the capacity of the client for intentional action. When both conditions have been met, we are required as professionals to actively seek to enable our clients to make informed decisions on their own behalf. Critiques of autonomy and self-determination cite the philosophically dominant Western context in which they have been developed, which clearly prioritises the rights of the individual over the collective (Reamer, 2006). Debate over the appropriateness of autonomy in more communal societies continues; however, in the contemporary Western context that informs health and human service practice in Australia, autonomy and self-determination remain central to our understanding of clients' rights.

As practitioners, when we engage with a client and start an assessment process, one of the first questions should be whether the client knows what is happening and why he or she is interacting with a professional (which relates to informed consent); what he or she expects or want to see happen as a result of this interaction; and whether what he or she wants is reasonable, realistic, safe and risk-free. Essentially, autonomy from our professional position is about respecting clients' right to make choices about issues that affect their lives. Autonomy comes with some restrictions, however, in that the making of choices cannot harm self or others, and needs to be within acceptable societal standards. Because of this, the concept of autonomy is socially constructed, and sits alongside a number of other principles that make up liberalist and existentialist philosophies (Alexander & Miller, 2009; Bowles et al., 2006). One of the highest forms of punishment for wrongdoing is the taking of someone else's life (capital punishment), followed by constraining someone's freedom through imprisonment. This clearly illustrates the significance of autonomy – to restrict a person's liberty and freedom is a harsh measure.

■ Self-determination in practice: questions of capacity

As we have already seen, however, what can appear simple in theory often becomes complex in practice. It might seem quite reasonable that people should be able to make their own decisions about issues that affect them, and not many would argue against this as a basic premise. The difficulty arises when we further examine liberty and agency in practice contexts. Despite the best of intentions, as practitioners, we can and do apply a controlling influence over the decisions that clients make. Most of us enter a profession with a desire to help, and it is this desire that can prove a barrier to the liberty of those we work with. The old saying 'Doctor knows best' is equally applicable to other helping professions. Given our professional training and the wisdom we build in practice, what do we do when we believe our clients are making the wrong decision, or if their decision is not wrong per se but not quite as good as another option? Additionally, consideration is needed of other parties who may exert controlling influence over clients. Partners, families, employers and the society itself can all influence the decisions we make. Although it is not realistic or even desirable to think that individuals will ever be completely free of some level of influence on their decisions, we must determine if any of these influences substantially diminish a person's freedom to self-determination.

In addition to liberty, autonomy also requires agency, or the capacity of the client for rationality and intentional action. As Garrett, Baillie and Garrett (2001, p. 32) state: 'Decision-making capacity is the patient's ability to make choices that reflect an understanding and appreciation of the nature and consequences of one's actions and of alternative actions, and to evaluate them in relation to a person's preferences and priorities'.

Agency has the potential to become extremely complex in practice, as there may be many situations where questions regarding a client's capacity for self-determination arise. To be competent to make decisions, an individual must be able to understand the relevant consequences of that choice, both on themselves and on others. There is much written on this issue, as the social, health and human service professions try to reconcile the need to protect clients from harm with the need to promote the rights of clients to determine their own choices. The codes of ethics of the helping professions provide guidance that promotion of autonomy is desirable, however detailed guidance on how to determine agency and competency is more complex. There is mutual consensus in the literature that all engagement with clients and patients must begin with presumption that individuals are competent to self-determine. Doing so avoids the potential for professionals to make assumptions drawn from previous encounters with clients presenting with certain behaviours or conditions. Competency is also subject to change, depending on certain factors. Take, for example, an elderly woman who is admitted to a medical ward confused, irritable and unable to give details of her financial affairs. In this state, she may well be assessed as not competent to manage her own affairs, and a referral made for intervention by the relevant guardianship authority. Some time later, after the woman has been treated for a previously undiagnosed urinary tract infection, she is found to be quite capable of managing independent living. It is important that we keep an eye to changing circumstances and conditions that can impact on capacity for self-determination.

REFLECTION 6.1

1 Can you identify examples of situations from within your professional discipline that might limit a client's capacity for self-determination?

2 How might you navigate through this situation? Who would you talk to? What documents or resources might be helpful?

■ Paternalism: moral offensiveness or justifiable action?

Paternalism refers to acting without someone's consent or overriding their wishes, wants or actions, in order to benefit them, or at least protect them from harm. Criticism of social, health and human service professionals has frequently involved the charge that care has historically been administered in a paternalistic fashion. Australian history, as with the history of most other countries, is littered with examples of governments forming policies and enacting laws on paternalistic foundations, using utilitarian rationales in an attempt to make these interventions more socially palatable. When Aboriginal children were stolen from their families and placed on missions between 1910 and 1970, the claim was that this was in their 'best interests'; when young pregnant unwed women were forced to give up children for adoption in the period 1930 to 1980, a similar rationale was used. These are examples of paternalism on the macro level. Coming down to the level of practice in hospitals, schools, and community agencies, we can see examples of paternalism that include taking a mentally unstable person to hospital against his or her will and administering anti-psychotic medication; sterilising a young woman with an intellectual disability; and placing an older person in a nursing home against his or her wishes. Paternalism is closely connected to 'duty of care', and these decisions are often made with a significant degree of discussion and discomfort, particularly where practitioners have good ethical literacy that allows them to understand the implications of overriding autonomy. Given the power imbalance between clients and professionals, charges of paternalism are not surprising as resisting the urge to 'know best' may prove challenging in complex practice contexts.

Paternalism can be either 'weak' or 'strong'. Weak paternalism refers to a situation where we might override the wishes of a non-competent person with a view to restoring the person to competence, whereas strong paternalism overrides the wishes of a competent person. Guillemin and Gillam (2006, p. 88) describe paternalism as one of the most common ethical issues in health care, and have said that: 'paternalism involves putting a higher ethical priority on doing good for patients and protecting them from harm, rather than respecting their autonomy'. In earlier chapters we have seen the definition of a 'professional' as someone professing to have expertise in a particular field. A doctor knows from experience and understanding of physiology that a person who keeps smoking after developing emphysema will suffer more towards their time of death than a person who decides to stop smoking. As a doctor's duty is to heal and restore health, it is understandably difficult to stand back and allow someone to make a decision that will cause them further harm. Where tensions emerge in interprofessional teams, it is often because of differences in perspectives on meaning attached to actions and decisions. A social worker might also have the same knowledge as medical colleagues about the dangers of continued smoking, but may also look at other factors such as the meaning the patient attaches to smoking, the relief of stress that smoking can bring, and the difficulties associated with withdrawal. If the smoker is a mother with significant life stressors, giving up smoking may be very low on a list of priorities when she also has to deal with homelessness, a mentally ill child, and a parent with dementia.

As another example, a teacher may look at a child who is disruptive in the classroom, lacks attention, and has poor impulse control, and advise that the parents seek a paediatric consult to confirm an attention deficit hyperactivity disorder diagnosis. When the ADHD diagnosis is confirmed, the teacher and paediatrician raise the option of stimulant medication. The parents may refuse to consider medication on the basis of potential side effects, and preference other interventions first. They are also not of the view that they have to do anything to make life easier for the teacher if a disrupted classroom is her primary concern. The guidance officer and paediatric occupational therapist may agree with the parents, but the school may then say that they cannot accommodate the child's needs at that school due to lack of resources. The child has no say, as they are not at the age of consent. Bringing all of these perspectives to the table and working out who has legitimate claims is not easy. In a case like this, the parent's autonomy and right to make a decision on behalf of their child is placed in jeopardy by an educational system that is under-resourced and possibly not able to accommodate the child's needs. For the child to continue in the education system, at a school that he likes and which the family are a part of, he may have to take medication, which he is unable to refuse, and the parents may have no other options if they are unable to change schools or home school their child. While it is not the professionals involved that are forcing the issue of medication, the structural issues strip autonomy from the family. A collaborative interprofessional approach would see all of these practitioners working together to find a way to maintain the child in the school, without resorting to medication in the first instance, thereby respecting the parent's wishes and ensuring maximum learning opportunities for the child and others in his class.

REFLECTION 6.2

1 Do you believe it is possible to justify paternalistic interventions? Why?

2 Have you ever personally experienced an interaction with a professional where you believe you did not have full information to consent to something? How did this feel?

3 Can you identify an experience where you believe you have behaved paternalistically? Was this appropriate in the circumstances? Why or why not?

Another example of how practitioners can see things from different perspectives is offered in this contribution from a social worker in disability services:

THROUGH THE EYES OF A PRACTITIONER

I worked for two years in a multidisciplinary therapy team, alongside other allied health staff – a speech therapist, a physiotherapist, an occupational therapist and a psychologist. We provided services to families with young children with a disability, and while the other therapists aimed to teach the parents skills so that they could provide therapy to their children, I worked as the social worker to support the parents. The richness of the diversity of views of the multidisciplinary team was an aspect of this job that I loved. One of these differences I noticed was that the other therapists were comfortable asking 'why' in relation to therapeutic questions, but seemed less inclined to be as curious about the reasons why families sometimes failed to engage with our service. I was reminded of this when I recently visited the Allied Health Team at a local hospital, and noticed a poster reminding patients to ring early if they could not make an appointment, so that the appointment could be offered to someone else. This seemed like an efficient strategy to maximise valuable therapist time. In our case, such strategies were also accompanied by an informal client classification process, whereby clients who were reliable in attending appointments were informally identified as being 'engaged', or 'committed'; and those who regularly missed appointments as 'hard to engage' or, at worst, 'difficult'. While strategies to educate service users about the importance of cancelling appointments early is worthwhile, my view is that it needs to also be accompanied by a curiosity about why a service user might regularly miss appointments. In the case of my last workplace, failing to attend appointments was sometimes an indicator of low mood, a loss of motivation generally, or a reluctance to leave the house and face the world. Failure to attend then becomes a reason to prioritise a service user for attention and support, rather than transitioning them (albeit informally) into the 'hard to engage' basket. My sense from that experience is that social workers can bring a value-driven curiosity to a multidisciplinary team that can shape and contribute to team functioning as much as it can contribute to direct client work.

(George Rosenberry)

■ Informed consent: a legal obligation

The process of ensuring that a client's right to autonomy is met prior to any intervention is referred to as informed consent. Notions of gaining informed consent in a documented and transparent way are a relatively recent development. Historically, healthcare professionals (most notably doctors) were not required to gain consent from patients and it was not unusual practice to conceal information from patients if it was determined by the healthcare professional that this would be in the best interests of the patient (Garrett, Baillie and Garrett, 2001).

Although autonomy can be clearly defined as an ethical issue, informed consent is primarily a legal doctrine (Johnstone, 2009). Gaining informed consent seeks to both prioritise clients' rights and to serve a protective function for professionals. The ability to demonstrate that a client gave his or her consent for an intervention provides some protection should that intervention come into question at some point in the future. Informed consent is essentially the process whereby professionals gain autonomous authorisation from the client to proceed with planned interventions.

Garrett, Baillie and Garrett (2001, p. 31) outline two conditions that must be present for informed consent to be lawful:

1 The patient must be competent and able to understand consequences of the consent, so that there is no undue coercion to consent (voluntariness).
2 All necessary information must be provided to allow the patient to give fully informed consent.

Establishing informed consent must therefore involve both an *information component* and a *consent component* and it must be given voluntarily. Practitioners must discuss with clients their rights and responsibilities and provide them with accurate information that outlines:

• the service being offered
• who will have access to recorded information about them

- the purpose, nature, extent and known implications of the options open to them
- the potential risks and benefits involved in the course of action
- their rights to obtain second opinions
- their avenues of complaint.

As professionals, we must present such information so that clients can understand it. This may require that we refrain from using jargon or terms that patients might not understand, and that we make very clear what is expected of people in terms of their responsibilities. Part of the value in having a number of practitioners involved with a client's care is the ability to check understanding of what is planned, and what are the likely consequences; for example, an elderly patient who 'consented' to being involved in a lengthy research trial of a drug to aid symptoms of Parkinson's disease, which would mean weekly trips to the hospital for blood samples over a 12-month period. An administrative staff person collected the consent forms but the occupational therapist discovered, on casually enquiring during a home visit how the research trial was progressing, that the patient thought he was only required for one blood test at the beginning of the trial and another at the end. The patient had limited finances and could not afford the taxi fares to the hospital each week; no financial compensation had been offered as part of the research trial.

■ Informed consent in practice

The procedures that we will be required to follow to demonstrate that informed consent has been gained will vary depending on the employing organisation, the client group and our own preferred working style. Consent forms for medical treatments are generally straightforward, outlining the procedures offered, the risks and benefits to the patient and the complaints procedures that patients can follow should they wish to do so. In addition to providing the above, informed consent forms used by psychologists, social workers and welfare workers are often more detailed, providing information on the agency offering the service and the qualifications and experience of the professional delivering the service. Many organisations have standard consent forms that require the signature of the client and are kept as part of the client's record. It is now common practice for informed consent documents to be written in a number of languages, and best practice dictates that verbal processes of explanation accompany completion of documents. For clients from culturally and linguistically diverse communities, the informed consent process may require the assistance of interpreter services, and we should be familiar with how to access and use them.

It will be clear by now that complexities abound when we apply principles to practice situations. Although there will be many occasions when gaining informed consent is relatively straightforward, there will be others where serious ethical concerns arise. Atkins, Britton and de Lacey (2011, p. 101) clarify medical situations in which consent is not required. These include life-threatening emergencies; involuntary detention of people suffering a serious mental illness who represent a risk to self or others; and community treatment or counselling orders that a magistrate has stipulated. Consent is required for routine medical and nursing care; complex invasive treatments; special procedures (e.g. sterilisation – Guardianship Tribunal or Family Court can consent on these cases); and 'not for resuscitation' orders (a doctor can consent if patient not competent). If our work is with children, adolescents, people with intellectual disabilities or impaired cognition, or those diagnosed with mental illness, we will need to be aware of the complexities of gaining informed consent with these groups. Professional codes of ethics, documents of the employing organisation and guidelines established in a range of government legislation on health will outline the process to follow when gaining informed consent from these groups. While such protocols may provide clear indication of the process to follow, they do not exempt us from needing to make a decision on whether the client is able to give consent. If we determine that a client is unable to provide informed consent, we may be required by law to gain consent from a substitute or surrogate who can act on behalf of the client. Parents frequently adopt this role for children, as do family members or people who hold power of attorney for patients in a medical emergency. This situation can be extremely challenging, as we may need to reconcile competing interests from conflict between potential surrogates. In cases where no surrogate is available, the court may appoint one. When we are working with clients who are unable to give consent, it is vital to ensure that a diminished capacity to consent to treatment in no way reduces the respect that a client must be afforded as an individual. Clients must not be regarded as lesser or in any other way diminished by their inability to give informed consent.

A further complexity arises when a patient refuses to consent to treatment that we as professionals deem necessary to save his or her life or remove them from harm. In such situations, institutional ethics committees, made up of groups of multidisciplinary healthcare professionals and community representatives, play a role in determining the course of action to follow. Working with involuntary clients requires that we are knowledgeable of the legal and professional requirements concerning informed consent with our client groups.

■ Privacy and confidentiality: defining 'the right to know'

Although many social, health and human service practitioners have long been concerned with protecting clients' rights to privacy and confidentially, formal documentation of these rights is most often associated with the development of professional codes of ethics and practice standards in the second half of the 20th century. As has been discussed in previous topics, the exploration of clients rights and the desire to enshrine them, serves the function of protecting both the client from harm and the professional from malpractice and liability risk (Reamer, 2006).

The social, health and human services have undergone much change in recent decades due to advances in technology. While the risks involved in protecting clients' information that exists in hard copy are considerable, the growth in online mediums for service delivery has brought with it a new range of concerns regarding the safeguarding of client information. As service delivery contexts continue to change, so too must our vigilance in keeping abreast of systems that are able to deliver on the rights of clients to privacy and confidentiality. If we expect professionals to work collaboratively together, we must set up systems that will allow for information about people to be respectfully transferred, but this must be in a context of appropriate disclosures based on 'the right to know'. As McMahon (2006, p. 603) points out: 'Somewhere between untenable promises of absolute confidentiality and unthinking disclosure of information lies the modern duty of confidentiality.' Some of the dilemmas of recording information are illustrated in the 'Through the eyes of a practitioner' insert.

THROUGH THE EYES OF A PRACTITIONER

Questions that often cropped up for me, as a social worker in a team of therapists working with children with disabilities, were what information to share with the team and what to do with the information not shared. The primary client was the child but in most cases social workers worked with other family members. In the course of this work, we were often privy to personal information that wasn't directly relevant to the child's therapy. This could be difficulty in family relationships, employment issues or past experiences. If I was in a counselling relationship with the person, we would have some agreement about the limits to confidentiality, which made the decision clearer for me, but 'counselling' was mostly a broad term that covered many things, and we may not have had that specific discussion. Commonly my decision was to 'not tell' the team. This meant that I then faced the issue of what else to do with the information. Client files were the children's files, so there was nowhere to record important details that might have been relevant to future social workers working with the family.

(Melanie Hemy)

■ Privacy and confidentiality: is there a difference?

While the terms 'privacy' and 'confidentiality' are often used interchangeably, the terms mean different things. Privacy is concerned with being in control of the access that others have to personal information and the capacity to protect oneself from unwelcome intrusion. Privacy has been situated as one of the human rights that people should be afforded (Connolly & Ward, 2008). Confidentiality concerns the treatment of identifiable, private information that has been disclosed to others, usually in a relationship of trust and with the expectation that it will not be divulged except in ways that have been previously agreed on (Freeman, 2000). Both privacy and confidentiality are informed by the ethical principles of respect for persons and beneficence.

Privacy is problematic to define. Philosophers throughout the ages have sought to adequately capture what is meant by privacy but little consensus exists on what is specifically meant by the term. This may reflect on the changing conceptions of what it has meant to be private in different historical and cultural contexts. For this reason, it is more appropriate to seek a definition of privacy that applies specifically to health and human service practice, located in our current cultural and political context. Freeman (2000, p. 147) cites Siegel's definition of privacy in the health and human services as 'freedom of individuals to choose for themselves the time and the circumstances under which the extent to which their beliefs, behaviours and opinions are to be shared or withheld from others'.

Privacy is the foundation for relationships in the helping professions, and particularly in the therapeutic relationship. Without the right to privacy, many clients would be reticent to consent to sharing personal aspects of themselves. While the definition above may prove less challenging to deliver on in the private therapeutic relationship, the reality is that current health and human service practice exists largely within bureaucratic agencies and organisations, which may significantly hamper efforts to deliver on the definition of privacy quoted above. For example, involuntary clients mandated to receive services might feel that their privacy has been violated by the very requirement to participate. In thinking about privacy, questions such as the extent to which an individual's beliefs and opinions should be protected from others, who may intrude on an individual's privacy, and under what circumstances this is to be decided, alert us to the fact that determining how to respect a client's privacy requires considerable deliberation (McMahon, 2006). Additionally, critiques of notions of privacy highlight the Western context that it has emerged from, which may prove inappropriate and in some cases damaging when working with more collectivist societies or cultures that have expectations that all information should be shared with family and community (Hugman, 2013).

As a general summary, the codes of ethics of social, health and human service professions provide information on what is meant by privacy and guidance on how to achieve it. In a general summary, they include:

- the requirement not to share client confidences, clarifying in which situations this may be overriden, such as legal prerogative or duty of care considerations
- the need to disclose client confidences, if required, in such a way that a client's rights to privacy are respected
- the requirement to exercise caution when keeping client records, to ensure that a client's privacy is privileged.

REFLECTION 6.3

1 What does privacy mean to you? How would you determine if your privacy had been violated?
2 Have you ever experienced a violation of your privacy? How did this feel?
3 Do you consider yourself a private person? What boundaries do you have around your privacy? What determines your decisions to reveal private information about yourself?
4 In a professional relationship, what information would you consider appropriate to share with a client? How do you determine this?

■ Privacy in practice

Although inclusion of the points relating to privacy in the various ethical codes clearly evidences the importance of practitioners giving due consideration to the client's right to privacy, there is agreement in the literature that the contemporary complexities of delivering on the above points are significant (Clifford & Burke, 2009). In addition to work with involuntary clients, privacy may be complicated by the need to collaborate with colleagues, by high staff turnover, by the requirements of the bureaucracy and the law and by the keeping of required records. At times, these requirements may conflict with the professional requirements in our codes of ethics. In the contemporary workplace, as an employee, we may be required to comply with privacy agreements set out by the government, the law, the employing agency and its professional associations. Clearly, we must understand what all parties require of us, if we are to navigate the challenges of upholding a client's right to privacy.

■ Confidentiality and its limits

Like privacy, our understanding of confidentiality and its applications to health and human service practice have undergone considerable change over time. Once viewed as absolute as a result of connections with the sacrosanct 'priestly confessionals', contemporary understandings of confidentiality have explored the many situations and contexts that arise whereby it is not reasonable or desirable to keep information private (Johnstone, 2009). Exceptions to the duty to maintain confidentiality have been enshrined in law, codes of ethics and documents of employing organisations and agencies. Even though there are many situations that call for confidentiality to be breached, it remains central to preserving the fiduciary nature of the professional–client relationship. As Johnstone (2009, pp. 171–2), writing from the nursing perspective, says: 'indiscriminate breaches of confidentiality can have morally undesirable and catastrophic consequences for patients/clients … it is crucial, therefore, that every effort is made to ensure that information disclosed in the professional-client relationship is kept secret.'

According to Bowles et al. (2006, p. 159), the notion of professional confidentiality implies four principles:

1   Information is not limited to that actually communicated by the client to the professional – it can include opinion derived from observation as well as the exercise of professional judgement
2   The duration of the obligation extends beyond the period when a person has ceased to be a client
3   The obligation can be overridden in some circumstances by other ethical considerations
4   The obligation is subject to compliance with the law, at least when the specific law in question is ethically defensible.

The tension between upholding a client's right to confidentiality and yet remaining vigilant to situations that may require us, by law or morality, to breach confidentiality, raises the risk of ethical conflict on this issue. Added to this is the debate on the appropriateness of upholding Western notions of confidentiality with clients from non-Western backgrounds. Protecting individual confidentiality can be seen as rude in less individualistic cultures, who may believe that the 'keeping of secrets' negatively impacts on the harmony of the group (Chenoweth & McAuliffe, 2014).

All professional codes of ethics in the social, health and human services promote the client's right to confidentiality and provide guidance on how to meet this requirement in practice. In summary, professional codes of ethics require that we ensure that clients

- consent to the use of their private information prior to such information being divulged
- know to whom their information shall be given and in what detail
- know from whom information about themselves may be requested
- are fully informed of their right to confidentiality and the limits of confidentiality, from the start of the professional relationship.

Additionally, codes of ethics typically provide detailed guidelines on when it is appropriate to breach confidentiality and what procedures must be followed if this becomes necessary. These circumstances may include disclosure of client information, if and when there is:

- a legal or ethical obligation to do so
- an immediate and specified risk of harm to an identifiable person or persons that can be averted only by disclosing the information.

When we determine that a breach of confidentiality is required on either legal or moral grounds, we need to deliberate and often consult extensively with others in order to decide how to best manage the process. Consulting the relevant professional code of ethics and seeking input from supervisors will help to ensure that the process followed is appropriate and justifiable. We may need to determine if and how to inform a client of a decision to break a confidence and will need to work with the client to establish how the professional–client relationship will proceed in light of the breach.

If a decision is made to break confidentiality and report suspected abuse or potential harm, this should be done in a way that respects the dignity of the client, regardless of what they have done or threatened to do. Suggestions on a process to follow to ensure respectful treatment of the client include:

- involving the client in reporting the incident
- discussing with the client why a report needs to be made, what the benefits and risks are to the client of making a report, what procedures will be followed once the report is made and what some possible outcomes might be
- inviting the client to ask any questions they may have
- ensuring the client has support throughout the process.

It is important, as we have seen previously, to discuss the limits of confidentiality during the engagement phase of service provision, so that if the need to report or disclose information arises, we can remind the client of this. Many beginning practitioners find it difficult to have the 'limits of confidentiality' discussion, for fear that it will inhibit the formation of a trusting and open relationship. Important research conducted by McLaren (2007, p. 37) in the context of forewarning in child protection indicates that such discussions should take place in order to establish a transparent relationship at the outset, and

> ensure that clients do not feel deceived into thinking that superior levels of confidentiality exist … it is recommended that if forewarning takes place it is accompanied with information about what that means for the client and the worker–client relationship should they disclose.

■ Challenges to upholding privacy and confidentiality

Work with certain populations and particular practice methods can provide for increased difficulty in maintaining privacy and confidentiality. As mentioned previously, the contemporary understanding of privacy and confidentiality in the social, health and human services is largely informed by Western notions of the importance of prioritising the individual over the collective. When working with Indigenous clients or those from non-Western cultural contexts, it is particularly important to be sensitive to alternative worldviews that place a higher priority on the family or community as a whole. In this circumstance, family members may not understand why we cannot share information with them about their relative, and they may believe that our withholding of such information is inappropriate. For this reason, when working with clients from different cultural backgrounds, it is desirable to work closely with colleagues from that culture to determine the most appropriate method of communicating the professional requirements with regards to confidentiality and privacy.

Working with couples or groups presents another challenge in relation to confidentiality and privacy. In these instances, it is especially important to inform all parties of what information will and will not be shared. To ensure that a client's rights to confidentiality are respected when conducting group work, we need to spend a reasonable length of time at the beginning of the process, and at the start of each subsequent session, outlining the procedures for ensuring the confidentiality of all participants (Chenoweth & McAuliffe, 2014). It is important that practitioners who facilitate groups understand the limits of their responsibilities. All the discussions in the world about the need for respect for people's privacy in a group context will not stop some people from inappropriately divulging outside the group personal information that belongs to others.

THROUGH THE EYES OF A PRACTITIONER

I work in a homeless adult person's residential community facilitating bush adventure Therapeutic programs. Confidentiality in these types of interventions requires conditions which include: participants voluntarily choosing to attend; practitioners being well informed about participants' histories; a clear understanding of the intentions of each individual; and the ability to facilitate formal and informal moments of connection with respect and care. Maintaining agreed confidentiality boundaries that the group created and consented to at the beginning and during the program guides the process.

(Amanda Smith)

A further area of practice that can provide for significant challenges in relation to this issue occurs in rural practice settings (Green & Mason, 2002). Complexities arise in rural practice when, for example:

- clients provide personal information in informal settings, such as at a community festival or school event
- practitioners in the community hold dual and multiple roles, such as acting both as a member of a community safety committee and a volunteer suicide-prevention counsellor
- the rural 'grapevine' affects client anonymity.

Possible solutions can include being clear and consistent regarding boundaries, strictly following agency procedures, ensuring that clients are only acknowledged in public with their prior agreement, and locating services in another town if clients would prefer.

■ Online platforms: the challenge to privacy and confidentiality

Special mention is required of how new technologies are affecting privacy and confidentiality. The past two decades have seen the movement of case records and communications to online platforms, which raises a particular set of security concerns. Most of us will have heard stories of emails being sent unintentionally to the wrong person, and of course computers contain sensitive information that can be lost or stolen. Privacy and confidentiality protocols in the social, health and human services have struggled to keep up with changes in technology, attempting to use the online environment to streamline service delivery while seeking to ensure that client information is protected. To this end, organisations need explicit procedures and protocols determining the appropriate use of computer records and client data. The ethical issues as they relate to information technology and the concept of 'e-professionalism' will be further explored in the following chapter.

THROUGH THE EYES OF A PRACTITIONER

In my experience, ethical concepts are like paintings. They seem straightforward and are easy to understand from a distance, but when you get too close they are all scruffy and blurry. I have worked for a decade in a rural child-protection setting. I have provided services to hundreds of families, worked with foster carers and many other stakeholders, seen my kids go through school, and had all the friends and neighbours that are a normal part of life. It just won't all stay separate! Issues such as confidentiality, privacy, dual relationships and boundaries are much harder to manage when your kids attend school with children in care and when you have social relationships with colleagues and social overlap with clients. You need to develop a keen sense of accountability, sometimes with a very overt response to people of 'I can't talk to you about that'. The hardest part is that you can't un-know what you know – if you learn something in a social context (such as the fact that a client has been involved in a violent incident), then you can't ignore this as a risk factor in a professional context. It goes both ways – if your kids ask to go play at a friend's house, then there are times when you know that this is not safe. However, rural practice also offers an amazing experience of congruence and achievement. If you are known to act with integrity, this is seen as both a personal and professional attribute. If you act compassionately and fairly towards clients, you develop a positive reputation, which leads into your work with other stakeholders and agencies. I would not do this job in any other setting, to be honest.

(Matthew Armstrong)

■ The 'duty of care' and 'duty to warn': how far should we go?

As social, health and human service workers, we have a range of obligations to clients, colleagues, employers, our professions and the law. The duty of care and duty to warn are two such obligations, which aim to protect both professionals and our clients. These two obligations are not exclusive to people with professional training. Many of us will have been aware of situations where we observed a behaviour that made us uncomfortable and led us to feel that we were in some way obligated to intervene. As private individuals, we may have seen a parent smack a child with force in the supermarket; overheard a man shout a violent threat at his partner; or listened while a friend shared suicidal feelings. What do we do in such situations? How do we decide on the right course of action? As practitioners, clients will engage with us with the expectation that we will exercise care in our relationships with them and that we will endeavour to protect their privacy. In addition to clients' expectations, the public also expect that professionals will protect them from harm should a situation arise that we assess may threaten their safety. The tensions that arise as a result of trying to both care for and protect clients and also consider safety for the public can be considerable. Fortunately, there are many resources that will assist with determining the most appropriate course of action to take when we feel duty bound to act, including the law, our employer organisation's regulations, our professional ethical duties and our own sense of morality.

The duty of care

The duty of care is a legal obligation imposed on an individual and that requires that they adhere to a reasonable standard of care when engaged in the performance of actions that could potentially harm another. Enshrining the duty of care in law is essentially a formalisation of the social contract that exists between individuals involved in some form of relationship or action. In order to prove negligence, it must be established that the duty of care has been breached. Establishing limits on who has a duty of care and under what circumstances it can be said to have been breached has been an ongoing legal debate. A significant development in contemporary understanding of duty of care law occurred during a case in the UK (House of Lords, 1990), in which three criteria were established to determine if duty of care has been breached:

- harm must be a 'reasonably foreseeable' result of the defendant's conduct
- there is a relationship of 'proximity' between the defendant and the claimant
- it must be 'fair, just and reasonable' to impose liability.

Sokol (2006, p. 1238) summarises the definitional concerns well:

> the phrase 'duty of care' is at best too vague, and, at worst, ethically dangerous. The nature and scope of the duty need to be determined, and conflicting duties must be recognised and acknowledged. Duty of care is neither fixed nor absolute but heavily dependent on context.

There has been a significant amount of litigation tying the concepts of negligence (primarily medical) and duty of care, and to this end it is important that we have a clear idea about what our obligations are in this respect. Codes of ethics tend to use phrases that are open to interpretation, such as 'reasonable care', 'reasonably foresee' and 'reasonable person'. At the end of the day, it could be said that we have failed in our duty of care if we knowingly refuse to take information about potential harm into account in assessing a situation that relates to a person with whom we have a professional relationship. If we work outside the scope of practice, or engage in work while in an impaired state, and a person is harmed as a result, there could also be questions about our observance of duty of care.

REFLECTION 6.4

1 Identify the current relationships that you have where you believe you have a duty of care. What does this mean to you?
2 What situations would need to arise for you to feel that you needed to take action on your duty of care? What sort of actions might you take?
3 Who do you believe has a duty of care towards you? In what circumstances can you imagine that they may be required to act on their duty of care?

The duty to warn and protect from harm

Somewhat more clarity is available on the 'duty to warn' obligation, which concerns the requirement to report information that indicates that there is a likelihood of harm occurring to a person or persons. In the fields of health and human services, the duty to warn can outweigh confidentiality requirements. Dolgoff, Loewenberg and Harrington (2009) suggest that it is helpful to rank ethical principles from the most important to the least important. Their 'ethical principles screen' clearly establishes that the most important principle is the protection of life. Coming in at sixth most important is 'privacy and confidentiality', which clearly corresponds to the notion that protecting individuals from harm outweighs the requirement to maintain confidential information. The ground rules regarding duty to warn were changed as a result of a much cited landmark legal case that concerned a murder that occurred in 1969. In *Tarasoff v. The Regents of the University of California*, a therapist was charged with neglect when he failed to warn of a threat his client had made to murder a former girlfriend. When the murder subsequently occurred, the parents of the murdered victim sued the therapist. This case was much debated at the time, as it challenged existing notions on the confidential nature of information shared between a client and his or her professional helper (Gostin, 2002; Reamer, 2006). The judge found that: 'public policy favoring protection of the confidential character of the patient–psychotherapist relationship must yield in instances in which disclosure is essential to avert danger to others; the protective privilege ends where the public peril begins' (*Tarasoff v. Regents of the University of California*, 1976, p. 340). This case determined a precedent that intended victims of potential violence must be warned, police notified, and any other reasonable steps taken to protect a potential victim. This ruling had considerable impact on the establishment of criteria and guidelines for determining when it was appropriate and indeed legally required to break confidentiality. Other court cases since the Tarasoff case have continued to have an impact on professional understanding of the duty to warn obligation, but criticisms remain that, like the duty of care, duty to warn obligations are not always clear (Reamer, 2006).

Determining when to warn clients of duty to warn obligations provides us with considerable ethical discomfort, as we saw in the discussion about forewarning, as to do so may break established confidences. In deciding on the most appropriate course of action, we can seek guidance from a range of sources, including:

- the law
- our professional codes of ethics
- the requirements of our employer organisation
- our own 'practice wisdom' (that is, knowledge built up over time from our experience – our intrinsic knowing of what works and what doesn't).

We suggest caution when proceeding with warning, recognising the implications for doing so on the practice relationship, and the need to ensure the safety of third parties.

Complexities arise when we are mandated to report certain forms of harm, such as sexual, physical or emotional abuse of children or, in some states or territories, exposure to domestic or family violence. Although there is a legal requirement mandating some professional groups (predominantly doctors, nurses, teachers and police) to report specific instances of potential harm, other groups are not required by law to do so. As these laws have undergone considerable changes over time and differ across states and territories around Australia, we need to remain informed of our legal requirements to notify. An example of this complexity is that in Queensland, teachers are required by school policy to report any suspected abuse or neglect, but under law are only required to report suspected sexual abuse. Some states and territories have very broad provisions, while others are more restricted; in some states and territories, dentists and pharmacists are listed, while in others they are not. The Australian Institute of Family Studies (AIFS) (2013) provides a comprehensive list of which professional disciplines are subject to mandatory reporting, for what types of abuse and neglect and under which legal provisions.

The implications for practitioners working together are that some members of a team may be required to notify by law, while others may not. Again, it is important to not only be aware of the requirements of our own discipline but also of the potential implications for others when we engage in discussions around suspicions of possible abuse. If the whole practitioner team agrees that a notification needs to be made, either one member of the team or individual members can do this. We encourage a collaborative approach, so that a process can be put in place to manage outcomes of the reporting. In rural communities, there is often fear that a process of elimination will identify notifiers and, in some cases, this can lead to significant stress. Collegial support is important when confronted with situations of this nature.

REFLECTION 6.5

1 What are the potential implications of mandatory reporting requirements in relation to the practitioner–client relationship?
2 What might you do to limit the potential negative effects if you choose to report?
3 Are you aware of what actions would follow once you had reported potential harm? What would these be?
4 Can you identify situations that might make you hesitant to warn? Why?

■ Documentation and client records: collaborative information sharing

The codes of ethics of the social, health and human services provide guidance on how to record information so that we respect the client's right to confidentiality. This includes ensuring that we:

- only record essential information
- share records appropriately, with prior client consent for sharing of information that relates to them
- store client records in a safe location for the required period (this is sometimes determined by law)
- destroy both electronic and paper records appropriately when required.

In some situations, we may have our client records subpoenaed for use in court proceedings, and records should always be written with the knowledge that this is possible. Even more important is the right that clients have to access information written about them, which means that care has to be taken to ensure that written records are accurate, respectful and focused on the purpose for which they have been written (Chenoweth & McAuliffe, 2014).

Documentation and writing in professional practice can take many forms (McDonald et al., 2011), including:
- critical incident recording
- intake summaries
- case notes and case records
- action sheets
- specified court reports
- letter writing
- minutes of meetings
- submission writing
- media releases.

In the context of interprofessional collaboration, it is very important that client records, reports and clinical documents provide a clear and comprehensive history of any assessments, interventions, outcomes and future plans. Records need to be written in such a way that discipline-specific jargon is minimised, acronyms spelled out clearly, and intentions for interventions are well defined. Language needs to be accessible and the reader needs to be able to follow the logic of an assessment that has been well structured, backed up with relevant literature if appropriate, and referenced accurately. Being able to write clearly, without use of derogatory or discriminatory language, is an ethical responsibility.

THROUGH THE EYES OF A PRACTITIONER

Social workers and human services practitioners write a lot and our writing has a major impact on people's lives. On any given day at work, we might write emails, reports, letters, briefs for our managers, case file notes, case plans, funding applications, and submissions – and so the list goes on. The single unifying feature of all that writing is its subject: 'the client'. That client might be a whole population cohort, such as people with disabilities in need of support services or Indigenous peoples living in remote areas; children at risk of family violence; or migrants seeking access to health services. Or the client might be a single individual – perhaps the next person on the 'must-contact' list. The complexity of the writing task arises because we must deal with confidential client information while usually writing not only for multiple audiences today, but also for prospective audiences in the future. This means that we must achieve more than the basics of sound technical writing skills and documentation protocols. If we do not clearly convey our observations, judgements and recommendations in our writing, serious repercussions can – and do – arise for clients. Practitioners must write well to pursue social justice with competence and integrity. Mindfulness in how and why we write, as well as what we write, reflects a commitment to the values and ethics of professional practice. Practitioners' writing practices must be undertaken in the social, political and ethical professional circumstances of our professional responsibilities. Ethical professional writing integrates three essential elements: reflective mindfulness of the client-centred focus of writing responsibilities; a sound understanding of the values and principles of their profession as highlighted in the unifying themes in codes of ethics; and a sound competence in compositional, rhetorical and technical writing skills.

(Donna McDonald)

■ Conclusion

This chapter has explored some of the ethical principles at the heart of social, health and human service practice. When we observe the importance of concepts such as autonomy, informed consent, privacy and confidentiality, and when we are well aware of the implications of circumventing the principles, there is a better chance that our practice will be respectful of clients' rights. It is perhaps more important to look at what happens when these basic rights cannot be realised for reasons that are often structural or that involve relationships with others. When paternalistic decisions have to be made, or when we have to override the principles of consent or confidentiality, it is important that we place top priority on our ethical responsibilities to the process of how we work with clients. Issues of duty of care, duty to warn and mandatory reporting obligations serve to highlight the very real problems that we face in our work. Some of the social problems – such as the sexual abuse of children or family violence – that plague many of the social, health and human services are so serious that laws have had to be enacted to ensure that these types of traumas are not silenced as they have been in past decades. The extent to which governments have taken control of professional discretion by enforcing mandatory reporting is a clear example of paternalism at the macro level. The next chapter will move on to explore professional integrity and those areas of practice that most affect interpersonal relationships.

7

Professional integrity and e-professionalism

■ Learning objectives

■ **TO EXPLORE** the differences between personal and professional boundaries as these relate to work with clients, colleagues and others

■ **TO CLARIFY** professional expectations of appropriate behaviours and conduct in managing dual and multiple relationships, personal self-disclosure, competence and imposition of values in different contexts and settings

■ **TO DEFINE** the concepts of 'e-professionalism' and 'digital literacy' and understand the ethical dilemmas associated with online communications and engagement with social media, and provision of services using online methods

■ Introduction

WORK IN THE social, health and human services is essentially relationship-based practice (the 'caring for' and 'caring about' dimensions discussed in earlier chapters), and this necessitates negotiation of the ways in which we deal with others in interpersonal, group and community encounters. As professionals, we have a duty of accountability for practice that is respectful, empowering, encouraging of autonomy, observant of power influences, and clear in relation to boundaries, confidences, disclosures and competence. The term 'professional integrity' encompasses a practice context of personal and professional conduct and appropriate expression of relationships. It deals with issues of trust, truthfulness and honesty, transparency and authenticity, personal and professional congruency, and awareness of the potential for imposition of values and beliefs and the consequences of that imposition for those in unequal positions of power. When practice becomes governed by rules, as it inevitably does in times of heightened management of risk, it is all too easy to forget that what we are engaged in is a *human* endeavour, and it is very important that we remain attuned to our own humanity as workers. We may sometimes catch ourselves wondering whether what we have just done was a truly humane response, or one governed by duty or rules. The message in this chapter is that when lines have to be drawn – and we do need to draw them clearly, in the interests of transparent and accountable practice – then we must be conscious of both our own moral compass and expectations of the professions to which we all belong, which will guide us in how we behave in our relationships with others.

■ The personal and professional: are they inseparable?

It is not uncommon for the concept of 'personal and professional' to be raised early on in education for the social, health and human services, but often this remains an abstraction that we do not realise until we experience the realities of practice. When you begin to work in the social, health and human services, you will come to understand that every encounter with a client involves some negotiation of the space that lies between the 'personal' and the 'professional'. This negotiation extends to work with colleagues, managers, and general members of the public. The question about the ability to keep distance between personal and professional – whether this is even possible, and whether it is advisable – is highly contested, and it is a good starting point for discussion about boundaries. O'Leary, Tsui and Ruch (2013) argue convincingly that our relationships with clients should be characterised by connection rather than separation, and that humane responses to development of relationships should emphasise collaboration in the setting of appropriate boundaries. At the very heart of this debate are the issues of authenticity, genuineness and congruence. Can a person be something in one part of their life and something else in another part? Is it any business of the 'professional' what someone does with the 'personal'? These questions have been played out in a public way when a person's private life has come to the attention of a professional body, such as the case in the UK of the social worker who was taken to task for working in the sex industry after hours while employed as a child-welfare worker by day. Should a secondary school teacher have the right to be a member of a bikie gang on weekends? Does it make a difference if the bikie gang has in the past been linked to organised crime, or it is more acceptable if the bikie gang is one that regularly does rides to raise money for charity? Does a young lawyer who attends rave dance parties and takes illicit drugs outside work hours bring the legal profession into disrepute? Should anyone be concerned if a youth worker engages in sadomasochistic activities in the privacy of their own home? Is this different if the youth worker belongs to a bondage club and attends public rallies that promote safe sexual behaviours? The question here is whether it is any business of employers what their staff do with their lives outside work time, and whether professions should be clearer about what is not acceptable, and what sorts of behaviours would bring a profession into disrepute.

The Royal Australian & New Zealand College of Psychiatrists (RANZCP) Code of Ethics (2010, p. 15) has a statement that incorporates the connection between personal and professional as follows: 'Psychiatrists shall maintain appropriate ethical standards in their professional lives, and also in their personal lives in so far as this may reflect on the integrity of the medical profession.' As we will see later in this chapter, the distinction between personal and professional has become much more blurred with advances in technologies, which have made people's personal lives more publicly accessible through social networking and social media.

REFLECTION 7.1
1 Do you believe that what you do in your personal life should have any bearing on what you do in your professional role?
2 Can you identify any activities that you have undertaken that you would feel uncomfortable with an employer knowing about?

■ Overlap between the professional and personal: caution required

It would be fair to say that most professional disciplines educate students to be cautious about the overlap between personal and professional. There is, however, a continuum that is largely ideological and based on philosophical understandings of the nature of the therapeutic relationship. Historically, schools of thought, particularly in the psychodynamic and psychotherapeutic tradition, advised that therapists or counsellors should observe strict and rigid boundaries to guard against transference and counter-transference. Transference refers to misplaced feelings from a client to a therapist, while counter-transference is described as the distortion of a therapist's reactions and responses to a client that can result in overprotectiveness, rejection, or development of sexualised or romantic feelings (Corey, Corey & Callanan, 2007). Constructing barriers between the therapist and client, by setting up a situation where there is no room for emotional involvement and the risk of emotional entanglement is minimised, has historically been a major part of the psychotherapeutic tradition. This, of course, has been challenged by those taking a more humanist, existential or narrative approach to therapeutic relationships, and has been directly critiqued by those coming from a feminist perspective, where the primary aim is to minimise power relations, not exacerbate them. A counterargument to the need for distance in therapeutic relationships is the need for authenticity and honesty in practice, which can translate into negotiated dual relationships when the issues are not of a sexual or intimate nature. Many counsellors and therapists argue for the benefits of engaging with clients in social settings to break therapeutic impasses, and the recovery movement in mental health services encourages workers to engage in community-based social and recreational activities with client groups.

Beddoe and Maidment (2009) have given a very useful delineation of the differences between professional and personal relationships. In professional relationships, the worker is paid for their time and must be prepared and competent, the relationship is time-limited and contracted, and there is a degree of structure where the worker has more responsibility and actual or perceived power, as well as responsibilities to multiple stakeholders. In personal relationships, the association is voluntary, spontaneous, and not limited by time or contract. Personal relationships do not involve unequal power, do not require preparation or training, and rely on mutual responsibility. The main questions for professional relationships are whether the worker has the skills and training to engage with the other, and whether they can work with them; for personal relationships the questions are whether people like each other and what moral responsibilities they might have. It is important to be clear that professional and personal relationships are very different and moving from one to the other (professional to personal, or personal to professional) will have implications and consequences for all concerned. Again, some will take the view that such movement is not consistent with ethical practice, yet we know that in many situations these changes to the status of a relationship do have to be negotiated. Any professional who has worked in a rural community will immediately relate to this as negotiated relationships are a part of living and working in a place where keeping boundaries rigid simply may not be possible. The next section explores relationships and boundaries around these in more detail.

■ Managing relationships: establishing clear boundaries in practice

It is the complex issue of boundaries and dual and multiple relationships that occupy much of the time of those who manage complaints about the conduct of professionals, as the lines between a therapeutic relationship and an intimate or social relationship blur easily in some contexts. This is an area on which much literature and research has focused in the understanding that practitioners do need clear guidelines about the appropriateness of relationships, and their boundaries and limits. There is benefit in educating practitioners from different disciplines together to enable cross-disciplinary communication about these important issues (Fronek et al., 2009). A clear distinction has been drawn between what are known as 'boundary crossings' and the more serious 'boundary violations'. Boundary crossings are those situations that are departures from commonly accepted practice but which may actually benefit a client, such as giving or receiving a gift, hugging a bereaved client, attending a special occasion, or engaging in a closure ritual. Boundary violations are serious breaches of acceptable behaviour, and in some cases law, that result in harm to another, such as sexual boundary violations, or financial entanglements. Codes of ethics do attempt to draw the distinctions but contextual factors often muddy the waters. Sexual and intimate relationships may in fact be clearer in many ways because of the accepted position that it is never appropriate for a professional worker to engage in sexual activity or sexualised conduct with a person who is in treatment, therapy or any other role where there is room for exploitation and there is a power dynamic at play (such as teachers or police officers). Much advice has been offered to those who contemplate such a boundary violation, and there is consensus among professions that intimate and sexual relationships with current clients or students (in the case of teachers or supervisors) is deemed inappropriate and should attract the highest of professional sanctions. Sexual contact and behaviour can be categorised into overt sexual contact (intercourse, oral sex, genital exposure); touching behaviour (hugging, holding hands, stroking); and suggestive behaviour (sexual humour, suggestive remarks) (Reamer, 2001b, p. 57).

The issue becomes less clear-cut when the intimate or sexual attraction relates to a former client, and even more blurred when it relates to a friend or family member of a client, a colleague, an ex-student, a research participant, or a person that might have received a service not therapeutic in nature (for example, assistance with completing housing forms, or a brief information exchange between a worker and a hospital in-patient). The whole issue of 'when a client is no longer a client', and when it might be acceptable for the relationship between two people to move from a therapeutic one to a social or more intimate one has been given much consideration. In psychology, there are clear guidelines set out in the code of ethics that a period of two years must elapse before a relationship can change in this way. The stipulation is that a psychologist who wishes to engage in sexual activity with a former client, after a period of two years from the termination of their practitioner–client relationship, must first explore with a senior psychologist the possibility that the former client may be vulnerable and at risk of exploitation, and must encourage the former client to seek independent counselling on the matter (Australian Psychological Society, 2007). In social work, although the Australian Association of Social Workers (AASW) does not stipulate a timeframe, we must seriously consider the question of potential harm; it is also expected that anyone considering moving into a friendship or intimate relationship with a former client must engage in professional consultation or supervision (AASW, 2010). The Occupational Therapy Code of Conduct (2012) stipulates only that sexual relationships with former patients are generally inappropriate, while recognising the context of care, but does not go further in placing responsibility on the OT to consult with anyone if considering such a relationship. The only discipline to take a definitive position on both current and former patients is psychiatry. The RANZCP Code of Ethics (2010, p. 5) clearly states that 'sexual relationships between psychiatrists and their current and former patients are always unethical'.

REFLECTION 7.2

1 How do you view the issue of relationships with former clients? Do you believe that it should be permissible after a certain period of time has passed, or is it never permissible?

2 Do you believe that codes of ethics should clearly establish rules on relationships with former clients? What might be the benefits of doing this?

The other side of this coin is the situation in which a friend or someone with whom the practitioner has had a personal relationship requests assistance in a therapeutic sense. An ex-partner, for example, wants to come and see a psychologist for counselling; a family friend seeks advice about the mental health status of their child; a man going into a serious operation requests that his brother do the surgery. The general rule is that it is not good practice for a professional to take on the care of someone with whom they have a current or past personal relationship. The issue is one of potential lack of objectivity and risk to relationships if care has to be discontinued. Again, psychologists are clear that it is not appropriate to engage someone as a client if there has been a prior sexual relationship (although no other types of relationships are mentioned); the Code of Conduct for Doctors in Australia (Australian Medical Council, 2009) states:

> Whenever possible, avoid providing medical care to anyone with whom you have a close personal relationship. In most cases, providing care to close friends, those you work with and family members is inappropriate because of the lack of objectivity, possible discontinuity of care, and risks to the doctor and patient. In some cases, providing care to those close to you is unavoidable. Whenever this is the case, good medical practice requires recognition and careful management of these issues.

(Reproduced with permission by the Medical Board of Australia)

Social work, similarly to psychology, takes the position that 'Social workers will not provide clinical services to individuals with whom they have had a prior sexual relationship, as there is potential for the individual to be harmed, and it is unlikely appropriate professional boundaries will be maintained' (AASW, 2010, p. 22).

Interestingly, most codes of ethics stop short of providing guidance on what should happen when colleagues develop a romantic or intimate relationship with each other. It is common for people who work closely together to move from the work to the personal domain, and there are certainly many examples in every workplace of people forming relationships that may be met with varying levels of approval from others. Freegard (2007) discusses this issue in some detail, concluding that romantic relationships in the workplace should be conducted with great care, including consideration of the impact on other colleagues and on perceived conflicts of interest, as well as potential for disruption to the workplace should the relationship end acrimoniously. A number of strategies are suggested for dealing with such relationships to enable the involved parties to focus only on work during work time. It is important to draw clear lines around our work and personal life, so that our professional judgement does not become impaired.

■ Dual relationships: harmful or helpful?

While codes of ethics and codes of conduct may be able to stipulate guidelines on many issues, as we have already seen, context is very important in social, health and human service work. For example, consider the situation of a mental health nurse who lives and works in a small rural community, whose children attend the local primary school, who is married to the local mechanic, and who is a cousin of the local police officer. This worker will have dual relationships with many members of this community and will need to negotiate these relationships openly and declare conflicts of interest where they might compromise professional practice. Dual relationships, defined as those relationships additional to the primary therapeutic relationship, are not always harmful to clients and colleagues. In fact some dual and multiple relationships can be mutually beneficial, constructive and empowering. Mentoring relationships, for example, involve a blending of many roles, which may include guidance, supervision, teacher and friend. The problem arises when the understanding of the potential for harm (an inherent part of a relationship that has its foundations in an unequal power dynamic) becomes obscured.

Research into strategies that professional workers employ when they live and work in small rural communities indicates that dual relationships can be managed quite effectively when there is open discussion about competing roles and clients are explicitly asked to respect a worker's privacy and place in the community (Jervis-Tracey et al., 2012). Communities are not only geographic, and professional workers also face conflicts when they are a member of a community of interest (such as a member of a faith community, member of the GLBT community), and take on a role within that community that exposes them to conflict. The 'Through the eyes of a practitioner' insert gives a good example of this.

THROUGH THE EYES OF A PRACTITIONER

I am an active member of a mainstream church. I am also someone who undertakes some of the investigations, mediations, risk assessments and victim–offender conferences for that church when there are allegations of sexual misconduct by clergy. This means that I am in both a pastoral and professional relationship with the church. As a member of the congregation I am in a different relationship than when I am in a role of investigator and so on. There are boundary issues with this – or there are perceptions of boundary issues with these mixed roles. Some would say they are complementary roles (who better to investigate and assess what is going on inside a church, than someone who knows the church intimately). Others would say it is unethical (or potentially unethical) to blur boundaries so much. It is true to say that I become emotive when I hear or read the media making sensationalist or inaccurate statements about the church. However, no one knows better than me the amount of abuse that has gone on within church. A particularly difficult ethical dilemma is the matter of notifying the police of child sexual abuse when the abuse occurred perhaps 40 years ago, the clergy is no longer in ministry and (this is the crucial point) when the victim does not wish the matter to go to the police because they want to retain their privacy and do not wish to become involved in a legal process.

(Patricia Meads)

Becoming entangled in ethical dilemmas that result from dual or multiple relationships can be very stressful and can lead us to develop personal moral codes that may well be self-protective but not necessarily good for sustainable practice. For example, Jervis-Tracey et al. (2012) conducted research, funded by a major Australian Research Council grant, with more than 800 professionals who lived and worked in rural and remote communities across a range of disciplines. These professionals indicated that survival strategies included isolating themselves and their families from the communities in which they lived, holidaying outside their communities so they could enjoy private time away from the community's gaze, seeking support only from close and trusted colleagues (who may or may not live close by), and sending children away to boarding schools so that they would not be subject to work-related tensions. Professionals who adopted these coping strategies were less likely to feel a part of their communities, and excluded themselves from important parts of community life. Incidentally, many of the professionals who discussed these types of strategies did not have a historical connection to the communities in which they were working, and were often on contracts, with a view to moving on after a certain period of time.

On the other hand, those professionals who adopted strategies that allowed them to be more integrated into their communities were up front with clients about the work/life dilemmas, were clear in their discussions with clients and colleagues about acceptable interactions outside of work relationships, and made their expectations clear about what was 'work time' and what was not. This was particularly important for professionals such as rural doctors, paramedics, and police officers, who are expected to be available 24/7 for emergencies. Many of these workers were long-term residents within their communities, and they intended to stay and continue to be a part of their community into the future. Their strategies for managing relationships and ethical dilemmas were therefore very intentional and purposive.

This research is important as it signals a clear message that preparation for work in community settings that are defined by either geography or interest must take into account the dual and multiple relationships that will inevitably confront workers. When a social work student goes to complete a field placement in a remote Aboriginal community, for example, there must be focus on how to manage ethical tensions in that context. When a medical student who is in a same-sex relationship completes an internship in a GLBT health service, he or she must learn to navigate the issues of being a part of the community that he or she is serving. When a student teacher goes back to the same school that he or she attended, and is working alongside people who formerly taught him or her, there is a need to negotiate these new collegial relationships. This leads us to discussion about disclosures and how we manage information about ourselves in the context of our work.

REFLECTION 7.3
1   Can you think of a time when you became friends with someone you knew first in a professional context?
2   Did you feel that this friendship was affected in any way by your earlier relationship?

■ Personal self-disclosure: to tell or not to tell?

When we consider the way in which the personal and professional move towards each other, and invariably intersect at some level and at some time during the course of a relationship, we can see that much relies on personal self-disclosure. It is quite common for clients to want to know something of our lives, as a trade for letting us know almost everything about them. The question of the appropriateness of self-disclosure is again linked to the personal/professional divide, and is another contested issue in the literature. One side of the argument is that the personal life and experiences of the worker have no place in the therapeutic relationship, as this takes the focus off the client and is simply irrelevant and distracting. The counterargument is that, for an authentic relationship to develop, there needs to be some mutuality of sharing, as the barriers that distancing raises do not help build good rapport. From a feminist perspective, it would be most acceptable for a worker who had been a survivor of domestic violence or sexual assault to share this with other women as a way of raising consciousness about the issues of power. The central question seems to be about appropriateness, and the focus should be on whether disclosure is in the interests of the other. Disclosure is not seen to be appropriate when it is done more in the interests of the worker. The social work Code of Ethics (AASW, 2010, p. 23), which is one of the few codes to mention this issue, states that:

> Social workers will use self-disclosure with circumspection, and only when it is reasonably believed that it will benefit the client. If unsure, social workers will seek professional consultation or supervision to review their intention to use self-disclosure.

THROUGH THE EYES OF A PRACTITIONER

Working as a counsellor in the area of violence against women it is very common for clients to ask the question 'Have *you* ever been a victim of domestic violence?' Sometimes the question is motivated by a sense of an exasperated 'you can't possibly understand what I am going through', or the client may simply be curious. The field of work is certainly not without professionals who have been drawn to this work because of their own experiences. Counsellors who are also survivors might be tempted to say 'yes', and I'm sure some do. A truthful response may be given in an effort to join with the client, to communicate a sense of shared understanding of the client's situation, or to convey hope that surviving and thriving is possible. It is easy to see, however, how even a simple 'yes' response could open a door which, once ajar, becomes very difficult to push closed. For counsellors who are not survivors, responding to the client's question with a simple 'no' may be equally fraught with difficulty. Suddenly the counsellor has declared herself to be without personal experience and this too may have an impact on the therapeutic relationship. In discussing this dilemma with a professional colleague we came up with a response worded along the following lines:

> As women I think we have *all* experienced power and control or abuse in a relationship at some time in our lives. But this discussion is about you and your experiences, and the unique impact that this is having on you.

I've found this response useful in diffusing the question and shifting the focus back onto the client. Broadly speaking it is a truthful response, as it covers situations such as being bullied at school or by an older sibling; being a victim of sexual harassment in the workplace; being denied access to birth control by church teachings; or being a victim of severe physical and emotional abuse in an intimate relationship. This response therefore also provides an opportunity to locate the abuse and control of women within a structural context, emphasising the broader problem of women often being marginalised, oppressed and disadvantaged in society. This captures the attention of many women despite their own difficult and sometimes dangerous personal circumstances. It seems we ask so much of our clients in counselling in terms of self-disclosure, and yet often give so little of ourselves, and this remains a complex issue to negotiate our way through as social workers.

(Joanne Williams)

■ What do we tell?

In considering personal disclosure, we should also be aware that this is not limited to verbal expressions of sharing of life experiences. We disclose things about ourselves in the clothes that we wear; the cars we drive; our accent or language; where we live or choose to work; the photos, books or ornaments we have in our offices; the groups to which we belong; the values that we hold; and the people with whom we associate. With today's widely used social networks and social media, it is now much more possible for people to find out about others simply by Googling them, interrogating social networking sites such as Facebook or LinkedIn, or following web links, which sometimes lead to unfortunate revelations. Many teachers, for example, have been caught up in scandals when students have discovered information in the public domain that should have remained private; while some people are motivated simply by curiosity, others may become cyber-stalkers. It is important then, that we decide where we sit on the issue of personal self-disclosure, and how far we are prepared to go in allowing others to know who we are and what our lives are all about.

THROUGH THE EYES OF A PRACTITIONER

In wanting to use Twitter to share my personal views, I have become incredibly mindful about needing to think about what I share and with whom. I have my account set up with a privacy setting that allows me to decide who can see my tweets. Some of my friends and colleagues don't, and have been surprised to realise that, as they post photos and comments about their family, their kids, meals they've cooked, their political views, their holidays and even their homes, some of their clients are following them or have clearly looked at their profile and have made comments about this during sessions. They are now realising that once such information is out there it is hard to control what you share and disclose with clients, and in some ways they have invited people into their lives unwittingly. Some have also sadly had the experience of attracting trolls, who have posted outrageous and vile responses to some of their tweets.

(Kerryn Pennell)

Armstrong (2006, p. 64) urges a degree of caution in self-disclosure and encourages counsellors to think about the following points:

- Why do you feel that self-disclosure is needed at this time?
- Why do you need to get closer to your client?
- What is it you hope to achieve through your self-disclosure?
- Will this disclosure detract from the client's issues?
- Will the self-disclosure disempower the client?
- Is there the possibility the self-disclosure will raise or lower the client's perceptions of the counsellor?
- Will the self-disclosure give the client information that may be used against the counsellor at a later date?
- Is the self-disclosure more about you than the client?
- Is the client emotionally stable enough to appreciate the disclosure in the way it is intended?
- What will happen if you do not disclose?

While these questions relate to counselling and therapeutic relationships, they are equally valuable for many others such as teachers, disability support workers, child protection practitioners, or corrective services staff. Disclosure can be intentional and deliberate, or unintentional and accidental. It is wise to be clear about the issues on which we feel comfortable talking or responding to questions, and those we do not feel it is appropriate to discuss. For example, we may feel more comfortable with a client knowing that we have children, that we have worked for so many years at the same agency, or that we ride a motorcycle to work; but less comfortable with the same client knowing that our brother is in prison for drug offences, that we have a history of depression, or that our children were the product of a surrogacy arrangement. Then again, depending on the relationship with our client, we may at some point divulge the information about our brother if our client is also facing a difficult situation with a family member in prison. Part of the issue here is also relevance. If a client asks if we have ever experimented with drugs, but discussion of drug use is not part of our therapeutic agenda, responding to this may not take the relationship any further in the intended direction. This also might not be something that we would consider disclosing even if we were dealing with drug-related issues in therapy. As a reflective activity that will better prepare us for dealing with these issues around self-disclosure, consider the following questions:

■ Competence: understanding scope of practice

Another area that is important to consider within the context of professional integrity is competence and understanding what has come to be known within some professions as 'scope of practice'. Education for professional practice at the undergraduate level prepares us with generic skills to provide a baseline for moving into the workforce. Once we are employed in a social, health or human service agency, we can specialise and pursue postgraduate study in more explicit areas of interest. A social worker or a psychology graduate who has completed a university degree does not immediately become a competent family therapist. A nurse who has worked in an acute-care paediatric unit will not necessarily have skills in working with drug and alcohol dependence. We have an ethical responsibility to ensure that we do not claim expertise that we do not (yet) have, and if called on to move into an area where we do not yet have competence, we have a responsibility to ensure adequate professional supervision and training. As Corey, Corey and Callanan (2007, p. 344) state:

> We see the development of competence as an ongoing process, not a goal that counsellors ever finally attain. This process involves a willingness to continually question whether you are doing your work as well as you might and to search for ways of becoming a more effective person and therapist.

Standards for ongoing continuing professional education and development are becoming a more integral part of accreditation requirements, which works well for those professional disciplines that are part of the National Regulation Accreditation Scheme (NRAS) but not so well for the unregulated parts of the industry. Practitioners who set up private counselling and psychotherapy practices, for example, fall outside requirements to continually update their knowledge and skills, and there are few checks on competency. These practitioners will only come to notice of an investigation body if a client follows through with a complaint, and we know that very few do so. Practitioners who become complacent with their own supervision, and who fail to update knowledge and skills, are much more likely to engage in practice that has poor boundaries, and may rely on methods of questionable validity. They may also exaggerate their skills and level of competence, increasing the level of risk for vulnerable clients. In the field of nursing, 'scope of practice' is defined by the following criteria:

1   the nurse's level of training and demonstrated competence
2   the context of practice and level of appointment
3   relevant legislation
4   the employer's policy framework.

Examples provided by Atkins, Britton and de Lacey (2011, p. 131) about nurses who move outside their scope of practice include a nurse without midwifery training giving advice about delivery; and a nurse in a coronary care unit inserting an intravenous cannula without specified training. In a different field, occupational therapy, an example of working outside scope of practice might include consideration of 'whether they have the appropriate qualifications and experience to provide advice on over the counter and scheduled medicines, herbal remedies, vitamin supplements' (Occupational Therapy Board of Australia, 2012, p. 2).

Social workers who are voluntarily members of the AASW are required to obtain Accredited Member status, or to become an Accredited Mental Health Social Worker, in addition to meeting obligations for ongoing continuing professional development (CPD) and supervision. Most ethical codes require practitioners to make all reasonable efforts to engage in supervision and further education and training, and also to share knowledge gained from practice and contribute to research and the building up of evidence for practice effectiveness. The contemporary employment environment is highly competitive in some sectors, which means that there is risk of employees padding out their résumés in the hope of gaining an edge in selection processes. Increasingly often, employers now conduct online screening of applicants for positions by searching their profiles on social networking sites such Facebook and LinkedIn, and by perusing Twitter accounts, to ascertain whether an applicant has falsified their qualifications or experience. Leaving aside questions of the ethics of these practices for the moment, it is clear that transparency about competence, scope of practice and qualifications is an ethical responsibility that will hold a professional reputation intact.

REFLECTION 7.5

1   Have you ever exaggerated your skills, experiences or qualifications on a work résumé?
2   What could you do if you were asked to undertake work for which you didn't feel qualified?
3   What additional training opportunities to gain specialist skills exist in your profession? Which of them are you interested in undertaking at some point in your career?

■ The imposition of personal values

It is not possible for people to come into work in this (or any) professional area with a clean value slate. Experiences in life shape and form value positions; socialisation processes are at work from early infancy; and prejudices, biases and cultural attitudes develop with age and maturity. It is important, as has been previously discussed, that we make a good attempt to 'know ourselves ethically' so that we can be consciously aware of when our own values intrude on our work with others. When we talk about professional integrity, we are referring to the way in which a practitioner maintains a moral congruence with their own values and beliefs and is able to show respect to others by allowing them to express themselves as authentically as possible without judgement. Situations will always arise in which something that goes against our own personal moral code confronts and challenges us. For this reason, most codes of ethics incorporate a section on 'conscientious objection' that essentially gives a practitioner in this position a way of retreating from a situation that they find morally reprehensible. Decisions not to engage or act on this basis cannot be taken lightly, and we are expected to be accountable for such decisions. Savulescu (2006, p. 294), writing about conscientious objection in medicine, has taken the strong view that

> If people are not prepared to offer legally permitted, efficient, and beneficial care to a patient because it conflicts with their values, they should not be doctors. Doctors should not offer partial medical services or partially discharge their obligations to care for their patients.

Medical interventions in health care that raise the issue of conscientious objection can include late-term terminations of pregnancy, the provision of emergency contraception in cases of rape, IVF treatment for single people or those in same-sex relationships, or requests for withdrawal of medical interventions that could prevent death. In clarifying this issue further, Magelssen (2012) has set out five criteria under which conscientious objection in health care could be acceptable:

1 serious violation of a deeply held moral conviction
2 a plausible moral or religious rationale
3 treatment not considered essential to the person's work
4 burden on patient is not extreme
5 burden to colleagues or health institution is acceptably small.

In accordance with these criteria, many of the other professions that have conscientious objection clauses embedded in their codes of ethics or conduct stipulate similar restrictions to ensure that practitioners are not simply denying service based on preference, fear or personal convenience.

It is generally in the area of religion and spirituality, as well as culture, that these contentious issues come to the fore. Some practitioners choose to work in the social, health and human services from a vocational position, bringing with them a genuine belief in divine interventions and the power of a higher being. They use prayer and ritual as interventions, and consider it appropriate to explore the meaning of life from a particular perspective. It can be very difficult for many professional workers who have a religious background to work constructively and without judgement with same-sex-attracted individuals and families, people who want to end their lives with dignity at a time of their own choosing, or women who want to exercise the right to not bring a child into the world if they have been raped or if other circumstances do not support this. As Chenoweth and McAuliffe (2014, p. 13) point out:

> People who seek to convert others to a particular religion or who impress beliefs and moral judgements on others are not acting from a position of respect and can do a great deal of harm. It is critical that practitioners whose lives are governed by religious or spiritual convictions keep these convictions from overshadowing the decisions of others. If they are unable to do so, their motivations for engaging in helping work become suspect and can inhibit trust. People who actively use spiritually influenced interventions in their work must do so within an ethical framework of practice, acting in ways that are transparent and accountable.

It is important to note that the issue here is value imposition, not the respectful sharing of spiritual beliefs and discussion about spiritual matters. In fact, it would not be ethical to dismiss a client's request to explore spiritual or religious issues if these were an important part of the reason for engagement. The 'Through the eyes of a practitioner' insert illustrates this well.

THROUGH THE EYES OF A PRACTITIONER

Spiritual beliefs tend to become more prominent at times of despair and crisis, providing a person with comfort and hope as well as assisting with coping. On the other hand, however, it can also induce distress and evoke confusion, raising questions around the meaning of life, including a loss of faith for some. This can become significant when a person is living with an incurable illness and facing the end of their life. The topic of spirituality should therefore be raised by a health professional such as a social worker, if involved, to ascertain if a person is indeed suffering spiritual distress or this domain of a person's life can provide a resource for support. As a social worker, working closely with palliative clients and their families, I regularly enquire about a person's spirituality, alert to their belief system being a source of comfort or a cause for anxiety. Persons have disclosed a gamut of responses that have become the basis for therapeutic discussion or an onward referral to a pastoral care worker of their particular faith. A feeling of disillusionment because church members have indicated they have lacked faith, hence why they are not healed, is one example. Another person disclosed they can see dead relatives beckoning them. One grieving parent yelled into my face, 'Why did God let this happen?' Others have expressed optimistic expectations of a better life in the hereafter. No matter what the client discloses, my values, thoughts and spiritual beliefs are irrelevant. The crucial factor is whether or not the person is comforted by their beliefs or distressed in any way. This can also include any existential concerns. To impose my spiritual views on a dying patient or a distraught family member could be a potential cause for harm. With consent, it may be necessary for me to involve members of their faith to provide additional support or to assist with certain rituals. However, in many cases just being wholly present, listening, normalising, validating their experiences and providing appropriate, therapeutic interventions in a calm, non-judging manner are often all that is required. Monitoring for spiritual concerns should continue throughout the entire disease trajectory, being aware of who to refer to if necessary. A person's responses may alter or become more poignant as they journey closer to death.

(Lise Johns)

■ Spiritual dimensions in practice

As cultural issues and identifications are so entwined with spiritual expressions, being culturally respectful demands attention to the spiritual domain. It is not possible to work in areas that involve grief, trauma, bereavement, or chronic illness without being attuned to the need for a spiritual dimension in conversations about life and death. It is important that we understand what the different professions have to say in the codes of ethics and conduct about imposition of values. Social work, for example, is very clear on this point, as the AASW Code of Ethics (2010, p. 17) makes the following statement: 'Social workers will be aware of and reflect on their personal beliefs and history, values, views, prejudices and preferences and refrain from imposing these on clients.' Later in the same code (2010, p. 32), it states that 'Social workers will recognise and acknowledge the religious, spiritual and secular world views of colleagues, within a framework of social justice and human rights'. The RANZCP Code of Ethics simply states that psychiatrists 'shall not impose their own values on their patients or their families' (2010, p. 4).

THROUGH THE EYES OF A PRACTITIONER

I recall working in a community centre many years ago when a group of young women were involved in a health promotion project about defining young women's rights. The group met weekly and decided to develop a poster campaign to raise awareness of issues important to them. The young women wanted to include information about women's rights to fertility treatment, safe-sex information, contraception and pregnancy termination. The youth worker who was supporting the project had a very religious background and actively discouraged any discussion about these topics. Eventually the young women stopped coming to the meetings, the project fell apart, and an opportunity was lost to continue what had been important engagement because someone was not able to keep her own views out of the picture.

(Donna McAuliffe)

Spano and Koenig (2007) have written an article related to social work that questions whether there are some personal worldviews that are simply incompatible with the views and values of the profession. In focusing on evangelical Christians, they set out an argument for practice that includes the following:

> For example, a gay couple may meet with the social worker to strengthen their emotional, spiritual and physical connections. If the social worker refuses to assist the couple in meeting their goal based on a personal worldview that defines homosexual relationships as inherently immoral, this represents a lack of professional integrity, runs contrary to the Code, and is an outright rejection of the clients' expressed goals. For social workers to be faithful to their professional obligations, they must be able to manage their disagreement with clients' worldviews and make decisions that limit the influence of their personal values on professional work.

> (Reprinted with permission of White Hat Communications from <www.jswvearchives.com>)

One of the aims of good ethics education at the tertiary level is to give you, the student, ample opportunity to explore personal values and worldviews and to make decisions about whether you are capable of working within a profession that holds a value position on respect for diversity, autonomy, human rights and social justice. If you identify that certain values and beliefs are likely to have an impact on your practice, you may need to consider very carefully whether there are areas of work that you should avoid or organisations for which you should not work. It would not make sense for a practitioner who has deeply held beliefs about the immorality of abortion to work for a family planning clinic, or a worker who believes that people with intellectual disability should be sterilised to work for a disability rights and advocacy organisation. The question of imposition of values and personal worldviews is challenging and should continue to be part of professional supervision, mentoring and ongoing dialogue.

REFLECTION 7.6

1 Can you identify any current values or views that you hold that might cause conflict in your professional role?
2 Are there organisations or client groups for which you feel it might be best not to work?
3 How would you respond if a client wanted you to pray with him or her? Would it make a difference if you shared the same religious beliefs as the client?

■ E-professionalism: professional integrity in online communications

In this chapter so far, we have been discussing professional integrity as this relates to our communications and connections with others. How we portray ourselves to the various parts of our world – family, social, educational, employment – contributes to our reputation and the trust that others then place in us to be a person of good repute, with sound moral character, and a reliable, responsive and trustworthy nature. These are just some of the qualities that we would want to see in a person who holds a professional position (to name just a few) such as a nurse, doctor, psychologist, teacher, social worker, lawyer, police officer or physiotherapist. The professional positions that we hold convey the message to others that we have training, competence and moral standards to ensure that people are not harmed, and that we will provide a good standard of care. The significant advances in technology over past decades have opened up potential for private lives to be open to public scrutiny in ways never before seen in professional domains. Our professional education has relied on training for interpersonal communications that are face to face, but there is now a growing shift to online assessments and interventions made possible by a range of new internet applications. There are two important areas that have ethical implications that will be explored in this section, firstly the appropriateness of online personal constructions of image, and secondly ethical issues in the practice of online service delivery. The overriding framework is what is becoming known as 'e-professionalism', defined as an extension of professionalism to all things electronic.

■ Risks on the rise

Social media and social networking have opened up new avenues for communication, with growing opportunities for connection, education, advocacy and action on multiple fronts. The advantages of the technological age are undisputed, as the global world has opened up and awareness grown about the many critical issues different countries face. Most professions have already started to engage with the significant potential risks to practitioners' reputations arising from inappropriate use of social media and social networks. The unprecedented rise in use of sites such as Facebook, MySpace, Instagram, Twitter, YouTube and LinkedIn has led academics to include curriculum content about how to preserve privacy, how to engage in a professional way with requests from clients to 'friend' them on Facebook, and how to ensure that online communications are respectful and not discriminatory. We explored the issue of self-disclosure earlier in this chapter, and raised the possibility that clients or students might use online searching to find out information about their teachers, psychiatrists, youth workers or counsellors. Similarly, employers and colleagues also search professional sites such as LinkedIn or ResearchGate to check profiles and explore people's contacts and connections. Practitioners are now advised to keep a close watch on what comes up about them under 'Google images', as tagging of photographs is common and images can appear without a person's knowledge or consent. Such images might have come from a conference or professional gathering, or from a less-than-professional social event. It is not an easy matter to remove digital images that have been posted by others, so we need to be vigilant to protect our reputations. Watling and Rogers (2012, p. 118) discuss the impacts of 'permanent digital footprints' and the need for practitioners to develop what they call 'digital literacy', a broad term that covers a range of knowledge and skills including:

- 'computer literacies': the ability to use technology
- 'information literacies': how to find and evaluate content
- 'media literacies': audio and visual skills
- 'communication literacies': the effective management of networks
- 'digital scholarship': understanding licencing and copyright issues.

They also use the term 'cyber-ethics' to define 'ethical standards and considerations which apply to information and interactions that take place on computers or computer networks' (p. 147).

There have been many reported stories of situations where professionals have used social media in inappropriate ways and have been disciplined in the legal system and by employers. The Fair Work Commission has heard an increasing number of cases that relate to social media, and has begun to establish precedents for cases that concern similar themes. These cases include a public servant who used a Twitter account under an assumed name to accuse her employer of bullying and denigrate government policy on detention centres; an employee who used Facebook to threaten a co-worker; an employer who dismissed an employee for excessive use of social media time while at work; and an employee who divulged patient information on a social media site. In the wake of these cases and with increasing publicity about adverse impacts for reputation, the different professions have started to provide guidelines to the use of social media and have begun to include provisions about online communications in codes of ethics and conduct. This area is destined for constant development, as the rapid pace of change in information technology means that new dilemmas are emerging almost daily.

REFLECTION 7.7

1 What social networking sites do you currently use, and how do you protect your privacy on them?

2 Is there any information or images on your social networking sites that an employer might find problematic if they saw them?

3 Do you think employers should be permitted to search employees' social networking profiles? How could they be stopped from doing so?

Russo, Squelch and Varnham (2010) outlined a number of such cases involving teachers who had inappropriately used MySpace and Facebook to conduct ongoing online relationships with students. Through these relationships, the students were exposed to inappropriate content and photographs, and the educational relationship was disrupted. These authors (Russo, Squelch & Varnham, 2010, p. 2) make the salient point that

> teachers might argue that their social networking sites are personal websites but they are ultimately very public spaces that leave an electronic trail that can have serious, albeit unintended, consequences for teachers who breach professional codes of conduct and educational laws.

Professional conduct standards for teachers in Australia have largely been state- and territory-based and have also been developed to specifically meet the needs of different sectors of the education industry, such as Early Childhood or Catholic Education. While the Australian Institute for Teaching and School Leadership has now developed national standards for professional conduct, these do not specifically mention social media. It has been left to groups such as the Science Teachers Association Queensland (STAQ) to write their own social media policy documents.

The fields of medicine, pharmacy and psychiatry have expressed concern for many years about student misuse of social media sites and its implications for reputation and harm to practitioner–patient relationships. The Australian Medical Association (AMA) in 2010 developed a comprehensive 'guide to online professionalism for medical practitioners and medical students', which covers a range of issues. One of the messages on this site is that 'The anonymity potentially afforded by online is no excuse for unprofessional behaviour' (p. 3). Notably, the Australian Health Practitioner Regulation Agency (AHPRA) has also now taken action to develop a social media policy for all health professions under its jurisdiction (as set out in Chapter 7), so a total of 14 professional disciplines will be governed by the same policy. This policy makes explicit the requirements that health professionals take all action necessary to ensure that their engagement with social media does not breach the Health Practitioner Regulation National Law. There are strict provisions around breaches of privacy of patients, including warnings on the use of case studies without consent, and on the posting of photographs or details of procedures that could identify a patient. While health, as a national industry, has taken this issue on board, other professions have been slower to follow. The legal profession, for example, does not have industry-wide guidelines for use of social media, although law societies in various states have put together their own guidelines.

The currently unregulated professions do not fall under the jurisdiction of AHPRA and are not subject to the National Law. The Australian Association of Social Workers (AASW) has for many years managed ethics complaints against social workers and has developed a suite of ethical guidelines on social media to respond to increasing queries and calls to the Ethics and Practice Standards Consultation Service for advice on ethical dilemmas related to social media. As these issues continue to cause concern over time, other professional bodies will no doubt follow suit.

■ Constructing a professional online persona, or 'managing digital dirt'

Now that we have explored the plethora of available information about what constitutes good and inappropriate online conduct and practice, we can draw up a general list of some of the main points that emerge across many social media policy documents. Here is a summary of the generally accepted recommendations for professions that engage with social media and social networking.

- Be vigilant about checking your profile and any associated links that might contain information about you. If material is found that is problematic, take all necessary steps to have this removed.
- Sign up for 'Google Alerts' so that you will be aware of what comes up on the internet about you.
- Be aware of the privacy settings and keep very good control over who can access your sites.
- Use professional online networks such as LinkedIn to manage your professional profile. Keep Facebook for personal posts, but limit who can access them.
- Don't not post material that could in any way be construed or interpreted as derogatory, inflammatory, discriminatory, offensive or disrespectful of others.
- Don't use your work computer or work time for personal engagement with social media.
- Don't use your real name or image if connected to groups that are likely to be seen as odd or controversial.
- Don't accept 'friend' requests from clients where this will invite a client to view material of a personal nature.
- Establish clear contracts with clients about what level of online communication you will have with them.

- Talk with your family and friends about the importance of your professional image, and request that they do not post content on their sites about you without permission.
- Don't repost or reblog material by other people without including appropriate attribution, or getting their permission where needed.
- Ensure that the images you choose to represent yourself online portray you in a professional way.
- Ensure that information about yourself on various sites is consistent and gives an accurate representation of your work history, skills and achievements.

THROUGH THE EYES OF A PRACTITIONER

The teaching profession is guided by the Professional Standards for Teachers with respect to professional conduct and ethical responsibilities. Teachers may also be guided by specific employer codes of conduct and expectations. Such documents, along with community expectations, give insight into the socially and professionally acceptable behaviours of teachers. Pre-service teachers look to these guidelines to help shape their emerging professional teacher identities and guide their actions. However, despite the myriad of guidelines and codes of conduct, separating the professional from the personal can be difficult at times and is often blurry. An example of this is the use of social media. The use of social media as an educational tool in the classroom is emerging as education catches up with technology, but its use as a personal communication tool is now well established, connecting people in ways never before experienced. The ease in which personal and professional information is shared can be difficult terrain to navigate. Schools, students and parents have unprecedented access into the private lives of teachers. This has implications for teachers with respect to professional conduct, privacy and security of information. At a minimum, pre-service teachers should use the highest security settings, making use of the built-in privacy and safety features. That said, perhaps the most important advice for using social media is to 'think before you post'.

(Paula Jervis-Tracey)

■ Engaging in online practice: further considerations

Thinking about our online presence and the way we present ourselves professionally to others is one part of the 'e-professionalism' domain. The other is the way that we might actually use technology to deliver services to clients, patients and members of communities. As was said earlier, developments and advances in technology have undisputed advantages in connecting people who need information, who may be isolated because of where they live or their social circumstances, or have a preference for online engagement. Services delivered in ways other than face to face are certainly not new: many of the large organisations that have shaped the social welfare landscape in Australia, such as Lifeline and Kids Helpline, have been pioneers of telephone counselling for people who needed anonymity or who could not access services. These organisations have now moved into the digital space of web counselling and email counselling, while maintaining telephone counselling services. More recently developed services that target specific populations or issues are based on these models. MensLine Australia (2013) is a service that offers telephone, online and video counselling (Skype) to men who request counselling assistance, who are at risk of suicide, or who live in rural or remote areas. The service is staffed by qualified counsellors, social workers and psychologists and is government-funded. Eheadspace (2014) is an online service for young people with mental health concerns. The Butterfly Foundation (2013) offers web counselling for Australians experiencing eating disorders.

REFLECTION 7.8

1 What online services are available in your professional discipline?

2 Do you feel equipped to offer services online? How might you go about becoming qualified to do this?

3 What do you think are the benefits and risks of delivering services online?

There are many considerations for organisations that have taken on services delivered in this way, and policy protocols are important to have in place. When a practitioner takes a job as a counsellor using electronic means of communication, attention has to be paid to responsiveness, language and privacy issues. If a young person, for example, uses his or her parent's computer to engage in email counselling without the parent's knowledge, and the history becomes available to the parent, there could be inadvertent disclosure of information that the young person might not want his or her parent to know. A counsellor would need to ensure that the young person is aware of these potential issues before engaging in counselling in this way. If there are concerns about duty of care or risk to a client's safety, people need to be aware of limits to confidentiality.

A study by Gedge (2002) found that there was a small but growing number of online counselling services in Australia, with the majority of these being set up within existing services. This article expressed the concern that some individuals were setting up e-therapy services with little security and scant information about the identity of the counsellors. More than a decade later, we are seeing many more people moving into private practice and setting up online services for counselling, therapy and group-work. It is reasonable to ask whether these online counselling services are more or less effective than the traditional face-to-face services that have dominated the history of psychological services. Evidence suggests, from major studies and extensive reviews of literature, that there are few substantial differences in effectiveness and outcomes between internet-based or online psychotherapeutic services and face-to-face therapy or counselling (Barak et al., 2008; Murphy et al., 2009). The ethical issues include the need to ensure privacy of communications, security of payment, and contracting around duty of care concerns. It is also important that people have information about face-to-face alternatives and emergency contacts.

As professionals in the social, health and human services, we must also now interact daily with electronic data collection and storage systems, case recording and electronic record-keeping. Interprofessional practice will require that we not only meet with other professionals in case conferences to discuss plans for clients and patients, but also to share information in written form through medical records and psychological and vocational assessments. Advances in technology now also allow professionals not only from different disciplines but also in different locations to discuss their cases and work through videoconferencing and Skype. Digital literacy, mentioned earlier, becomes important when we are called on to use technology in our communications with colleagues and clients.

■ Conclusion

This chapter has explored the concept of professional integrity through a number of examples of practice situations in which practitioners need to exercise caution and have good awareness of their own boundary positions. As our work in the social, health and human services is essentially relationship-based, it is important that we are clear about what constitutes acceptable and appropriate behaviour and conduct in our disciplines. Not all codes of ethics and conduct, as we have seen in this chapter, give explicit guidance on all the issues that may arise. Some issues, such as conducting a sexual relationship with a current client, are canvassed very well in all professions; but others, such as self-disclosure, may not be given such clear attention. In due course, it is expected that social media guidelines will become more uniform, as the professions continue to determine their respective positions on what is and is not acceptable. The next chapter will now move on to explore the nature of professional collaborations and collegial relationships in the workplace, extending some of the issues we have looked at in this chapter into a practice context.

8

Ethics in the workplace

■ Learning objectives

■ **TO EXPLORE** interprofessional collegial relationships, responsibilities to colleagues, and sources of conflict in the workplace

■ **TO UNDERSTAND** the responsibilities of organisational managers and appropriate responses to systematic and structural workplace issues

■ **TO CLARIFY** professional and workplace expectations around impaired practice, vicarious trauma and stress-related responses to difficult work

■ Introduction

MOST SOCIAL, HEALTH and human services work takes place within organisations, so consideration of how professional ethics operates within the organisational context is an important topic to explore. We have already seen how important it can be to choose a place of employment where values will not be unduly compromised, and even though mission statements of organisations might be clear, it is not always possible to gauge the cultural climate from an external position. The value positions of people in a workplace will be many and varied, depending on people's professional socialisation, previous work and life experiences, and religious, spiritual and cultural backgrounds. Even if a number of people in a workplace have different knowledge, skills and values, a culture of inclusiveness and respectful relationships can nurture collegiality. It is largely the responsibility of managers to monitor the cultural climate of a workplace, and employees should feel comfortable raising concerns without fear of negative personal repercussions. This chapter focuses on how we work together with others, what responsibilities colleagues have to each other, and what should happen in the event of a colleague being observed to engage in unprofessional behaviour or misconduct. It is important to clarify at this point that people working with each other as part of a team, in one organisation, sharing an employer, is only one part of interprofessional practice. The concepts we are discussing transcend organisational and workplace boundaries, and so, apply equally to communications we might have with people who work in different agencies, even in different parts of the country, but in relation to a similar (or same) client, whether this be an individual, family, group or community. The final part of this chapter will focus on self-care and our ethical responsibility to attend to personal or workplace problems that can result in impaired practice or stress-related responses to our work, which is often difficult, complex and emotionally taxing.

■ Different workplaces, different experiences

Diversity of fields of practice is often cited as one of the benefits of a career in the social, health and human services, and it allows us to choose to some extent when we are deciding where to seek employment. Working within this sector may mean that we can find a good fit between our personal values, professional working style and those values embodied by an organisation, which may be a large government department or organisation such as a hospital, housing department or school; a small community agency such as a neighbourhood centre; or a sole worker private practice. Organisations communicate messages about their values, the activities they carry out and the people they work with and for in a variety of ways (Chenoweth & McAuliffe, 2014). From their websites to their waiting rooms, identifying what an organisation 'feels' like is generally not a difficult task. One way of trying to minimise the likelihood of a potentially problematic fit between your professional working style and that of your employer is to attempt to choose a place to work that broadly matches with your ideas of what ethical practice means. For example, if you know that you are ethically uncomfortable with the procedures for managing involuntary clients under statutory mental health legislation, then it is likely that working in a mental health unit in a hospital setting might create ethical challenges for you. If you are an avowed atheist, you might not be able to work as a teacher in a Catholic school. If you fundamentally believe that children should never be removed from their family of origin, you might find working in child protection difficult but be able to work very well in preventative parenting and family support programs. Likewise, choosing to work for a faith-based health organisation when your spiritual beliefs clash with those of the organisation may not be a wise choice.

We can ask questions to help us identify the 'mission', 'vision' and 'values' of an organisation (Sluyter, 1998, p. 40). 'Mission' refers to identification of who the organisation has been established to serve (the client or customer target group) and why it has been developed, what outcomes are important, and how it measures effectiveness. 'Vision' relates to the organisation's direction, and describes the ideal picture. 'Values' are the traditions, principles and beliefs that govern employee behaviour and set the benchmark for the organisation's reputation in the community. Spending some time identifying the potential ethical conflicts that may arise within an organisational setting will maximise your chances of ensuring a good ethical fit between you and your employer.

REFLECTION 8.1

1 Think of an organisation or area of professional practice in which you may be interested in working. Why are you attracted to this work? How much do you know about the values that inform practice in this organisation or area of practice? How might you find out more?

2 Can you identify an organisation or field of practice that you believe would not be a good fit with your values and beliefs? Why do you think this is, and on what information are you drawing? Can you ever see the fit changing?

■ Interprofessional collaboration: identifying possibilities and tensions for teams

In recognition of the importance of extending ethical practice to include relationships with colleagues, all codes of ethics of the social, health and human service professions outline the responsibilities practitioners have to their colleagues. These responsibilities generally have their own space within ethical codes, distinct from responsibilities to clients or to the workplace. To provide guidance on how to maintain positive working relationships, the codes of ethics and conduct, as a general summary, outline responsibilities to colleagues in the following ways:

- treat each other with respect, integrity and courtesy
- seek to understand differences in values and perspectives
- utilise the expertise of other professionals to the benefit of clients
- cooperate with other professionals to expand knowledge and skills
- remain open to constructive comment by other professionals
- address suspected professional misconduct appropriately.

As the number of interdisciplinary working environments grows, so too does the importance of behaving ethically towards those with whom we work. We need to share our knowledge of the ethical requirements of our profession with colleagues from other disciplines. In this way, we can attempt to create a collegial environment, where practitioners support each other to foster healthy ethical workplaces. Bronstein (2003) identifies the components of successful interdisciplinary practice as interdependence, flexibility, collective ownership of goals and reflection. Further, she identifies the role that the history of collaboration within the organisation plays in contributing to successful teamwork. Each of these components would be difficult to deliver on if the practitioner did not draw on an ethical foundation, written into ethical codes and standards of conduct. Positioning collegial relationships as an ethical responsibility elevates them to an expectation that these relationships will not be neglected, as to do so may have a negative impact on client outcomes. It also means that, if we do not uphold our ethical responsibilities, we may be in breach of our discipline's code of ethics, which gives added impetus to our need to put effort into building and strengthening relationships.

Smith (2009, p. 136) has identified a number of factors that present potential challenges to interprofessional relationships in settings where people from different disciplines work closely together. These are often the unspoken questions that, if left unaddressed, can create tension:

- boundary disputes: 'whose job is this?'
- status issues: 'you don't have the right to tell me what to do'
- language barriers: 'is this individual a patient or a service user?'
- competing practice models: 'which is more valid, the "social" or the "medical" model?'
- complex accountabilities: 'who will take the blame if this goes wrong?'
- decision-making rights: 'who takes the lead here?'
- social factors: gender, ethnicity and culture.

These are all quite legitimate questions, and they cut to the core of interprofessional collaborative practice. Medical doctors and psychiatrists, who generally act as team leaders in multidisciplinary mental health settings or medical units, are quite likely to see themselves as the ones who will be answerable in terms of accountability should there be an adverse incident with a patient. The role of team leader carries with it a degree of higher responsibility on the questions of accountability and decision-making, and professional socialisation through medical education fosters this tendency to adopt a position of authority. Similarly, nurses and allied health disciplines are professionally socialised to defer to the medical authority, on the basis of status and claims to expert knowledge.

■ Contesting territory: clarifying roles

As discussed in Chapter 1, questions of status can cause many problems in teams. Boundary disputes and disagreements about the primacy of competing practice models are often a result of lack of clarity around roles in a team and lack of understanding of the philosophy of other disciplines. While nursing, as an example, may have traditionally been seen to align with the medical model, there is now a strong emphasis in nursing education on critical reflection, narrative, and strengths-based approaches to care. Counsellors and psychotherapists are engaging more with neuroscience, and interventions are evidence-based and grounded in empirical research. Unless psychologists and social workers engage in mutual discussions about their respective practice models, they may not understand that not all psychologists take a psychoanalytic approach to treatment and not all social workers embrace only structural and critical positions. There is much to be said for interprofessional teams spending time addressing the points raised above, to establish a shared starting point for working together, and to consider honestly questions of role, status and authority. If these issues are not addressed, there can be serious consequences.

THROUGH THE EYES OF A PRACTITIONER

In a study I conducted about the Children's Court, the polarised positions of social workers and lawyers about the rights of various parties in child protection proceedings were very evident. Often lawyers and human services professionals come at issues from different rights perspectives – for example, legal rights, evidence and due process compared with rights of the child to protection. These actually are different perspectives on social justice. It can be viewed as both the lawyers and the human services workers taking an ethical stance. Human services workers tended to think that if lawyers were defending parents, or questioned a case plan they thought best for the child, then the lawyers were acting against the rights of the child. This binary thinking is unhelpful in navigating ethical issues. It is important to recognise the ethical dimension of these cross-disciplinary encounters, because there are no easy answers when there are competing rights – the rights of children and parents have to be balanced, both recognised. Even when children's rights are paramount, parents still have rights that should be defended. Critical reflection on the different disciplinary backgrounds, knowledge bases, responsibilities, and power differentials that contribute to different viewpoints is required, rather than one profession taking the high moral ground. The poor working relationships and lack of mutual respect between the two professional groups working in the Court were much to the detriment of children and families whose lives are so affected by Court processes and decisions.

(Clare Tilbury)

◼ Workplace responsibilities: colleagues and managers

Just as we, as workers, have ethical responsibilities to each other in a collegial sense, so too are we required to behave ethically towards our employers. We saw in the preceding chapter that employees have been dismissed (and these decisions upheld by the Fair Work Commission) for making derogatory comments about their employers on social media, and it is common for workplaces to expect staff to show corporate loyalty and support for organisational initiatives and policies. This expectation can cause very real problems when workers feel that they are not valued by their employers, that their jobs are not secure, or that the organisation is not acting consistently with professional values. In this country, members of the workforce have the right to join industrial unions, so that there is external protection in the event of discrimination, unfair treatment or workplace conflict. This right is written into some professional codes of ethics as a 'reciprocal right', so that practitioners can legitimately be afforded this protection. The social work Code of Ethics (AASW, 2010), for example, states that social workers have the right to 'hold membership of a union and/or obtain industrial advice'. Broadly, the provisions of ethical codes across the social, health and human service professions outline the ethical responsibilities in the workplace, including:

- acting in compliance with the aims and objectives of the employing organisation
- being accountable for practice behaviours within the workplace
- using the resources of the workplace appropriately
- engaging in action to improve workplace practices.

Additional responsibilities covered in the codes relating to what to do when organisational values clash with those of the professional's code of ethics will be discussed in more detail later in this chapter. Most employing organisations and government departments also have codes of conduct that cover all staff, including legislative requirements, such as public-sector and anti-discrimination laws. Employees are often required to sign agreements about confidentiality and are expected to refrain from making comment in the public sphere in a way that could be interpreted as the view of the organisation, except when someone is speaking legitimately as an appointed organisational spokesperson. For example, in connection with social media, a Queensland organisation was prepared to take disciplinary action against any of its staff who 'liked' a web page that criticised funding cuts to a sexual-health service for very vulnerable people.

REFLECTION 8.2

1 What does your professional code of ethics have to say about your responsibilities as an employee?
2 What does it say about the responsibilities of managers in your profession?
3 Are there any restrictions or cautions in your professional code of ethics or workplace documents on what you can say publicly about your employer? If so, how do you feel about these? Are they necessary or do they limit your rights to free speech?

Organisations generally communicate their ethical expectations of staff members within their policies and procedural documents. These documents can include codes of conduct, codes of behaviour, codes of practice, statements of corporate values and codes of ethics (Sinclair, 1996). They serve to guide the behaviour of practitioners, provide protection for service users and allow employers to identify and take action should employees not behave in accordance with expected behaviours. Organisational codes developed alongside the rise of large corporations during the 1950s and 1960s and were associated with rising interest in what constituted best business practice. In Australia, the 1980s saw a range of corruption investigations that contributed to the strengthening of many government codes, in an effort to make the responsibilities of public servants more explicit. Given the prevalence of organisational codes today, it would be reasonable to assume that they serve an important function in communicating expected behaviours and procedures. However, it is debatable how effective organisational codes are in influencing the behaviour of employees; although such documents and manuals are often the first item new employees receive from their employer, we might question how seriously employees take them. Criticisms of organisational codes include the 'shallow' nature of the information included in them and their irrelevance to daily practice issues (Sinclair, 1996).

We can see the growth of organisational codes of ethics and/or codes of conduct as both a benefit and a challenge. Using such documents to build our awareness of what is expected of us as employees will help us identify when our behaviour does not align with organisational expectations. Given that professionals in the social, health and human services may be required to follow both our professional and workplace codes of ethics, situations may arise where the codes conflict and we must choose what to do. This may result in multiple loyalties, often framed by the realities of needing to maintain employment in difficult economic circumstances. As we saw in Chapter 5, a sound model of ethical decision-making is critical when we are confronted with dilemmas of this nature.

In recognition of the additional tasks that social, health and human service managers undertake, several of the codes of ethics also address specific guidelines to management, including:

* maintaining adequate staffing levels and working conditions
* providing ongoing training opportunities for the professional development of staff
* providing support for staff where debriefing is necessary
* appropriate use of organisational finances.

These ethical requirements of managers construct a set of responsibilities that link closely to competence and professional integrity, as discussed in the previous chapter.

It is not difficult to see where potential ethical dilemmas might lie for managers who have responsibility for both resources (physical and financial) and people. Managers need to be aware of how teams function and where tensions that exist within groups may affect service delivery. They need to know if there are interprofessional conflicts (or the potential for these) and may need to become involved in mediating between members of different disciplines, or people within the same discipline. Breakdowns in communication, or outright hostility between members of work groups, can have a major impact on staff morale and can contribute to a culture of intimidation and, in serious cases, bullying or overt discrimination. A manager can be held liable for the actions of employees when it is reasonable to expect him or her to know about certain practices by virtue of his or her supervisory role. It is also important to remember, however, that staff who feel threatened or unsure of what they are doing in their work will often take the path of avoidance, and actively obscure their practice from the managerial or supervisory gaze. McAuliffe and Sudbery (2005) found that social workers who did not engage in supportive consultation with their managers or supervisors when faced with ethical dilemmas cited a fear of being seen as somehow 'unprofessional', which left them unwilling to expose themselves to critique of their work or decisions. This resulted in isolation, stress and poor management of decisions that led some to leave work in the human services, and others to develop mental and physical illnesses. Interviews with social workers (McAuliffe, 2005b) who did not make good use of supervision or management support while experiencing an ethical dilemma revealed that:

- I had really classic stress-related symptoms. I was edgy, nervy, often tearful. I know I cried a lot, just through tiredness too. It was a stress thing for me. And I'd lock my office door and have a cry and didn't want to take phone calls…
- I was a bit hypervigilant, a bit paranoid. I knew I was paranoid but I also knew I had a right to be paranoid. I was tense, my blood pressure shot through the roof. I felt really betrayed, really vulnerable and fragile.
- I felt I was isolated. I was very much alone at the time. I had a real sense of being disconnected from what was happening around me.

All those interviewed were certain that they would have handled their responses differently had they been able to seek good support from colleagues or managers. The importance of collegial relationships to act as a buffer for work-related stress is clear.

REFLECTION 8.3
1 Have you had the experience of being a part of a 'toxic' work environment? What was its impact on you as a worker?
2 Were the issues resolved and if so, how?
3 What role did managers in the organisation take to address the tensions?

Buckingham and Coffman (cited in Freegard, 2007, pp. 172–3) outlined 12 dimensions of a good workplace, and identified what managers can do to maintain morale and a functional culture. These dimensions include:

- providing clear expectations
- accessing necessary tools and resources
- using people's talents
- providing recognition and praise
- caring about each individual
- encouraging development
- valuing opinions and input
- creating a sense of purpose
- making a commitment to quality
- valuing personal relationships and friendships
- acknowledging individual team members goals and progress
- encouraging innovation and new perspectives.

■ Competing values: when organisational and professional values collide

At times, as practitioners in the social, health and human services, we may feel constrained by our employers' policies, procedures and practices. Much has been written concerning the changes in service delivery that occurred as a result of neoliberal economic policies in the 1980s and beyond. This ideology has been associated with funding cuts, restrictions on entitlements and the loss of professional autonomy (Banks, 2004). Health and human service practice in the contemporary context operates largely from within a business model, requiring that employees tailor their practice behaviours accordingly (Hugman, 1998). As a result, we may find at times that we are required to act in ways that inhibit our ability to deliver on the ethical requirements set out in our professional code of ethics. There are many examples of this: we have only to look at immigration detention centres, or some Indigenous communities, to see demonstrations of dedicated medical, nursing, legal and welfare staff working in situations that daily challenge their values and wreak havoc on their ability to maintain professional integrity. Navigating these situations can prove extremely difficult, as practitioners weigh up the competing loyalties with the reality of their need to hold their jobs, or to continue working within systems to effect even small changes. In the previous chapter, we looked at the issue of 'conscientious objection', which relates to the extreme case of a practitioner deciding that they cannot in good faith engage in a particular job for moral reasons. In recognition of the growing frequency of organisational and professional tensions, the codes of ethics of the health and human services include guidance on what to do when dilemmas arise. The AASW Code of Ethics (2010, p. 33) clearly establishes that the professional code has priority over the requirements of the employing organisation. It states that:

> Social workers will uphold the ethical values and responsibilities of this Code, even though employers' policies or official orders may not be compatible with its provisions. Attempts to resolve conflicts between ethical values and organisational policies and practices will remain consistent with the values and responsibilities outlined in this Code.

An apt example of an ethical dilemma of this sort would be a Catholic hospital that has a clear policy that staff will not actively provide information to women about termination of pregnancy. When a client requests such information, a practitioner has a professional responsibility to provide all possible information that will allow a client to make a fully informed choice about a course of action; not to do so would be negligent. The worker's options are: to provide the information and go against organisational directives; not to provide the information and go against professional code of ethics responsibilities; or to take the middle ground and refer the client on to another service that can provide the requested information. Most practitioners appear to take the latter option, at the risk of the relationship with the client.

A growing body of research explores the growth of covert actions that workers undertake to reconcile the tensions between their organisational and professional obligations (Abramovitz, 2005; Aronson & Smith, 2009; Baines, 2001; Carey & Foster, 2011; Greenslade, McAuliffe & Chenoweth, (2014 in press); Gregory, 2010; McDonald & Chenoweth, 2009). The most recent research in this area establishes that some workers will prioritise their professional requirements, choosing to take actions in conflict with workplace directives. Greenslade (2013) reports that workers turn a blind eye to client behaviours that their employer does not endorse; tamper with record keeping to protect clients; stretch the truth to optimise the likelihood that clients will receive a service; and even break the law to protect clients. Obvious risks occur when workers purposely decide to disobey the rules of their employing organisation, and yet increasing numbers of workers are making such decisions.

■ Blowing the whistle

When social, health and human service practitioners encounter serious wrongdoing and ethical misconduct by their colleagues, management or organisation, a decision may be made to report such conduct. This process is referred to as 'whistleblowing', a term which derives from the practice of English police who would blow their police whistles when they observed a crime in progress. The majority of whistleblowers report misconduct to their superiors and are therefore known as 'internal' whistleblowers. A smaller group, unable to confine the misconduct to internal complaint mechanisms, are known as 'external whistleblowers'. It is difficult to estimate the number of whistleblowing cases, as the majority do not come to the attention of those outside the organisation. Miller, Roberts and Spence (2004) outline the forms of corruption or illegality that might warrant whistleblowing:

- any illegality or infringement of the law
- fraudulent or corrupt conduct
- substantial misconduct, mismanagement or maladministration
- gross or substantial waste of resources
- endangerment of public health or safety and the environment
- dishonest or partial performance of duties
- breach of trust
- misuse of information.

For social, health and human service practitioners, the decision to report colleagues we believe have engaged in wrongdoing is a difficult one. We should not take this step lightly, and we should have evidence of the alleged misconduct or illegal activity.

Further, it is advisable to join with others rather than take on large and powerful organisations single-handed. DeMaria (1997) explored the ramifications of whistleblowing for the complainant and found that reporting unethical conduct can lead to workplace bullying, demotion and, potentially, loss of employment. Given that the result of reporting unethical conduct can be considerable personal stress and trauma, the decision to proceed can be seen as evidence of courageous practice. In recognition of the difficulties encountered when proceeding with a complaint, many organisations have developed whistleblowing policies that aim to protect complainants from undue harm and to support them through the process of investigation. There have been many high-profile whistleblowing cases in Australia, and some significant research projects on the incidence, significance and outcomes of whistleblowing. Kerridge, Lowe and McPhee (2005) reported on studies with medical students that showed that 65 per cent had witnessed some form of unethical conduct in healthcare teams, and 80 per cent admitted to having behaved unethically in some way themselves. It was common for these observations and acts to remain covert, leading Kerridge, Lowe and McPhee (2005, p. 106) to conclude that: 'students often react with a policy of silence when they observe or take part in ethically suspect actions ... keeping quiet becomes a habit and it represents a failure in teaching, learning and caring'. Despite witnessing unethical behaviour, most practitioners are aware of the serious ramifications for both their colleagues and themselves and are therefore reluctant to complain (Reamer, 2006). A large Australian Research

Council funded project conducted between 2005 and 2009 interviewed more than 10 000 public-sector employees about reported wrongdoing, the results of which also demonstrated people's reluctance to report for fear of repercussions (Roberts, Brown & Olsen, 2011). This project resulted in a detailed set of guidelines and strategies for managing whistleblowing in the public interest.

REFLECTION 8.4

1 Revisit your professional code of ethics and identify any sections that offer guidance on what to do should the requirements of the employing organisation clash with your ethical responsibilities to your profession. How useful do you believe your code of ethics is in addressing this issue?

2 Does your code of ethics include a statement on conscientious objection? Can you identify any circumstances or actions within your professional setting that might violate your moral beliefs? What might you do in such circumstances?

3 What might be the ramifications of choosing to conscientiously object? What might be the ramifications for you, personally and professionally, of choosing not to conscientiously object on an issue you feel strongly about?

■ Regulating the professions

As previously outlined in Chapter 4, a range of integrity and regulatory bodies exist at both state and federal levels to manage the process of investigating complaints of professional misconduct. AHPRA now handles complaints about professionals across 14 discipline areas. Organisations such as the Crime and Misconduct Commission (Queensland), Human Rights and Anti-Discrimination Commissions, Federal and State Ombudsmen, Health Quality Complaints and Health Rights Commissions, Children's Commissions, Child and Adult Guardians, Public Advocates, Guardianship and Administration Tribunals, provide mechanisms for managing the process of whistleblowing complaints. It is important that, as practitioners, we have good knowledge of these integrity bodies, as the time may come when we are called on to support a client through the process of making a complaint against another health worker; when a complaint is made against us; or when we need to make a complaint against someone else.

■ Impaired practice and fitness to practice: ethical responsibilities of self-care

Due to the complex nature of our work in the social, health and human service sectors, it is widely recognised that we need to use strategies to continue working in a competent and ethically sound manner. Good ethical practice requires that we remain free from impairment. The term 'impaired practice' means that a professional is unable to meet the requirements of their code of ethics and workplace policies and procedures due to some problem with cognitive, interpersonal or psychomotor skills (Raia, 2004). Another definition of impairment is 'any physical or mental condition which detrimentally affects, or is likely to detrimentally affect, his or her capacity to practice their profession' (Kerridge, Lowe & McPhee, 2005, p. 129). It is also made clear that impairment is related to risk to the public.

The three most commonly identified problems that social, health and human services staff present with in the workplace are substance abuse, mental health issues, and problems related to discrimination, such as racism (Segal, Gerdes & Steiner, 2010). All of these problems can have a negative impact on the quality of service we provide to clients. We and our colleagues alike are responsible for raising any concerns about the fitness of individuals to function in the work environment. This is a very important issue for employers to manage with sensitivity and care, as failure to do so can result in difficult collegial relationships if staff feel that they have to cover for a colleague who is having difficulties maintaining an acceptable standard of work. Some of the most difficult situations in workplaces relate to poor management of this issue.

The codes of ethics and conduct of most (but not all) professional disciplines that we have discussed so far mention impairment and the ethical responsibility to maintain a high level of awareness of any potential problems that could have a negative impact on practice. Different disciplines take their own focus: the codes for pharmacy and chiropractic, for example, refer to the need for work–life balance and to ensure that we understand the impact of fatigue. The discipline of psychology, in contrast, focuses more on what should happen in terms of cessation of services should a psychologist be unable to ensure competency. The code for dieticians states that practitioners should not work outside their scope of competency, but does not directly mention practitioner impairment, while those for social work, nursing and most other allied health professions very clearly state practitioners' ethical responsibility on impairment.

■ Staying fit to practice

There is an extensive research literature on the issue of fitness to practice (Walker et al., 2013). This issue is taken very seriously, and has now been written into National Law for all the professions under the jurisdiction of AHPRA, who, since adoption in 2010, has a mandatory responsibility to notify the respective Board of any person who poses a risk to the public. Notifiable conduct includes:

- practising while under the influence of alcohol or drugs
- engaging in sexual misconduct in connection with practice

- placing the public at risk of substantial harm because of impairment
- placing the public at risk of harm due to practice that constitutes a significant departure from accepted professional standards.

This means that if a nurse observes an occupational therapist do something harmful to a patient, or if a medical radiologist has evidence that a physiotherapist has mistreated a patient, he or she needs to report it. A psychologist who is engaged in therapy with a doctor, and who has concerns about his or her fitness to practice, may be mandated to notify the Medical Board. The onus of responsibility on colleagues is very high under this requirement, particularly when the level of impairment has obscured reason or insight, making it difficult for us to address problems first in the hope of avoiding notification.

Statistics from AHPRA show that the number of notifications is increasing each year, but there is still a high percentage of cases in which no further action is taken after investigation. Professions that fall outside AHPRA, such as teaching and social work, have other regulatory strategies to monitor and respond to impaired practice. In the education sector, if a teacher has their registration revoked following an investigation into a breach of professional conduct, then they cannot teach. If a social worker, however, is found by the AASW ethics complaint management system to have breached the code of ethics, they can lose eligibility for membership of the AASW, which may have some implications for employment in government; but they can still continue to practice as social work is not yet a registered profession. This 'Through the eyes of a practitioner' insert highlights the growing evidence of harm in the counselling and therapy professions.

THROUGH THE EYES OF A PRACTITIONER

Uncomfortable, important, but often overlooked questions for professionals are 'what happens if something I do harms my client?' and 'what do I do if I have concerns that a colleague is doing something harmful?' In my undergraduate education several decades ago, these questions were not focused on, and I certainly was not well informed about the regulatory and complaint mechanisms applicable to a range of professions. There was also a sense that the medical professions can harm patients because there is a risk of physical injury or death, but those that provide 'talking cures', such as counselling, psychotherapy, group work, community work or casework, could not be harmful. The other common myth has been that sexual-boundary violations are the main form of harm. We now have an increasing body of evidence that harm can arise from psychological manipulation, dependency, over- and under-servicing, practices which lack a robust evidence base, poor assessments and powerful decisions by professionals, in a manner that is just as serious, if not more enduring and complex in its impacts (and more difficult to prove), than physical harm alone. There is also evidence in literature that no profession is immune from impaired practice (the impairment rate is estimated at 5–11 per cent), nor from the risks of exploiting the considerable power we hold. What I found, through researching these sensitive topics, was that we can improve our practice if we strive to improve our ethics literacy and our ability to speak about taboos such as risks of harm to clients, and our willingness (backed up by organisational resources) to be well qualified and supervised in our work.

(Deborah Sauvage)

When exploring the sources of impairment, we see a complex combination of issues that can result in one practitioner working with resilience and empathy, or another succumbing to stress, isolation or cynicism and hostility towards others. In the next section, we examine the sources of impairment.

Psychiatric illness or disability

Many people can work quite well in a range of different professions with diagnosed and treated mental health conditions, or physical or intellectual disabilities. In Australia, it is illegal to discriminate against employees on the basis of disability, and all reasonable arrangements should be put in place to assist people to maintain productive employment to the best of their ability. There is always the potential for instability with psychiatric illness in particular, and if a person is non-compliant with medication, has fluctuating mood, or is emotionally labile, there can be implications for work stability. It is important that a person in need of mental health or disability support has a plan in place to assist in the event of recurring ill-health. There are many ethical issues around disclosure of psychiatric illness, and people have a right to privacy concerning their own mental health status. This needs to be balanced against the requirement for transparency and accountability, so that employers can work in partnership with staff who do need support and plan flexible working arrangements if required. An excellent resource has been developed by Mental Health First Aid Australia (MHFA) for organisations to help plan employees' return to work. This guide sets out explicit strategies to manage support, disclosure issues and reasonable work adjustments, including plans for rehabilitation in cases of substance misuse or dependency (see the MHFA website at <www.mhfa.com.au/cms/home>). It is particularly common for professionals working in the health field to develop substance misuse problems, as drugs are accessible and self-prescription not difficult. The Medical Council of NSW is an example of a statutory body that investigates complaints about doctors (as part of AHPRA), but also provides a health and performance program service to doctors who may require intensive help to overcome substance abuse and addictions. The management response to problems of this nature should be one of protection of the public as a primary duty. Suspected substance abuse problems should not be ignored, but should we suspect that a colleague is self-medicating, diverting medication or under the influence of drugs or alcohol at work, it can be difficult to know what to do, particularly as reporting will most likely have serious consequences. We need to be well educated about the signs of possible substance misuse, which may include medication errors; discrepancies in medication records; offers to medicate co-workers' patients; increased narcotic sign-outs; changed mood following breaks; or isolation from peers. Physical signs may include tremors or shakiness; unsteadiness of gait; watery eyes or dilated or constricted pupils; slurred speech; frequent use of mouthwash; or weight gain or loss. Behavioural changes may include defensiveness; lack of concentration; mood changes; angry outbursts; decreased judgement in performance; and frequent lying.

Personal problems unrelated to work

None of us is immune to difficulties in life, and many of us will at some point experience the illness or death of a loved one, a traumatic experience, a major change of circumstances, a breakdown of relationship, or personal ill-health. We tend to be more forgiving of impaired practice when the circumstances are outside someone's control, and it is common for colleagues to cover for each other in the event of a family tragedy, an unexpected illness or a period of depression following difficult life events. The management strategy in these cases should allow for clear contractual arrangements about reduction of load, flexible work arrangements, a clear expectation that professional assistance be accessed, and a reassurance that impairment can be accommodated in the short term but not for an unreasonable length of time. Colleagues who become aware that a co-worker is struggling should encourage him or her to access an Employee Assistance Program (EAP), seek medical care, or take a period of leave. Unfortunately, not all workplaces are sympathetic to personal problems that intrude on work, so we should support colleagues to access appropriate assistance at an early stage, which may prevent a situation worsening.

Problems related to work

Impaired functioning can be the result of ongoing problems in a workplace that leaves an employee anxious, depressed, lacking in morale and suffering from questionable productivity. Mangers have a responsibility to read the climate of a work group, be familiar with the needs of staff, and guard against complacency. We should ideally discuss problems related to work with the appropriate line manager or supervisor in the first instance. There may also be an advantage in accessing an external supervisor; that is, someone from outside who can look objectively at what is happening and challenge assumptions. Again, EAPs can be of great benefit in assisting practitioners to manage work-related conflicts, clarify role definitions, and balance workload. EAPs have now become an integral part of most organisations and businesses, to the point where there is now the Employee Assistance Professional Association of Australasia (2009). The EAPAA, as a peak body, has its own code of ethics and complaint process.

Vicarious trauma

This is a specified stress response to accumulated stories of pain, hardship and unfairness. Figley (1995, p. 7) has defined it as 'the natural, consequent behaviours and emotions resulting from knowledge about a traumatising event experienced by a significant other – it is the stress resulting from helping or wanting to help a traumatised or suffering person'. If you spend your work hours listening to stories of trauma, violence, loss and grief, you are particularly susceptible to vicarious trauma (VT). It can be almost impossible to avoid in fields like sexual assault, family violence, child protection, resettlement work with asylum seekers, or disaster responses. It is important that we realise that VT is a normal response to cumulative exposure to trauma material, and that it is not a personal failing or weakness. People respond to VT in different ways, but they should receive support in the workplace regardless of how their VT symptoms manifest. Some will have intrusive reactions, such as dreams or obsessive thoughts; others will have avoidant reactions, such as feeling numb and disconnected; while some will become hypervigilant. Organisations have a responsibility to ensure that employees have access to supports, debriefing and supervision or mentoring, where the nature of the work means that practitioners are at risk of VT. Many other practical strategies can be put in place, such as ensuring diversity of workload, access to peer support, and flexible working arrangements. VT has also been called 'compassion fatigue', and is linked to burnout in cases where proactive strategies have not been employed to guard against the impacts of stress. Working closely with colleagues in a team environment can give good insight into our susceptibility to VT, and all members of a team should be alert to signs of this type of emotional fatigue. If we fail to manage VT effectively, it may start a practitioner on a spiral to impaired practice, but we can avoid that situation with good awareness and collegial support. The importance of managers being aware of these issues is illustrated in this 'Through the eyes of a practitioner' insert.

■ Caring for ourselves well

Developing a realistic and achievable self-care strategy, committing to following it seriously, and reviewing it regularly with supervisors or mentors will give us a sound foundation to ensure we function well in the workplace. Part of interprofessional collaboration is being prepared to observe how others are coping with the demands of complex and difficult work and to notice the positive and negative impacts of work on others. While there may be a humane and moral obligation for this observation and noticing, we have an associated ethical obligation to act if a colleague shows signs of impairment, stress, VT or emotional fatigue. This ethical obligation becomes a legal one if there is evidence of harm or risk to others from the conduct or behaviour of a professional practitioner. It is generally advisable that any observations be raised first with the colleague in question, and if there is denial or lack of insight that sustains or increases risk, the next step is to take the matter to a higher authority.

Self-care strategies often need to be learnt and practised to be effective; they are conscious efforts designed to balance emotional responses, maintain physical and mental health and wellbeing, and increase resilience and strength. These strategies need to take account of the emotional, physical and spiritual domains, and we should integrate them into our daily activities and dedicate time to practising them.

Strategies for good self-care

- Stress management and physical wellbeing activities, such as engaging with regular exercise and physical activity through the course of a day. This also includes paying attention to nutrition and diet, and being aware of over-reliance on caffeine, alcohol, smoking or recreational drug use.
- Planning holiday periods, during which we can focus on recreation and spending time with significant others. This includes making a conscious effort not to take work with you on holiday, so that you can remove yourself for a time from the responsibilities of your job.
- Being very careful about work–life balance and understanding clearly what this means. Intrusions of work into family life can have dire consequences for healthy relationships with partners, extended family, children and friends. Work needs to be kept in its place, as difficult as that can be at times.
- Acknowledging the small and bigger successes in your work and life, and developing rituals to celebrate when you achieve your goals.
- Engaging with your community in an active way, such as joining a local action group, or doing some volunteer work, so that you can channel energy into something other than the work you are paid to do.
- Maintaining clear boundaries between your work and home life, and reaching conclusions about your stance on issues such as self-disclosure. This may include making conscious decisions about how to engage with social media and social networking, and how to preserve privacy and safeguard reputation.
- Seek out professional supervision or mentoring and use it wisely, ensuring that all agreements are in place about limits of confidentiality in the event of observable concerns about fitness for practice. If you need to engage in counselling or therapy, do so. Do not use supervision to focus on personal issues; these are different processes with different aims.
- Develop a professional reputation and a persona that reflect your capacity for humour and your ability to maintain good judgement and make objective appraisals of people, dynamics and organisational culture.

THROUGH THE EYES OF A PRACTITIONER

My main self-care strategy is to have a good relationship with myself. I know my tender points and how to care for them/me if I become triggered. I prioritise myself and my happiness. If I don't look after these things for myself, chances are that someone else will have to! I think that to work with people who have a trauma history means that we need to be extra-focused on looking after ourselves. So here are some of the things I love to do. I meditate morning and night, just to spend some quiet time with myself, see how I'm going and become still and present in the moment. I exercise every day by walking my two beautiful Labradors after work and sometimes going to the gym. Exercise clears my head and helps to release any built up tension in my body at the end of the day. I find ways to express myself and my creativity through writing, singing and making music. I consciously do at least one nice thing for myself every day. It doesn't have to be a big deal – enjoying a bath, or taking my shoes off and walking in the grass. I always have something in my diary to look forward to, usually some time away in nature with my partner and my dogs.

(Jenny Gilmore)

REFLECTION 8.5

1 Do you currently participate in activities that you feel help you keep a good balance in your life? Are you able to maintain these even when life stressors intrude?

2 Can you identify a range of self-care strategies that might work for you? How might you go about developing a sustainable self-care routine?

■ Ethics consultation, advice and information

The complexity of practice and the continued revision of ethical guidelines, codes and standards of conduct have resulted in many of the professions being proactive in the development of consultation services to assist practitioners to work through situations of ethical tension. While AHPRA has largely taken over control of investigations into alleged professional misconduct for a growing number of disciplines, there is still room for a more consultative approach to ethical decision-making. In Australia, the St James Ethics Centre (based in Sydney) provides assistance to organisations that seek to address ethical issues within their workplaces. It also provides individual assistance to people who are struggling with ethical dilemmas in practice. In the area of law and justice, the Queensland Law Society Ethics Centre provides ethical advice to lawyers, and provides advice on any professional conduct issues. The Australian Association of Social Workers (AASW) provides a National Ethics and Practice Standards Consultation Service, which enables members to talk through ethical dilemmas with an experienced ethics adviser. There are now a number of Ethical Guidelines documents on the AASW ethics site, covering issues such as mandatory reporting, responding to subpoenas, case note recording, international practice, private practice, using client material for teaching and education, and working with children. The Australian Psychological Society has a similar consultation service, which provides advice on how to interpret its code of ethics and practice guidelines. As we mentioned at the start of this book, ethical literacy is an important part of becoming an aware professional. When we develop the confidence to consult with others, to test out our thinking and justify decisions based on values, we can help ensure our competence to manage complexity. It is incumbent on professional associations, as demonstrated in the contribution below, to provide consultation services such as mentioned in this section, so that practitioners can exercise their ethical responsibilities to engage in appropriate discussions and dialogue.

THROUGH THE EYES OF A PRACTITIONER

When a social worker contacts the Ethics and Practice Standards Consultation Service, they are generally looking for advice about how to manage an ethical or practice issue that they have not been able to resolve themselves. It has been the experience of ethics staff that most people who contact this service do so because they are genuinely committed to practising in accordance with the Code of Ethics and Practice Standards. The service offers the opportunity to process, unpack and think through the considerations relevant to each particular situation. The service has also developed ethical and practice guidelines that further explore those issues and dilemmas that arise most frequently in practice.

(Kym Daly)

■ Conclusion

In this chapter, we have ascertained that clients and patients benefit from our work in multidisciplinary and interprofessional teams when we practise open communication, respect, and a willingness to listen – but there are also potential problems. We should look for work in places that will not compromise our integrity to the extent that we are continually at loggerheads with our employers. We have seen that workplaces are many and varied in the social, health and human services and, to this end, it is important that managers take seriously the responsibility of reading the climate of the organisation and being attentive to the needs of staff as they negotiate working relationships. The issue of impaired practice, in particular, requires a systematic approach that can be both fair and harsh in the interests of public safety, while self-care is an ethical responsibility that we all need to take very seriously. In the final chapter, we will bring the threads of this book into cohesion and explore the question of how we can keep ethics on the agenda at multiple levels in the interprofessional context.

9

Keeping ethics on the agenda:
strategies for future practice

■ Learning objectives

- **TO PROVIDE** a summary of important points from earlier chapters and identify core themes for ongoing learning
- **TO DEVELOP** a professional development plan for integrating ethics into future practice
- **TO IDENTIFY** challenges for the future and explore ways to keep ethics on the agenda within workplaces
- **TO PROMOTE** a commitment to ongoing critical reflection and interprofessional collaboration for future practice.

■ Introduction

WRITING A TEXT about ethics and professional practice is a challenge. This is because no other area in professional education has so much potential for controversy, difference of opinion, and outright conflict when people's values simply do not align. The primary difference between this text and others that are discipline-specific or that cover moral philosophy in a more general way is that we have focused on interprofessional learning and education, based on an understanding that multiple perspectives exist by virtue of educational socialisation. We have seen how ethics education has traditionally been taught in single-discipline silos, and we have discussed the possibilities that open up when students and practitioners make a conscious effort to learn from, with and about each other. The concept of interprofessional education (IPE) is not new, and its benefits are well documented for a number of professional groups, even though there are calls for a nationally coordinated and research-informed approach (Matthews et al., 2011).

While interprofessional practice is perhaps most visible in the field of health, we have provided many other examples, throughout this book, of practitioners working together in the legal and justice, education, youth work, disability, community work, child and family, and housing sectors. Heather D'Cruz, co-author of another text on a similar topic, has contributed the following analysis, in which she explores the challenges inherent in any attempts to bring together disciplines in a collective way for academic and educational purposes. D'Cruz writes that:

> Interprofessional practice, variously conceptualised as team work, multidisciplinarity, interdisciplinarity and transdisciplinarity, is valued by helping professions and their employing organisations for its contribution to holistic service provision and effective and efficient use of resources. Our experiences as co-editors of *Knowledge-in-Practice in the Caring Professions: Multidisciplinary Perspectives* (D'Cruz, Jacobs & Schoo, 2009) gave us some insights into the underlying dynamics associated with multidisciplinarity. Our book proposal for chapters by authors from a range of professions/disciplines attracted criticism as to its 'unmarketability' because professionals and educators would only read the chapter(s) 'relevant to their profession'. We viewed this criticism as exemplifying a practical problem associated with a conceptual problem of IPE for practice. Our approach aimed mainly to stimulate discussion and offer insights to open-minded and critically-aware readers, although being aware of the challenges of how to encourage this in practice. Having gained a contract, our next challenge as editors was how to make sense of what were clearly disparate chapters: in structure, content, and writing style. We concluded by offering the insights that our experiences with the process were much like participating in a 'textual multidisciplinary team meeting', in which the writing equated with verbal expressions of knowledge that may alienate those 'outside' a particular profession. Presenting problems may be identified differently, ranging from those discernible by the senses to those that are less tangible. Interventions may range from technological to 'talk'. Claims of efficacy may vary between professions because it may not be possible to make causal or correlational associations between problem, intervention and outcome. These differences in knowledge influence hierarchies of expertise and differences in duty of care and legal liabilities, and the degree to which service users may participate in decision making, for different professional groups within teams.

In this concluding chapter, we will bring together the primary themes discussed in the text, before concluding with a series of recommendations for the most important 'take-home messages', which will serve to keep ethics 'on the agenda'. It is about ways of 'being' that integrate knowledge, skills and values into a framework for ongoing professional practice. Our focus on 'being' is important because it moves us beyond simply *having* values, beliefs and views of the world, to a state of action that plays out in our relationships with others.

■ Being ethically literate: speaking the language of ethics

In the first few chapters of this book, we explained why students and practitioners need to develop a strong understanding of content about ethics as a field of study, and moral philosophy as a foundation for ethics. The proposition was put that work in the social, health and human services is essentially a 'moral endeavour' and that it is not possible to avoid ethical dilemmas, problems and issues when working with people who use our professional services. Being ethically literate involves more than just knowing that there is a code of ethics for your discipline, or having a basic understanding of policies such as those on privacy or clients' capacity to provide informed consent. It is useful to use a correlation with a definition of health literacy to explain the point. Zarcadoolas, Pleasant and Greer (2005, pp. 196–7) define health literacy as 'the wide range of skills and competencies that people develop to seek out, comprehend, evaluate, and use health information and concepts to make informed choices, reduce health risks and improve quality of life'. We can look at a parallel definition in relation to ethical literacy. This could be defined as the skills and competencies that people develop to seek out, comprehend, evaluate and use information about values, to make informed choices, reduce ethical risks and improve quality of practice. Being literate means being knowledgeable, informed and educated in a particular area, so it is therefore imperative that ethics education be incorporated in professional training. Campbell and Hare (1997) present a very clear definition of what ethical literacy should include, with reference to the field of gerontology and geriatric education. They clarify that ethical literacy is about: 'recognising an ethical issue; stimulating the ethical imagination; fostering critical thinking and analytical skills; cultivating ethical responsibility; and resolving and tolerating ethical ambiguity' (1997, p. 3). We have covered all of these issues in different sections of this text.

Strategies for developing and maintaining ethical literacy

- Buy at least one good textbook on moral philosophy and ethical theory and add this to your professional library. Having a good reference text close to hand can provide you with a resource to anchor decisions.
- Become familiar with the academic journals that focus specifically on professional ethics, either in your discipline or more broadly (some examples are *Ethics and Social Welfare*; *Science, Technology and Human Values*; *Ethics and Behaviour*; *Journal of Buddhist Ethics*; *Medical Ethics*; *Journal of Social Work Values and Ethics*). Set up a 'TOC email alert' so that you can keep up with new articles in selected journals.

- Make a conscious effort to use the language of ethics when having conversations with colleagues. Being able to identify and name theoretical positions, discuss culturally diverse worldviews and refer with confidence to ethical principles will integrate this language more closely with your practice repertoire.
- Choose an issue that you feel passionate about and set up a 'Google alert' so that you will have a continuous stream of current developments on that issue (for example, refugee children in detention centres; mandatory alcohol rehabilitation; marriage equality). Practice reading these articles using an 'ethical lens' and try to identify the different ethical positions that are evident in government responses, public opinion and other critical forums.
- Ensure that when you document case notes, write reports, or produce assessments, you use ethical language and present ethical dimensions for consideration. When you are able to write about autonomy, to query informed consent, and to identify potential breaches of privacy, you can bring ethical issues to the fore in documentation that will be shared with others.

■ Being ethically congruent: knowing oneself ethically

A clear message that has been repeated many times through this text is the importance of taking the time to engage in critical reflection on values, beliefs, attitudes and views of the world, humanity, and the meaning of life. Not only is it important to examine our motivations for deciding to pursue a career path that is about people rather than objects or the inanimate, we should look to messages conveyed by parental or authority figures in our early years to explore patterns of socialised responses to moral issues (Chenoweth & McAuliffe, 2014). Views about controversial issues such as euthanasia, capital punishment, abortion, same-sex parenting, genetic modification of foods and animal rights have their roots, generally, in either experiences of self or others, religious doctrines, or persuasive arguments. The first step to living a life that is ethically congruent is to acknowledge the influences of history, significant others, and learning (both scholarly and from experience), as this enables us to make decisions that will not compromise our values. In this text, we have explored the difficulties that can arise if we work in a field of practice or an organisation where we are confronted with situations that we find morally abhorrent. Placing ourselves in situations where our values are constantly challenged can be exhausting and can lead us to disengage from colleagues. It is easy to lose sight of the purpose of the work. Continually trying to refer on or regularly excusing yourself from cases on the grounds of conscientious objection is not a constructive way to practice.

Strategies for developing and maintaining ethical congruence

- Use professional supervision, mentoring, or even therapy if need be, to explore personal and professional value positions and uncover early influences and acknowledge their potential power.
- Ensure that you are not working in a situation where you are constantly being challenged on a moral level because of a poor fit between your values and those of your workplace. This has the potential to result in exhaustion and disconnection, and can result in burnout and stress-related responses over time. This is not to say that a good sense of moral outrage on issues of injustice should not be applauded, but rather that internal incongruence is difficult to sustain.
- Be clear about your own ethical positions on controversial topics, and practice giving a rationale for this position; be prepared to defend your position on other grounds than the emotive. Seek out knowledge, evidence and research, as well as the lived experiences of those who have been in situations that exemplify what you wish to defend.

■ Being digitally aware

There is no longer any doubt that the age of the internet, social media and digital communication is now part and parcel of our lives professionally as well as personally. We have discussed the concept of e-professionalism in this text, highlighting some of the many ethical and reputational dilemmas that can arise as a result of engagement with others using online communications. We have an ethical responsibility to manage e-communications in a way that maintains respect for others, acknowledges the limits of lack of face to face contact, and upholds all of the other ethical principles, such as privacy, consent and veracity. There are many situations in which people are made vulnerable in ways not previously experienced, such as cyber-bullying, cyber-stalking, trolling, and deliberate invasions of privacy. As professionals,we need to take very active steps to manage our 'digital footprint', and we have to consider seriously how our online persona might impact on our reputations, credibility, and standing in the community. Equally important is understanding the power of the internet, social networking and online communications to push social activist agendas forward in previously unheard-of ways. The capacity for advocacy and lobbying for social change is immense, as evidenced by social movements such as GetUp! (Action for Australia). It is doubtful that campaigns such as those for marriage equality, opposition to coal seam gas mining, action on climate change, and protection of the Great Barrier Reef, would have had such political impact were it not for the reach of social media. The rapid rise of 'crowdfunding' – a way of raising money for specified projects by calling for donations through the internet – has resulted in many worthy causes and charities receiving much-needed resources.

> ## Strategies for staying 'digitally savvy'
>
> - Accept that the digital world is here to stay. Make engaging with the basics of technology a priority and work out what you need to know to carry out your work competently. Understand passwords, encryptions, privacy settings, data security and online protocols.
> - Interrogate your 'digital footprint' and consider the implications of having personal information on social networking platforms such as Facebook. Make it a priority to understand and manage your privacy settings.
> - Be clear about your expectations of how others should engage with you in the online world. Develop your own personal policies on the 'friending' of people (including clients and colleagues) on Facebook. Maintain appropriate professional boundaries in online communications.
> - Use online sites that are set up for professional networking, such as LinkedIn, to promote your professional profile, rather than sites such as Facebook. Be aware that clients, their families and associates, colleagues, potential employers, and students will search for you online, and will trail back to look for information about your history. If you need to deal with your 'digital dirt', do it now.

■ Being collegial: rhetoric or reality?

The interprofessional focus of this text provides a unique vantage point from which to explore the ways in which practitioners from different disciplines can work together for better outcomes for people who engage with social, health and human services. It has been firmly established that benefits do exist for clients when there is good teamwork, consensus on decisions, and consistency of approaches. It is, however, taken for granted (in an idealistic world) that practitioners are expected to get on with their colleagues, and if there are difficulties then the expectation is that these are managed.

Unfortunately, there are many situations where relationships in a workplace are anything but collegial, and there are many reasons for tensions and clashes of values. In this text, we have examined in detail what can happen in the interprofessional space when values collide, including the impact of such collisions on our ongoing relationships. The tightening of some regulatory frameworks now means that it is mandatory for a practitioner to report a colleague if there is evidence of impaired practice. In considering ethical decision-making, we have strongly encouraged the practice of consultation with others, as a means of ensuring that decisions are inclusive of others where appropriate, and that as many vantage points on the issue as possible have been obtained. Collegiality means not only feeling comfortable in approaching others for support, but also being willing and prepared to extend support to others when they seek it. Mutual sharing of the ethical space can create a culture where dialogue becomes the norm rather than people holding onto information in a self-protective way and becoming isolated as a result. It is well known that good collegial relationships form the best buffer against work-related stress. Learning how to work as a productive and constructive member of a team will result in more negotiated outcomes, better discussion about professional responsibilities, and increased awareness of potential areas of conflict. The 'Through the eyes of a practitioner' insert in this section is by a (now graduated) student who studied a postgraduate course in interdisciplinary professional ethics. One assessment task students completed on this course involved developing an ethical question, which they then discussed with two people from different disciplines, with the aim of exploring different ways of understanding ethical perspectives.

THROUGH THE EYES OF A PRACTITIONER

I found the process of doing the assignments (including interviewing other professionals) very useful when I subsequently had to work in an interdisciplinary environment. I had to listen deeply and open myself up to the different ethical frameworks of the professionals I interviewed and their relevant ethical standards. In particular, it was useful for me to avoid falling into the trap of dismissing certain professions as 'too narrow', as I came to understand more about the values underpinning their approaches. It also reinforced in me a stronger appreciation of social work ethics, and confidence to articulate these in meetings. Knowing more about other professions' ethics has also been useful if I need to make my point persuasively; I can refer to mutually complementary ethical standards (or do the research beforehand if I am not familiar with their standards).

(Sophie Staughton)

Strategies for valuing the input and perspectives of colleagues from other disciplines

- Make time to sit with colleagues from disciplines different to your own and ask them about their training, their regulatory framework (or lack thereof), their code of ethics, and their understanding of foundational values for their discipline. Be genuinely interested in what others do, where the similarities and differences in your values and work lie, and identify the areas of common ground.

- Consider initiating a peer-mentoring group so that in-depth discussions can take place about commonly experienced ethical dilemmas. This forum can be used to work through a case using an ethical decision-making model. Different codes of ethics can be used to work through dilemmas from different professional perspectives.
- Explore possibilities for interprofessional training and professional development within the workplace. Use this training as a way to find out more about others in your workplace within a more contained space.
- Ensure that you have good knowledge about how to manage situations where you might hear about or witness ethical misconduct in relation to a colleague. If you find yourself in a position of needing to report such information or observations, ensure that you have evidence to support your allegations. If you find yourself on the other end of a complaint about your practice by a colleague, ensure that you know how to respond to this in a way that is respectful on potentially ongoing work relationships.

■ Being wise, brave and human

One of the most difficult things about working in the field of professional ethics is reaching the understanding that there are few situations that are black and white. Most are shades of grey – and *all* depend on context. Every situation should be examined from the standpoint of 'it depends', so that the concept of context can become ingrained and every situation can be explored for what it is that is unique from any other situation. Even those situations that require a deontological approach where rules or laws are clear, will have their own context to take into account. A wise practitioner will always engage with critical reflection so that they take nothing for granted; so that they remain aware that no two situations will automatically demand the same response; and so that they explore every situation for evidence of structural disadvantage or potential injustice. A brave practitioner will not remain silent when there is a need to speak out, or take a stand, on a principle that upholds professional ethical responsibilities.

We have looked in this text at the ways in which the neoliberal agenda can work to silence activism, which can lead workers to choose covert ways of supporting clients in efforts to ensure that their needs are met. The requirement for moral outrage and courage in leadership and advocacy has been put forth as a reasonable (if not expected) response to human rights abuses and oppressive social systems. The political call from deposed Prime Minister Gough Whitlam in 1975 to 'maintain your rage' continues to resonate with those who uphold the values of respect for diversity; protection of human dignity; freedom from torture, trauma, unsafe living situations and fear; and fair and equitable access to the resources necessary to sustain both physical and psychological quality of life. Being brave is to find ways to put these values into actions that speak louder than words.

Finally, being human requires professionals to pay close attention to what is meant by the construction of personal and professional boundaries. An earlier section of this text explored and offered a critique of this construction, and concluded that there are many situations in which professional boundaries work to protect and safeguard the interests of others, but also many that deny some of the basic human requirements for physical connection and emotional attachment (O'Leary, Tsui & Ruch, 2013). Being human as a professional sometimes means working in ways that allow the connection with another to uncover information that is critical to positive growth and change. Being human is to acknowledge one's own history; the impact of our experiences; our biases and prejudices; our socialised value patterns and emotional triggers; and our capacity for vulnerability and fears about insufficient knowledge or skill. Being human allows practitioners to engage with others at a deeper level so that collectively they can become, in the timeless words of Aristotle, 'a whole greater than the sum of its parts'. This is the primary aim of interprofessional practice in essence.

Strategies for becoming wise and brave and staying human

- Surround yourself with people in your life who believe in the capacity for people to grow, change and move forward in their lives. Your ability to sustain difficult work in the fields of social, health and human services will rely on how well you can maintain a respect for people and a belief that change is possible. Consult wisely with chosen associates and colleagues, ensuring that they are open to exploring situations from different positions and to promoting decisions that are not based on self-interest or self-indulgence.
- Decide which battles you will take on and which you will leave for another day. If there are particular issues that you are passionate about, make it your business to connect with others that share this passion. Seek work in fields that will sustain your energy and enthusiasm, and broaden your networks to include people from different discipline backgrounds who can expand your knowledge and complement your skills and interests.
- Engage in professional supervision, mentoring or discussions with colleagues about how to manage professional boundaries in ways that will enable you to remain congruent with your own values. Give careful consideration to personal disclosures, conduct of relationships, and conflicts of interest.
- Take care of yourself. Develop a clear plan for self-care, including building in time for critical reflection so that you can monitor your responses to difficult or complex ethical situations and check your moral compass for consistency and congruence. Acknowledge that you won't get everything right all of the time, and that this is all part of being human. The ability to learn from mistakes, moving forward with confidence to the next challenge, is the mark of a good practitioner.

■ Conclusion

Keeping ethics on the agenda is a critical part of every professional's role. Integrating ethics into our work at all levels ensures that we keep a watchful eye on situations that can disadvantage people or undermine their rights. We believe, and have argued in this text, that professional ethics is best explored, learnt and taught in an IPE context because this is the context that mirrors the realities of practice. The many examples provided in this text have illustrated connections between practitioners from different disciplines, who share a common purpose in their interest in working with people who are in need of some form of service provision, or in organisations that prepare the policies and laws to support funding for and provision of those services. These services may include legal, housing, education, financial, disability or mental health support, aged care, health, income support, community connection and intervention, therapeutic counselling, or disaster relief. Across all these fields of practice or methods of intervention, the one constant is that ethical issues will arise *often* in some fields, and *always* in every field. If you prepare an ethical toolkit, stocked with your understanding of all the knowledge, skills and values discussed in this text, you will be well placed to respond appropriately and humanely to ethical issues, problems and dilemmas. Professionals who work together to collaborate, activate, and learn with and from each other can help create a better social, health and human service workforce.

References

Abramovitz, M. (2005). The largely untold story of welfare reform and the human services. *Social Work, 50*(2), 175–86. doi:10.1093/sw/50.2.175.

Alexander, A. & Miller, S. (2009). *Ethics in practice: Moral theory and the professions.* Sydney, Australia: UNSW Press.

Ali, A.Y. (1998). *The Qur'an: Text, translation and commentary.* New York: Tahrike Tarsile Qur'an.

Alinsky, S. (1971). *Rules for radicals.* New York: Random House.

American Psychological Association. (2008). *Report of the APA Presidential Advisory Group on the implementation of the petition resolution.* Retrieved from http://www.apa.org/ethics/advisory-group-final.pdf.

Appiah, A. (1989). *An introduction to philosophy: Necessary questions.* Englewood Cliffs, NJ: Prentice-Hall.

Armstrong, P. (2006). Counselling skills. In N. Pelling, R. Bowers & P. Armstrong, *The practice of counselling* (pp. 46–75). South Melbourne, Australia: Thomson.

Aronson, J. & Smith, K. (2009). Managing restructured social services: Expanding the social? *British Journal of Social Work, 40*(2), 530–47. doi:10.1093/bjsw/bcp002.

Atkins, K., Britton, B. & de Lacey, S. (2011). *Ethics and law for Australian nurses.* Port Melbourne, Australia: Cambridge University Press.

Australian Association of Social Workers (n.d.). *Introduction of a national code of conduct for unregistered practitioners.* Retrieved from http://www.aasw.asn.au/document/item/4695.

Australian Association of Social Workers. (2010). *Code of ethics.* Canberra, Australia: Australian Association of Social Workers.

Australian Association of Social Workers. (2013a). *Practice Standards.* Retrieved from http://www.aasw.asn.au/document/item/4551.

Australian Association of Social Workers. (2013b). *By-laws on ethics: Revised 2013.* Retrieved from http://www.aasw.asn.au/document/item/91.

Australian Association of Social Workers. (2014). *Australian Association of Social Workers.* Retrieved from http://www.aasw.asn.au.

Australian Community Workers Association. (2012). *Australian Community Workers Association*. Retrieved from http://www.acwa.org.au.

Australian Institute of Family Studies. (2013). *Mandatory reporting of child abuse and neglect*. Retrieved from http://www.aifs.gov.au/cfca/pubs/factsheets/a141787/index.html.

Australian Medical Association. (2010). *Social media and the medical profession: A guide to online professionalism for medical practitioners and medical students*. Retrieved from https://ama.com.au/social-media-and-medical-profession.

Australian Medical Association. (2012). *In the beginning*. Retrieved from https://ama.com.au/about/history/the-beginning.

Australian Medical Association. (2014). *Australian Medical Association*. Retrieved from https://ama.com.au.

Australian Medical Council. (2009). *Good medical practice: A code of conduct for doctors in Australia*. Retrieved from http://www.amc.org.au/images/Final_Code.pdf.

Australian Nursing and Midwifery Federation. (2014). *Australian Nursing and Midwifery Federation*. Retrieved from http://anmf.org.au.

Australian Professional Teachers' Association. (2010). *Australian Professional Teachers' Association*. Retrieved from http://www.apta.edu.au.

Australian Psychological Society. (2007). *Code of ethics*. Retrieved from http://www.psychology.org.au/Assets/Files/APS-Code-of-Ethics.pdf.

Australian Psychological Society. (2014). *Australian Psychological Society*. Retrieved from https://www.psychology.org.au.

Baines, D. (2001). Everyday practices of race, class and gender: Struggles, skills, and radical social work. *Journal of Progressive Human Services*, 11(2), 5–27. doi:10.1300/J059v11n02_02.

Banks, S. (2004). *Ethics, accountability and the social professions*. London: Palgrave Macmillan.

Banks, S. & Nohr, K. (2012). *Practicing social work ethics around the world: Cases and commentaries*. London: Routledge.

Barak, A., Hen, L., Boneil-Nissim, M. & Shapira, N. (2008). A comprehensive review and meta-analysis of the effectiveness of internet-based psychotherapeutic interventions. *Journal of Technology in Human Services*, 26(2), 109–60.

Barnett, J. & Johnson, W.B. (2011). Integrating spirituality and religion into psychotherapy: Persistent dilemmas, ethical issues, and a proposed decision-making process. *Ethics and Behavior*, 21(2), 147–64.

Baskin, C. (2007). Conceptualising, framing and politicizing Aboriginal ethics in mental health. *Journal of Ethics in Mental Health*, 2(2), 1–5.

Beauchamp, T.L. & Childress, J.F. (1979). *Principles of biomedical ethics*. New York: Oxford University Press.

Beck, U. (1992). *Risk society*. London: Sage.

Beddoe, L. & Maidment, J. (2009). *Mapping knowledge for social work practice: Critical intersections*. South Melbourne, Australia: Cengage.

Bernard, T. (1947). *Hindu philosophy*. New York: Philosophical Library.

Billington, R. (1997). *Understanding Eastern philosophy*. New York: Routledge.

Bowles, W., Collingridge, M., Curry, S. & Valentine, B. (2006). *Ethical practice in social work*. Crows Nest, Australia: Allen & Unwin.

Briskman, L. (2008). *Recasting social work: Human rights and political activism – Eileen Younghusband Lecture*. Durban. Retrieved from http://info.humanrights.curtin.edu.au/local/docs/Recasting_Social_Work.pdf.

Briskman, L., Latham, S. & Goddard, C. (2008). *Human rights overboard*. Brunswick, Australia: Scribe Publications.

Briskman, L. & Uriz Peman, M.J. (2012). Respecting rights: Introduction. In S. Banks & K. Nohr (eds), *Practicing social work ethics around the world: Cases and commentaries* (pp. 69–76). London: Routledge.

Bronstein, L. (2003). A model for interdisciplinary collaboration. *Social Work*, 48(1), 297–303.

Butterfly Foundation. (2013). *Web counselling*. Retrieved from http://thebutterflyfoundation.org.au/web-counselling.

Campbell, C. & Hare, J. (1997). Ethical literacy in gerontology programs. *Gerontology & Geriatrics Education*, 17(4), 3–16.

Carey, M. & Foster, V. (2011). Introducing 'deviant' social work: Contextualising the limits of radical social work whilst understanding (fragmented) resistance within the social work labour process. *British Journal of Social Work*, 41(3), 576–93. doi:10.1093/bjsw/bcq148.

Carus, P. (2009). *Lao Tze's Tao-Teh-King*. Charleston, SC: Bibliolife.

Centre for the Advancement of Interprofessional Education. (2002). *Defining IPE*. Retrieved from http://www.caipe.org.uk/resources/defining-ipe.

Chenoweth, L. & McAuliffe, D. (2014). *The road to social work and human service practice* (4th edn). South Melbourne, Australia: Cengage.

Civil Liberties Australia. (n.d.). *Welcome to Civil Liberties Australia*. Retrieved from http://www.cla.asn.au/News.

Clark, P.G., Cott, C. & Drinka, T. (2007). Theory and practice in interprofessional ethics: A framework for understanding ethical issues in health care teams. *Journal of Interprofessional Care*, 21(6), 591–603.

Clifford, D. & Burke, B. (2009). *Anti-oppressive ethics and values in social work.* Basingstoke, UK: Palgrave Macmillan.

Coates, J. (2013). Ecospiritual approaches: A path to decolonising social work. In M. Gray, J. Coates, M. Yellow Bird & T. Hetherington (eds), *Decolonising social work* (pp. 63–86). Aldershot, UK: Ashgate.

Congress, E. (1999). *Social work values and ethics: Identifying and resolving ethical dilemmas.* Chicago, IL: Nelson Hall.

Connolly, M. (2013). Values and human rights. In M. Connolly & L. Harms (eds), *Social work: Contexts and practice* (3rd edn) (pp. 48–59). South Melbourne, Australia: Oxford University Press.

Connolly, M. & Ward, T. (2008). *Morals, rights and practice in the human services.* London: Jessica Kingsley.

Corey, G., Corey, M.S. & Callanan, P. (2007). *Issues and ethics in the helping professions.* Belmont, CA: Brookes/Cole.

Cumming, S., Fitzpatrick, E., McAuliffe, D., McKain, S., Martin, C. & Tonge, A. (2007). Raising the Titanic: Rescuing social work documentation from the sea of ethical risk. *Australian Social Work*, 60(2), 239–57.

Dalai Lama XIV. (2011). *Beyond religion: Ethics for a whole world.* London: Random House.

Davis, M. (2003). What can we learn by looking for the first code of professional ethics? *Theoretical Medicine and Bioethics*, 24(5), 433–54.

D'Cruz, H., Jacobs, S. & Schoo, A. (2009). *Knowledge-in-practice in the caring professions: Multidisciplinary perspectives.* London: Ashgate.

DeMaria, W. (1997). Flapping on clipped wings: Social work ethics in the age of activism. *Australian Social Work*, 50(4), 3–19.

Dickens, J. (2013). *Social work, law and ethics.* London: Routledge.

Dolgoff, R., Loewenberg, F. & Harrington, D. (2009). *Ethical decisions for social work practice* (8th edn). Belmont, CA: Thomson Brooks/Cole.

Downie, R. & Calman, K. (1987). *Healthy respect: Ethics in healthcare.* London: Faber & Faber.

Eheadspace. (2014). *Eheadspace can help.* Retrieved from https://www.eheadspace.org.au.

Employee Assistance Professional Association of Australasia. (2009). *What is an employee assistance program?* Retrieved from http://www.eapaa.org.au.

Featherstone, B. (2010). Ethic of Care. In M. Gray and S. Webb (eds), *Ethics and value perspectives in social work* (pp. 73–84). New York: Palgrave Macmillan.

Figley, C. (1995). *Compassion fatigue: Coping with secondary traumatic stress disorder in those who treat the traumatized.* New York: Bruner/Mazel.

Fortune, T. & Fitzgerald, M. (2009). The challenge of interdisciplinary collaboration in acute psychiatry: Impacts on the occupational milieu. *Australian Occupational Therapy Journal*, 56(2), 81–8.

Freegard, H. (2007). *Ethical practice for health professionals*. South Melbourne, Australia: Thomson.

Freeman, S. (2000). *Ethics: An introduction to philosophy and practice*. Belmont, CA: Wadsworth/Thomson Learning.

Fronek, P., Kendall, M., Ungerer, G., Malt, J., Eugarde, E. & Geraghty, T. (2009). Towards healthy professional–client relationships: The value of an interprofessional training course. *Journal of Interprofessional Care*, 23(1), pp. 16–29.

Garcia, J., Cartwright, B., Winston, S. & Borzuchowska, B. (2003). A transcultural integrative model for ethical decision-making in counseling. *Journal of Counseling and Development*, 81(3), 268–77.

Garner, H.G. & Orelove, F.P. (1994). *Teamwork in human services: Models and applications across the lifespan*. London: Butterworth-Heinemann.

Garrett, T., Baillie, H. & Garrett, R. (2001). *Health care ethics: Principles and problems*. New Jersey: Prentice-Hall.

Gedge, R. (2002). *Online counselling services in Australia – the challenges of a new vehicle for an old art*. Retrieved from http://ausweb.scu.edu.au/aw02/papers/refereed/gedge2/paper.html.

Giddens, A. (1990). *The consequences of modernity*. Cambridge: Polity Press.

Gostin, L. (2002). *Public health law and ethics: A reader*. Berkeley, CA: University of California.

Gray, M., Coates, J. & Yellow Bird, M. (eds) (2008). *Indigenous social work around the world: Towards culturally relevant education and practice*. London: Ashgate.

Gray, M. & Webb, S. (eds) (2010). *Ethics and value perspectives in social work*. New York: Palgrave Macmillan.

Green, R. & Mason, R. (2002). Managing confidentiality in rural welfare practice in Australia. *Rural Social Work*. 7(1), 34–43.

Greenslade, L. (2013). *Social work activism: Resistance at the frontier* (Unpublished Thesis). Griffith University, Brisbane.

Greenslade, L., McAuliffe, D. & Chenoweth, L. (2014 in press). Social workers' experiences of covert workplace activism. *Australian Social Work*.

Greenwood, E. (1957). Attributes of a profession. *Social Work*, 2(3), 45–55.

Gregory, M. (2010). Reflection and resistance: Probation practice and the ethic of care. *British Journal of Social Work*, 40(7), 2274–90. doi:10.1093/bjsw/bcq028.

Gretter, L.E. (1893/2014). *Florence Nightingale Pledge*. Retrieved from http://nursingworld.org/FunctionalMenuCategories/AboutANA/NationalNursesWeek/MediaKit/FlorenceNightingalePledge.html.

Guillemin, M. & Gillam, L. (2006). *Telling moments: Everyday ethics in health care*. Melbourne, Australia: IP Communications.

Hall, P. (2005). Interprofessional teamwork: Professional cultures as barriers. *Journal of Interprofessional Care*, Supplement 1, 188–96.

Hanh, N.T. (1998). *For a future to be possible: Commentaries on the five mindfulness trainings*. Berkeley, CA: Parallax Press.

Harrington, D. & Dolgoff, R. (2008). Hierarchies of ethical principles for ethical decision making in social work. *Ethics and Social Welfare*, 2(2), 183–96.

Hart, M.A. (2010). Indigenous worldviews, knowledge and research: the development of an indigenous research paradigm. *Journal of Indigenous Voices in Social Work*, 1(1), 1–16.

Hawley, G. (2007). *Ethics in clinical practice: An interprofessional approach*. Harlow, UK: Pearson Education.

Hill, M., Glaser, K., & Harden, J. (1995). A feminist model for ethical decision-making. In E.J. Rave & C.C. Larsen (eds), *Ethical decision-making in therapy: Feminist perspectives* (pp. 18–37). New York: Guilford Press.

Hinman, L.M. (2008). *Ethics: A pluralistic approach to moral theory* (4th edn). Belmont, CA: Thomson.

House of Lords. (1990). *Caparo Industries v Dickman*. Retrieved from http://oxcheps.new.ox.ac.uk/casebook/Resources/CAPARO_1.pdf.

Houtman, D. & Aupers, S. (2010). New Age Ethics. In M. Gray and S. Webb (eds), *Ethics and value perspectives in social work* (pp. 207–18). New York: Palgrave Macmillan.

How Kee, L., Martin, J. & Ow. R. (eds) (2014). *Cross-cultural social work: Local and global*. Melbourne, Australia: Palgrave Macmillan.

Hugman, R. (1998). *Social welfare and social values: The role of caring professionals*. London: Macmillan.

Hugman, R. (2005). *New approaches in ethics for the caring professions*. New York: Palgrave Macmillan.

Hugman, R. (2012). Human rights and social justice. In M. Gray, J. Midgley & S. Webb (eds), *The SAGE handbook of social work* (pp. 372–86). London: Sage Publications.

Hugman, R. (2013). *Culture, values and ethics in social work: Embracing diversity*, New York: Routledge.

Ife, J. (2012). *Human rights and social work: Towards rights-based practice*. Melbourne, Australia: Cambridge University Press.

Ife, J. (2013). *Community development in an uncertain world: Vision, analysis and practice.* Melbourne, Australia: Cambridge University Press.

Jamrozik, A. (2009). *Social policy in the post-welfare state.* Frenchs Forest, Australia: Pearson Education Australia.

Jervis-Tracey, P., Chenoweth, L., McAuliffe, D., O'Connor, B. & Stehlik, D. (2012). Managing tensions in statutory professional practice: living and working in rural and remote communities, *Australian and International Journal of Rural Education,* 22(2), 97–126.

Jessup, R. (2007). Interdisciplinary versus multidisciplinary care teams: Do we understand the difference? *Australian Health Review,* 31(3), 330–1.

Johnson, D. (2011). *Socrates and Athens.* Cambridge, UK: Cambridge University Press.

Johnstone, M.-J. (2009). *Bioethics: A nursing perspective.* Sydney, Australia: Churchill Livingstone.

Keown, D. (2005). *Buddhist ethics: A very short introduction.* Oxford, UK: Oxford University Press.

Kerridge, I., Lowe, M. & McPhee, J. (2005). *Ethics and law for the health professions* (2nd edn). Sydney, Australia: Federation Press.

Klaczynski, P.A., Byrnes, J.P. & Jacobs, J.E. (2001). The development of decision making. *Journal of Applied Developmental Psychology,* 22(3), 225–36.

LaFollette, H. (1997). *Ethics in practice: An anthology.* Oxford: Blackwell Publishers.

Law Council of Australia. (n.d.). *Law Council of Australia.* Retrieved from http://www.lawcouncil.asn.au/lawcouncil.

Lewins, F. (1996). *Bioethics for health professionals.* South Yarra, Australia: Macmillan Education.

Lovat, T. (2010). Islam and ethics. In M. Gray & S. Webb (eds), *Ethics and value perspectives in social work* (pp. 207–18). New York: Palgrave Macmillan.

Magelssen, M. (2012). When should conscientious objection be accepted? *Journal of Medical Ethics,* 38(1), 18–21.

Marston, G., McDonald, C. & Bryson, L. (2014). *The Australian welfare state: Who benefits now?* Melbourne, Australia: Palgrave Macmillan.

Matthews, L.R., Pockett, R.B., Nisbet, G., Thistelwaite, J., Dunston, R., Lee, A. & White, J.F. (2011). Building capacity in Australian interprofessional health education: perspectives from key health and higher education stakeholders. *Australian Health Review,* 35, 136–40.

Mattison, M. (2000). Ethical decision making: the person in the process, *Social Work,* 45(3), 201–12.

McAllister, M., Morrissey, S., McAuliffe, D., Davidson, G., McConnell, H. & Reddy, P. (2011). Teaching ideas for generating critical and constructive insights into well-functioning multidisciplinary mental health teams. *Journal of Mental Health Training, Education and Practice*, 6(3), 117–27.

McAuliffe, D. (1999). Clutching at Codes: resources that influence social work decisions in cases of ethical conflict. *Professional Ethics*, 7(3/4), 9–24.

McAuliffe, D. (2005a). Putting ethics on the organisational agenda: the social work ethics audit on trial. *Australian Social Work*, 58(4), 357–69.

McAuliffe, D. (2005b). I'm still standing: impacts and consequences of ethical dilemmas for social workers in direct practice. *Journal of Social Work Values and Ethics*, 2(1),1–11.

McAuliffe, D. (2010). Ethical decision making. In M. Gray & S. Webb (eds), *Ethics and value perspectives in social work* (41–50). New York: Palgrave Macmillan.

McAuliffe, D. (2012a). Challenging and developing organisations: introduction. In S. Banks & K. Nohr (eds), *Practicing social work ethics around the world: Cases and commentaries* (pp. 147–52). London: Routledge.

McAuliffe, D. (2012b). Ethical decision making. In M. Gray, J. Midgley & S. Webb, (eds), *The SAGE handbook of social work* (pp. 316–27). London: Sage.

McAuliffe, D. & Chenoweth, L. (2008). Leave no stone unturned: the inclusive model of ethical decision-making. *Ethics and Social Welfare*, 2(1), 39–49.

McAuliffe, D., Sauvage, D. & Morrissey, S. (2012). Integrity provisions in response to practitioner sexual boundary violations in Australia: a comparative analysis. *Psychiatry, Psychology and Law*, 9(1), 45–59.

McAuliffe, D. & Sudbery, J. (2005). Who do I tell? Support and consultation in cases of ethical conflict. *Journal of Social Work*, 5(1), 21–43.

McDonald, C. & Chenoweth, L. (2009). (Re) shaping social work: an Australian case study. *British Journal of Social Work*, 39(1), 144–60. doi:10.1093/bjsw/bcm094.

McDonald, C., Craik, C., Hawkins, L. & Williams, J. (2011). *Professional practice in human service organisations*. Crows Nest, Australia: Allen & Unwin.

McLaren, H. (2007). Exploring the ethics of forewarning: social workers, confidentiality and potential child abuse disclosures. *Ethics & Social Welfare*, 1(1), 23–40.

McMahon, M. (2006). Revisiting confidentiality. In I. Freckleton & K. Petersen (eds), *Disputes and dilemmas in health law*. Sydney, Australia: Federation Press.

MensLine Australia. (2013). *MensLine online and video counselling*. Retrieved from http://www.mensline.org.au/register.html.

Miller, S., Roberts, P. & Spence, E. (2004). *Corruption and anti-corruption: An applied philosophical approach*. Upper Saddle River, NJ: Pearson Prentice Hall.

Millsteed, J. (2006). Regulation of the Professions. In H. Freegard (ed.), *Ethical practice for health professionals* (pp. 93–108). South Melbourne, Australia: Thomson.

Minch, M. & Weigel, C. (2009). *Living ethics: An introduction*. Belmont, CA: Wadsworth, Cengage Learning.

Miner, M.H. (2006). A proposed comprehensive model for ethical decision-making. In S. Morrisey & P. Reddy (eds), *Ethics and professional practice for psychologists* (pp. 25–37). South Melbourne, Australia: Thomson.

Morrison, A., Morrissey, S.I. & Goodman, D. (2006). Researching ethical decision making in Australian psychologists. In S. Morrissey & P. Reddy (eds), *Ethics and professional practice for psychologists* (pp. 50–63). South Melbourne, Australia: Thomson.

Munro, E. (2012). Risk assessment and decision making. In M. Gray, J. Midgely & S. Webb (eds), *The SAGE handbook of social work* (pp. 224–35). London: Sage.

Murphy, L., Parnass, P., Mitchell, D., Hallett, R., Cayley, R. & Seagram, S. (2009). Client satisfaction and outcome comparisons of on-line and face-to-face counselling methods. *British Journal of Social Work*, 39(4), 627–40.

Neitzke, G. & Fehr, F. (2003). Teachers' responsibility: A socratic dialogue about teaching medical ethics. *Medical Teacher*, 25(1), 92–3.

Nipperess, S. & Briskman, L. (2009). Promoting a human rights perspective on critical social work. In J. Allan, L. Briskman & B. Pease (eds), *Critical social work: Theories and practices for a socially just world* (2nd edn) (pp. 58–69). Crows Nest, Australia: Allen & Unwin.

Norman, I.J. & Peck, E. (1999). Working together in adult community mental health services: an interprofessional dialogue. *Journal of Mental Health*, 8(3), 217–30.

Occupational Therapy Australia. (2014). *Occupational Therapy Australia*. Retrieved from http://www.otaus.com.au.

Occupational Therapy Board of Australia. (2012). *Code of conduct for registered health professionals*. Retrieved from http://www.occupationaltherapyboard.gov.au/Codes-Guidelines.aspx.

O'Leary, P., Tsui, M-S. & Ruch, G. (2013). The boundaries of the social work relationship revisited: towards a connected, inclusive, and dynamic conceptualisation. *British Journal of Social Work*, 43(1), 135–53.

Olson, B., Aalbers, D. & Fallenbaum, R. (2009). APA takes a stand on torture: an update. *The Just Word*. XV(1), 2.

O'Sullivan, T. (1999). *Decision-making in social work*. London: Macmillan.

Preston, N. (2007). *Understanding ethics*. Sydney, Australia: The Federation Press.

Professions Australia (2013). *Definition of a profession*. Retrieved from http://www.professions.com.au/defineprofession.html

Rafiee, B. (2004). *Ethics in Islam*. London: Al-hoda International.

Raia, S. (2004). Problem of impaired practice. *New Jersey Nurse* 34(6),8.

Ray, B. (1950). *Gandhian ethics*. Ahmedabad, India: Navajivan Publishing House.

Reamer, F. (1993). *The philosophical foundations of social work*. New York: Columbia University Press.

Reamer, F. (2001a). *The Social Work Ethics Audit Risk Management Tool*. Washington, DC: NASW Press.

Reamer, F. (2001b). *Tangled relationships: Managing boundary issues in the human services*. New York: Columbia University Press.

Reamer, F. (2006). *Social work values and ethics* (3rd edn). New York: Columbia University Press.

Reamer, F. (2013). Codes of Ethics. In M. Gray, J. Midgely. & S. Webb (eds). *The SAGE handbook of social work* (pp. 299–315). London: Sage Publications.

Reel, K. & Hutchings, S. (2007). Being part of a team: interprofessional care. In G. Hawley (ed.), *Ethics in clinical practice: An interprofessional approach* (pp. 137–53). Harlow, UK: Pearson Education.

Roberts, P., Brown, A.J. & Olsen, J. (2011). *Whistling while they work: A good-practice guide for managing internal reporting of wrongdoing in public sector organisations*. Retrieved from http://epress.anu.edu.au?p=144611.

Robison, W. & Reeser, L.C. (2000). *Ethical decision making in social work*. Boston: Allyn & Bacon.

Rowson, R. (2006). *Working ethics: How to be fair in a culturally complex world*. London: Jessica Kingsley.

Royal Australian & New Zealand College of Psychiatrists. (2010). *Code of ethics*. Retrieved from https://www.ranzcp.org/Files/ranzcp-attachments/Resources/College_Statements/code_ethics_2010-pdf-(1).aspx.

Russo, C.J., Squelch, J. & Varnham, S. (2010). Teachers and social networking sites: think before you post. *Public Space: The Journal of Law and Social Justice*, 5(5), 1–15.

Sargent, J., Loney, E. & Murphy, G. (2008). Effective interprofessional teams: "Contact is not enough" to build a team. *Journal of Continuing Education in the Health Professions*, 28(4), 228–34.

Sauvage, D. (2014). *Experiences of complaints about counselling, psychotherapy and casework: Voicing the need for accountability and care* (Unpublished Thesis). Griffith University, Brisbane.

Savulescu, J. (2006). Conscientious objection in medicine, *British Medical Journal*, 332(7536), 294–7.

Scharfstein, B. (1998). *A comparative history of world philosophy*. Albany, NY: State University of New York Press.

Segal, E.A., Gerdes, K.E. & Steiner, S. (2010). *An introduction to the profession of social work: Becoming a change agent* (3rd edn). Belmont, CA: Brookes/Cole.

Sherwin, B.L. (2000). *Jewish ethics for the 21st century: Living in the image of God*. Syracuse, NY: Syracuse University Press.

Shun, K. & Vong, D. (2004). *Confucian ethics: A comparative study of self, autonomy and community*. Cambridge, UK: Cambridge University Press.

Sicker, M. (2008). *The ten commandments: Background, meaning and implications from a Jewish perspective*. Bloomington, IN: iUniverse publishing.

Sinclair, A. (1996). Codes in the workplace: Organisational versus professional codes. In M. Doady & S. Bloch (eds), *Codes of ethics and the professions* (pp. 88–108). Melbourne, Australia: Melbourne University Press.

Sluyter, G.V. (1998). *Improving organisational performance: A practical guidebook for the human services field*. London: Sage Publications.

Smith, R. (2009). Inter-professional learning and multi-professional practice for PQ. In P. Higham (ed), *Post-qualifying social work practice* (pp. 135–47). London: Sage Publications.

Sokol, D. (2006). Virulent epidemics and scope of healthcare workers' duty of care. *Emerging Infectious Diseases*, 12(8), 1238–41.

Spano, R. & Koenig, T. (2007). What is sacred when personal and professional values collide? *Journal of social work values and ethics*, 4(3). Harrisburg: White Hat Communications.

Stenmark, C. (2013). Forecasting and ethical decision making: what matters? *Ethics and Behavior*, 23(6), 445–62.

Streng, F. (1973). The ethics of moral coercion: Gandhi and political revolution. *Philosophy East & West*, 23(3), 283–90.

Suzuki, D.T. (1959). *Zen and Japanese culture*. Princeton, NJ: Princeton University Press.

Tarasoff v. Regents of the University of California. (1976).

Walker, S., Dearnley, C., Hargreaves, J. & Walker, E. (2013). Risk, fitness to practice, and disabled health care students. *Journal of Psychological Issues in Organisational Culture*, 3(4), 46–59.

Waller, B.E. (2005). *Consider ethics: Theory, readings and contemporary issues*. New York: Pearson Longman.

Watling, S. & Rogers, J. (2012). *Social work in a digital society*. London: Sage.

Webster, P. (2010). Codes of Conduct. In M. Gray and S. Webb (eds), *Ethics and value perspectives in social work*. (pp. 31–40). New York: Palgrave Macmillan.

Wronka, J. (1992). *Human rights and social policy in the 21st century: A history of the idea of human rights and comparison of the United Nations Universal Declaration of Human Rights with United States federal and state constitutions*. Lanham, MD: University Press of America.

Yu, J. (2007). *The ethics of Confucius and Aristotle: Mirrors of virtue*. New York: Routledge.

Zarcadoolas, C., Pleasant, A. & Greer, D. (2005). Understanding health literacy: an expanded model. *Health Promotion International*, 20(2), 195–203.

Index

and social justice, 54
 three generations of, 50–1
human rights practice frameworks, 47
 benefits of, 54
 elements of, 51–2
humanism, 27
humanity, 181–2
Hume, David, 27
Hursthouse, Rosalind, 28
Hutchings, S., 15

ideologies and ethical codes, 36
Ife, J., 48
impaired practice, 164–5, 170–1
 common issues, 165
 notifiable conduct, 165–6
 personal problems unrelated to work, 168
 problems related to work, 168–9
 psychiatric illness or disability, 167–8
 substance abuse, 167
 vicarious trauma,
inclusive model of ethical decision-making
 accountability, 96–8, 100
 consultation, 98, 99, 103
 critical analysis and evaluation, 102
 critical reflection, 99–100
 cultural sensitivity, 98–9, 101
 development of alternative approaches
  and actions, 102, 103
 engagement of all stakeholders, 101
 and ethical literacy, 104
 gathering of information, 101
 identification of the problem, 100–1, 103
 identification of who has authority to
  move forward, 100
 mapping of legitimacy, 101
 platforms for interprofessional work, 100
 process of, 100–2
 stages of, 100–2
 traps, 103–4
inclusiveness, 153
 see also inclusive model of ethical
  decision-making
Indigenous communities, 99–100, 120
Indigenous worldviews, 35
 mino-pimatisiwin, 35
 principles of, 35–6
industrial revolution, 27
inequality and inequity, 56
information, management of, 4
informed consent, 20–1, 112–13
 complexity of, 113
 conditions necessary for, 112
 consent component, 112
 development of, 112
 information component, 112–13
 in practice, 113–14

 procedures for demonstration of, 113
 refusal of, 114
 voluntary nature of, 112
interdisciplinary ethics course, 1
interdisciplinary work teams, 15, 155
 definition of, 15
interprofessional activism, 63–4
interprofessional care
 definition of, 15
 inclusive model of ethical decision-
  making, 96–100
interprofessional collaboration, 111, 155–6,
 170
interprofessional education, 63, 174,
 180, 181
 benefits of, 14–15
 contribution of, 175
 definition of, 14
 emergence of the concept, 1
 outcomes of, 14
 principles underlying, 14
 rationale for, 18–20
interprofessional practice
 benefits of, 102
 definition of rights, 106
interprofessional relationships, 4
 challenges to, 156
 clarity of roles, 156–7
 questions of status, 156–7
interprofessional space, definition of,
 15–17
Islam, pillars of, 33, 36

Jacobs, J.E., 86–7
Jacobs, S., 9
Jagger, Alison, 28
Jervis-Tracey, Paula, 101, 135, 150
Johns, Lise, 143–4
Johnson, W.B., 98
Johnstone, M.J. 118
Judaism, ethical principles, 33–4
justice, 46–65, 84
 distributive justice, 56
 natural justice framework for responding
  to complaints, 83–4
 social justice, 54–6

Kant, Immanuel, 27
Kantian ethics, 40–1
Kemp, Michelle, 96
Kerridge, I., 163
Kids Helpline, 150
Klaczynski, P.A., 86–7
Koenig, T., 145
law, and ethics, 3
Law Council of Australia, 71

leadership, 2, 72, 181
League of Nations, 48
Lenette, Caroline, 37–8
liberty, 106
Lifeline, 150
Locke, John, 27
Loney, E., 16
Lovat, T., 32
Lowe, M., 163
Lowenberg, F., 89–90, 94, 124

Magelssen, M., 142
Magna Carta, 48
Maidment, J., 131
management responsibilities, 159
mandatory detention legislation, 62
Marston, G., 92
Marx, Karl, 27
McAuliffe, Donna, 38, 78–9, 98, 160
    courage, 60
    ethical decision-making, 89
    ethical dilemmas, 102–3
    ethics audit tool, 91
    spiritual dimensions in practice, 144–5
    value differences among professions,
      13–14
McCawley, Anne-Louise, 22, 170–1
McDonald, C., 53
McDonald, Donna, 126–7
McLaren, H., 119
McMahon, M., 115
McPhee, J., 163
Meads, Patricia, 135
Medical Council of NSW, 167
MensLine Australia, 151
Mental Health First Aid Australia, 167
mentoring, 5, 171, 181
metaethics, 39
Middle Eastern philosophy, 32
Mill, John Stuart, 27
Miller, Roberts and Spence, 163
Millsteed, J., 69
moral hazard, 75
moral obligations of professionals, 8
moral philosophy, 24–45, 176
    Buddhist philosophy, 31–2
    Chinese philosophy, 32
    classical Greek philosophers, 26
    contributions of women, 28
    Eastern philosophical traditions, 29–34
    ethical codes of non-geographical groups,
      36–7
    and ethics education, 26–8
    Hellenistic philosophers, 26
    Hindu philosophy, 30–1
    history of, 24, 26–8
    Indigenous worldviews, 35

    and the industrial revolution, 27-8
    Judaism, 33–4
    metaethics, 39
    Middle Eastern philosophy, 32–3
    modern philosophy, 28
    Roman and Christian philosophy, 26–7
    Western philosophies, 29
moral rights, and human rights, 49
multidisciplinary work teams, 1, 8, 15, 17, 22,
    111–12
    definition of, 15
    dysfunctional, 21
Munro, Eileen, 90
Murphy, G., 16

National Aboriginal and Islander Child Care
    Secretariat, 73
National Alliance of Self-Regulating Health
    Professionals, 73
National Disability Insurance Scheme, 70
National Ethics and Professional Practice
    portfolio, 80
National Registration and Accreditation
    Scheme, 4, 79, 81, 140
needs, 56
negotiation of professionals working together,
    7–8
neoliberalist construction of welfare, 92, 161, 181
New Age movement, 36
Nietzsche, Friedrich, 27
Nightingale Pledge, 74
Nipperess, Sharlene, 48, 55
Noddings, Nel, 28
Nohr, K., 40
non-consequentialism, 40–1
Norman, I.J., 16
Nussbaum, Martha, 28

Occupational Therapy Australia, 70–1, 133
O'Leary, P., 129
online communications, 146
    advantages of, 146
    impacts of digital footprints, 147, 178
    responsiveness, language and privacy
      issues, 151
    risks of, 146–9
online platforms and privacy and
    confidentiality, 121
online practice, 150–2
Orelove, F.P., 15
organisational cultures, 9, 59
organisational structures, 9
organisations
    codes of ethics, 159
    mission, vision and values of, 154
    policies and procedures documents, 159

paternalism, 109–11
    strong, 110
    weak, 110
Peck, E., 16
peer support, 5
Pennell, Kerryn, 138
People's Inquiry into Detention, 62–3
    Human Rights Overboard publication, 62
Percival's Medical Ethics, 74
personal and professional relationships, 4, 20,
    135, 182
    boundary crossings, 132
    boundary violations, 132
    caution necessary, 130–1
    deliberate or accidental, 139
    differences between, 131
    dual relationships, 134–6
    establishment of clear boundaries, 131–4
    and friends or personal relationships, 133
    negotiation of in practice, 129–30
    and personal self-disclosure, 136–7
    in rural practice settings, 134
    sexual and intimate relationships, 132
    survival strategies, 135, 136
personal self-disclosure, 136–7
    caution needed, 139
    content of, 138–9
    relevance, 139
personal values, 142–3, 145
    and cultural considerations, 142, 144
    and religion and spirituality, 142, 143–4
Plato, 42
Pleasant, A., 176
Plotinus, 26–7
POEM (philosophy, ontology, epistemology and
    method), 2
policy decisions, 57
Poor Law (England), 56
power, 24, 52–3, 82, 134
Preston, N., 38
Prince, Diana, 64–5
privacy, 20–2, 46, 114–15
    challenges to upholding, 120–1
    and confidentiality, 115–17
    definition of, 116
    and online communications, 151
    and online platforms, 121
    in practice, 117
    in rural practice settings, 121
    Western notions of, 116, 120
professional associations, 69–73
    advocacy role, 72
    collaboration between, 73
    complaint mechanisms, 78–9, 80, 83–4
    development of, 69–72
    leadership role, 72
    policy role, 72
    voluntary membership, 79

professional conduct, courses on, 14
professional culture, 69–73
professional development, 140, 181
professional education
    continuing, 140
    disciplinary silos, 19
    ethics, 145
    induction processes, 90
    internships and field placements, 18
professional ethics, journals on, 176
professional identity, 69–73, 76
    human rights perspective in, 49
professional integrity, 128, 159
    competence, 140–1
    dual relationships, 134–6
    establishment of clear boundaries,
        131–4
    imposition of personal values, 142–3
    and online communications, 146
    personal self-disclosure, 136–7
    spiritual dimensions in practice, 144–5
professional practice, 174–83
    diversity of, 154–5
    documentation and record keeping,
        126–7
    integration of knowledge, skills and
        values, 175
    and moral philosophy, 24
    understanding the scope of, 140–1
Professional Standards for Teachers, 150
professionalisation, 9
    see also professional development
professionalism, 146
professionals
    career shifts, 11–12
    profession of knowledge and wisdom, 10,
        110
    reputation, 146
    socialisation of, 9
professions
    complementarity of, 7
    counselling and therapy, 166–7
    critical view of, 68
    definition of, 8, 10–11, 67–9
    development of training courses, 18
    disciplines included, 9–10
    doing no harm, 66
    ethical decision-making models, 93–5
    ethical differences between, 8–9
    functionalist view of, 68
    legitimacy of, 10
    regulation of, 66–85
    tensions between, 19
    value clashes among, 12–13
Professions Australia, 8
professions, unregulated, 149
psychiatric illness or disability, disclosure of, 167
psychologists, 63